Christendom

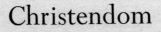

ROLAND H. BAINTON

Christendom

A Short History of Christianity

and

Its Impact on Western Civilization

Vol. II

From the Reformation

to the Present

HARPER TORCHBOOKS

Harper & Row, Publishers

New York, Cambridge, Hagerstown, Philadelphia, San Francisco
London, Mexico City, São Paulo, Sydney

To an inheritor of the Reformation,
Wilhelm Pauck

CHRISTENDOM: VOLUME II

Copyright © 1964, 1966 by American Heritage Publishing Co. Inc.

The text of this book was first published in *The Horizon History of Christianity* in 1964 by American Heritage Publishing Company and is here reprinted, revised and expanded, by arrangement. The illustrations have been selected for this edition by the author.

Library of Congress catalog card number: 64-19638

82 83 84   20 19 18 17 16 15

Contents
Volume II

Illustrations

The illustrations pertaining to each chapter
will be found in groups following pages 46,
96, 126, 160, and, for chapter XIII, two
groups following pages 168 and 196.

IX

The Age of Reformation

MENACING forces of dissolution in the Church during the late Middle Ages appeared to have been dispelled in the early years of the sixteenth century. Sectarianism and heresy had largely been crushed. Savonarola had been burned, leaving behind him no following. The conciliar movement had been subordinated to papal control, and the schism had been terminated. Spain, long torn between the crescent and the cross, was now definitely aligned with Christendom; the rigors of the Inquisition could be relaxed. As a consequence, Christendom enjoyed in the first quarter of the century a period of relative tranquility and liberalism.

Yet there were unrest and dissatisfaction within the Church, and they were justified. Corruption in the Church was rampant, and many high-minded churchmen throughout Europe bemoaned her derelictions and clamored for reform. Complaints centered on three points: immorality among the clergy, severe financial demands imposed upon the faithful, and neglect of the parishes. As noted earlier, the enforcement of clerical celibacy had led in many instances to clerical concubinage. How widespread the practice was cannot be statistically determined, and figures given by reformers may be exaggerated. But complaints about clerical incontinence were heard in every country of Europe; the papacy itself was among the most notorious offenders. Fortunately society did not discriminate against priests' bastards and some, like Erasmus, became persons of great distinction.

The financial exactions of the Church had long been regarded as a grievance. Although the people gave voluntarily, with immense generosity, they acutely resented paying tithes when nonpayment meant excommunication. By various forms of exaction, the Church at every level acquired sufficient wealth to arouse criticism by the faithful. The sale of offices was widespread. So, too, was the traffic in indulgences. The unpopularity of papal taxes was aggravated by resentment over the way this money was spent. Why should the faithful in Germany, or England, or France, finance the siege of Bologna by Pope Julius II? And why contribute to the rebuilding of St. Peter's at Rome when one could not afford to patch the roof of one's own parish church?

The most severe strictures were directed against the sorry state of parishes. Many of the lower clergy were almost totally uneducated. Moreover, so much money was drained off for the support of the national church or the universal Church that priests were unable to live on the revenues from a single parish; hence, several parishes were combined (a system called pluralism), to the inevitable neglect of each. Pastors and bishops were often not in residence and committed the cure of souls to vicars living on a pittance. When bishops became cardinals, they were withdrawn from their sees to Rome. Catholic reformers in all lands were demanding that celibacy be enforced among the clergy, that the financing of the Church be overhauled, and that the flock be properly tended.

There were two types of Catholic reform, at first not sharply differentiated. One was liberal, undogmatic, ethical, relying on education to achieve its ends. The other was doctrinal and disciplinary, demanding the precise formulation of the faith and rigorous enforcement of the rules, with recourse to the secular arm to do so if need be. Both types were found in all Catholic lands and for some decades supported each other. Yet it may not be too much of an exaggeration to describe the first type as Dutch and the second as Spanish, because their roots were grounded respectively in the Netherlands and Spain.

Erasmus

The great exponent of liberal reform was the Dutchman Desiderius Erasmus (1466 or 1469–1536). He was educated by the
Brethren of the Common Life in the Humanist tradition and early
became passionately devoted to classical and patristic studies.
Upon the death of his father, his guardians persuaded him to enter
a monastery, but eventually a dispensation relieved him of the
obligation of residence, so that he might be free to follow his
vocation as a Christian scholar in whatever centers manuscripts
and printing presses were to be found. He was influenced from
Italy by Lorenzo Valla regarding methods of historical and biblical scholarship and by the Florentine Academy in disparaging the
sensory and external aspect of religion. His great achievement lay
in making available the treasures of classical and Christian antiquity, but in addition his devotional and satirical tracts made him
the ideal of international Humanism and the epitome of liberal
Catholic reform.

Erasmus was acutely aware of the evils within the Church of his
own time. *The Praise of Folly*, written while he was a guest in
London of St.Thomas More, was a cutting satire on the foibles of
monks, priests, popes, theologians, and mankind in general, including himself. The central note in his piety was his emphasis on
inner experience rather than on external devotions and ceremony.
"Oh, the folly of those who revere a bone of the Apostle Paul
encased in glass and feel not the glow of his spirit enshrined in his
epistles!"[1] he ejaculated. What, he asked, is the point of fasting?
To gain a reputation for piety, or to discipline the body for fruitful
endeavor? As for the cult of relics, he scoffed at the miracles
allegedly wrought by those of Thomas à Becket, one of whose
slippers, he observed with irony, would do more after the saint
was dead than his whole body while still alive. Erasmus criticized

[1] Desiderius Erasmus, *Enchiridion Militis Christiani*, 5th rule. English in
Christian Classics (Philadelphia, 1953), XIV, 338.

the monastic orders as superstitious, contentious and addicted to matters external, whereas the spirit alone matters, and this may actually be more manifest in family life. The dietary prescriptions of the Catholic Church appeared to him as a new Pharisaism.

With regard to dogma, he was anti-speculative, like the Brethren, maintaining that the essential of religion consists not in ratiocination but in piety and charity. He introduced a distinction between the dogmas essential to salvation and those nonessential. To be necessary for salvation, he insisted, a dogma must be simple enough to be universally understood, for God would surely not damn men for not believing what they cannot grasp. Dogma must be universally accepted, because that which is controverted cannot be certain. Erasmus reduced the essentials to the Apostles' Creed, though as a matter of fact some portions even of the Creed meant very little to him; for example, the clause "suffered under Pontius Pilate." For Erasmus the suffering of Christ was not necessary to appease God's wrath or to satisfy his justice.

From such a position, one might easily infer that Calvary was not a sacrifice and that the Mass was therefore not, as orthodox dogma maintained, a repetition of such sacrifice. In accordance with a tradition of long standing in the Netherlands, Erasmus looked upon the doctrine of transubstantiation as an unwarranted scholastic sophistry and interpreted the presence of Christ in the sacrament as spiritual. But he was not prepared to dogmatize and would not go counter to the consensus of the Church.

He was greatly concerned to correct morals, curb ambition, and stimulate piety, not only by ridicule but by the dissemination of learning. Much of his life's work consisted of editing and translating the texts of Christian antiquity. Above all, he was eager to make known the Bible; the essence of his reform was a return to the simplicity of the Gospel, especially to the Sermon on the Mount. His greatest contribution in this area lay in the publication for the first time of the Greek text of the New Testament, at the press of Froben at Basel, in 1516. Erasmus worked hastily, relying on only a few manuscripts and these not the best. Unhappily, his version was for too long the *textus receptus*, the received text. Nonetheless, it was a great achievement, the more so because Erasmus accompanied the text by a Latin translation, revealing errors in the Vulgate of St.Jerome. Henceforth, any scholar who could read Greek could study the New Testament for himself at first hand, and anyone acquainted with Latin could perceive mistakes in the version that had been authoritative throughout the Middle Ages.

Any program of reform by education required harmony in the Church and concord in the state. In tracts, biblical commentaries, and letters, Erasmus constantly preached peace. The new spirit of nationalism knew no sturdier foe. Why should Englishmen, Frenchmen, and Spaniards, he argued, consider themselves natural enemies when in fact they are brothers in Christ? Erasmus looked back with nostalgia upon a society comprised within a universal empire and a universal Church, a world which in fact had never existed. It was better represented in his day by the Church than by the empire and that was one reason for his refusal to leave the Church. How deeply was he grieved in 1521, when the banning of Luther divided the Church and the outbreak of war between the most Christian king of France and the Holy Roman emperor further disrupted the universality of the empire!

Such evangelical Humanism was not confined to the Netherlands but had exponents throughout Europe. In England, there were John Colet, the dean of St.Paul's, and More, Henry's lord chancellor and the author of *Utopia*; in France, the great biblical scholar Jacques Lefèvre d'Etaples, and John Standonck of the College of Montaigu, a residence for clerical students at the University of Paris, where both John Calvin and Ignatius Loyola were to live at different times. For a decade or more, while the Netherlands were under Spanish rule, Erasmus had a great vogue in Spain. When Charles, who had been reared in the Low Countries, became the king of Spain in 1516, he brought in his entourage counselors from the Netherlands of an Erasmian temper.

In Italy, the great exponent of such Humanism was Juan de Valdés, a Spaniard living in Naples, then a dependency of Spain. Thus, by way of the Iberian Peninsula the currents from the Netherlands flowed to Italy. Valdés, like Erasmus, stressed inwardness and sometimes suggested that the death of Christ was more an educational device on the part of God for the sake of man than a propitiation.

Italy had also an indigenous company of reforming churchmen, some of whom were members of an association called the Oratory of Divine Love, which convened in Rome until the sack of the city in 1527. These ardent churchmen included bishops who had reluctantly become cardinals and suffered themselves to be drawn away from their sees to Rome. Cardinal Giacomo Sadoleto, for example, who composed the bull against Luther, spent all the time the pope would permit attending to his episcopal duties in the Provence. There was Gasparo Contarini, a nobleman of Venice, who, because of his integrity, was rapidly advanced from the status of a layman to that of a cardinal. He utilized his high office to seek agreement with the Protestants on justification by faith. There were many more of like temper: Cardinal Giovanni Morone; Pietro Carnesecchi, the papal secretary; Reginald Pole, the English cardinal in exile; and many women of the aristocracy, such as Vittoria Colonna, who inspired some of the sonnets of Michelangelo.

Imbued with the ideals of the Oratory and aided by the influence of some of its members at the papal court, the Italian reform movement in these years of crisis gave birth to several new religious orders, most importantly the Theatines. Living a strict and holy life, preaching in the streets of Italian cities, serving the poor and the sick, the prostitutes, and the prisoners, the Theatines were a powerful example, alike to the laity and fellow priests. From the ranks of the Theatines in particular, the papacy was to draw numerous reforming bishops—more than two hundred in the first century of their existence. Another order, the Capuchins, sought to revive the program of the Spiritual Franciscans. Devoted to utter poverty, the Capuchins were at first averse to learning, but a generation after their founding introduced a program of study.

Reform in Spain

Reforms in Spain were attended by a unique combination of circumstances: the political situation and the appearance at a crucial juncture of Francisco Ximénez de Cisneros, commonly called Ximénez, one of the most remarkable religious leaders in the nation's history. In the fifteenth century, Spain was in the last throes of a long struggle for religious and political consolidation, in the course of which the land, once the most tolerant on the Continent, became the most intolerant. The old Visigothic pattern of rigid orthodoxy was revived, and a close union of Church and state grew up, characterized by marked independence from the papacy.

Late in the fifteenth century, Church and state in Spain had become convinced that all remnants of non-Christian faiths must be stamped out, not only among the *conversos*—the converted Jews—but as well among the *moriscos*—the converted Moors. The Inquisition was established in Spain in 1480, and three years later a Dominican named Tomás de Torquemada was appointed grand inquisitor. Backed by Ferdinand and Isabella, Torquemada over the next fifteen years subjected no one knows how many heretics to torture and the stake. He came to perceive, however, that he would never eradicate all remnants of Judaism from among the *conversos* so long as any unconverted Jews remained in the land to seduce them. Ferdinand was loath to expel the unconverted, who were still sufficiently numerous and wealthy to finance his war against the Moors; but after Granada finally fell in 1492, he could dispense with their help. In the very year in which Columbus sailed westward across the Atlantic, all unconverted

Spanish Jews were exiled. Ten years later the Moors shared the same fate.

Ximénez, who was to become not only the primate of Spain but a cardinal of Rome and a regent of the realm, was a man of a different stamp. In him we see an amazing combination of the old spirit of orthodoxy and the new Humanism. When he was about fifty, after practicing law in Rome and serving as vicar general of the diocese of Siguenza in Spain, Ximénez became a friar. His extreme austerity attracted large crowds of penitents. In 1492, the year Ferdinand expelled the Jews, Ximénez was called to the royal court as confessor to Queen Isabella and three years later he was named archbishop of Toledo and thus became the primate of all Spain.

In that capacity, he launched a thoroughgoing reform of the Spanish clergy, both secular and regular, including the branch of the Franciscans to which he himself belonged. Yet he was also a patron of the new learning. In 1500, he founded a new university at Alcalá to provide for clerical education at all levels. In addition to two colleges of liberal arts, there was a school of theology to promote the study of the Fathers, the Scriptures, and the requisite languages, Hebrew and Greek. Meanwhile, popular religious books in the vernacular were issued from the university press. With the aid of several scholars, Ximénez edited the Complutensian Polyglot, the first edition of the entire Bible in the original tongues, together with the Vulgate translation of the whole and the Greek Septuagint of the Old Testament.

The life of this extraordinary man was one of sharp contrasts. He wore a hair shirt beneath his cardinal's robes, but as primate of Spain he controlled the wealth of the Church and did not hesitate to finance a crusade against the Moors on the African side of the Straits of Gibraltar, accompanying the troops in person and haranguing them like a new St.Bernard. A strict reformer, he enlisted the best scholars of the Renaissance in his campaign to renew the life of the Church.

Luther

Curiously, the reform that was to convulse Christendom was initiated by a Catholic monk and priest interested only in reforming himself. Martin Luther, the son of a copper miner, was born on November 11, 1483, in the little village of Eisleben in Saxony. He took his Bachelor's degree in 1502 at Erfurt, Germany's greatest university, and three years later his Master's degree. In that same year, when he was returning to the university from a visit with his parents, he was overtaken on the road by a thunderstorm so violent that he feared for his life. Then and there he made a vow: if God preserved him, he would become a monk. Two weeks later he fulfilled the vow by entering the Augustinian monastery at Erfurt. He was not quite twenty-two.

Luther was one of those medieval Christians who took very seriously the "four last things"—death, judgment, heaven, and the eternal fire. He was tormented by terror of the wrath of God, by dread of the judgment of Christ, by panic at the power of Satan. For a time he experienced surcease in the cloister. Then the old torments returned, precipitated by his first saying of the Mass. This was—is—an ordeal for any new priest, for who would not tremble at sacrificing upon the altar the very God and Saviour of the world? All went smoothly until Luther came to the words in the Mass "We offer unto thee the living, the true, the eternal God." He related afterward: "At these words I was utterly stupefied and terror-stricken. I thought to myself, With what tongue shall I address such majesty, seeing that all men ought to tremble in the presence of even an earthly prince? Who am I, that I should lift up my eyes or raise my hands to the divine majesty? The angels surround him. At his nod the earth trembles, and shall I, a miserable little pygmy, say, 'I want this, I ask for that'? For I am dust and ashes and full of sin, and I am speaking to the living, the eternal, and the true God."[2]

[2] Translation by R. H. Bainton of a conflation of three accounts by Luther

The words "dust and ashes and full of sin" convey at once Luther's deep sense of man's creatureliness and unworthiness. How should a worm confront the divine majesty, and how should a sinner stand in the presence of the divine holiness? Only in harmony with the Ultimate can man find peace, but what harmony can there be between the finite and the infinite, between the unclean and the holy?

The first answer offered by the Church was that man should seek to purge himself of sinful inclinations by acts of self-denial. Luther chose the castigation of the flesh. But the thought constantly obsessed him that he could never be hungry enough or poor enough to merit God's favor, and that whatever good works he might do, his thoughts were forever tainted by self-love. This discovery did not leave him hopeless, however; the Church addresses herself as much to sinners as to saints and in the sacrament of penance offers absolution to all who transgress, provided they fulfill the three conditions of contrition, confession, and satisfaction.

Luther had come to feel that no satisfaction man can make is enough, nor can he be sure that his contrition is heartfelt. But confession was open to him, and he set himself to exploit it to the utmost of his memory. He believed, together with the leading theologians of his day, that sins, to be forgiven, must be recalled, confessed, and absolved one by one. Luther proceeded to confess for six hours on end and was utterly disconcerted to find that after leaving the confessional, he recalled some trivial offense he had overlooked. Then he would return again and again until his confessor grew impatient and told him to go and do something worthy of being confessed, such as killing his father or his mother. But Luther's problem was not whether his sins were big or little, but whether he had confessed them all.

More devastating to him was the insight that many sins are

---

in Otto Scheel, *Dokumente zu Luthers Entwicklung* (Tübingen, 1929), see Index *sub* Primitz.

not even recognized as such. So deep is man's corruption that no scrutiny will ever bring him to recognize all that is amiss. Hence, he must seek not the forgiveness of this sin or that, but the redemption of his nature. But experience shows that, in this life, nature is never wholly redeemed and remade. Therefore, man can only hope that God in his mercy will treat man as if he were good, although actually he is not.

Luther did not arrive at such uneasy peace by a placid series of deductions. He was distraught by what he found in himself, and even more by what he had come to believe about the nature of God. For him, God was a God of terror, who suffers men to be crushed by disasters, racked by fantasies, plagued by doubts, driven to desperation by fears. Do not the Scriptures say that some men God justifies and some he rejects, according to his good pleasure? What justice is there in this? Luther's confessor told him he was making the way of salvation too hard. He need only love God. But Luther answered, "I do not love him. I hate him." His confessor could not understand this. And then came to Luther the severest of all trials, the loneliness of uniqueness. If an experienced confessor did not understand, could it be that Luther alone in all history had been so plagued?

Now, his confessor, perceiving that this monk would destroy himself through introspection, sought to call him further out of himself by assigning him to a chair of biblical studies at Wittenberg; to this task were added preaching assignments as well, and the cure of souls in the parish church. In 1512, he took the degree of Doctor of Theology; it was on the basis of his doctorate that he later justified his work as a reformer. Beginning in 1513, he engaged in a series of lectures on the Psalms and the Epistles of St. Paul to the Romans, the Hebrews, and the Galatians.

In the course of these lectures he was confronted by the Passion of Christ, in particular by his words upon the cross, "My God, my God, why hast thou forsaken me?" Christ forsaken by his Father in heaven—this was precisely how Luther felt, and he had thought himself unique. Now he saw that Christ was tempted even as we are, and to the point of utter alienation. But why? Surely not because Christ had sinned. Rather, being without sin, he had taken on himself the sins of us all, nailing them to the cross and thereby manifesting the utter love of the Divine Father. What a different view of Christ this presented! He was not the implacable Judge, but the derelict upon the cross. And what a new picture of God, for the all-terrible was the all-loving, too. On the cross, his wrath and his mercy met in the wonder of redeeming love.

What then is required of man? Luther asked himself. Only this, he concluded, that he relinquish all reliance upon himself, that he come to terms with his continuing unworthiness, that he accept God's goodness with faith, trust, and commitment. This, Luther perceived, was what the Apostle Paul meant when he quoted the prophet Habakkuk: "The just shall live by faith." The insight opened for Luther the gates of paradise. This is the meaning of justification by faith, and it is the foundation stone of what came to be known as Lutheranism.

Faith, for Luther, was above all else objective. Christianity, he believed, is a religion of history resting upon something done by God in time—the Incarnation and the Redemption—and done once and for all. This is known to us solely through the Scriptures open to interpretation by any Christian under the guidance of the Holy Spirit. Acquaintance with the original languages of the Scriptures is needful, and theological education should be concerned exclusively with these tools and with the understanding of the Scriptures. To bring this to pass was initially the sole object of Luther's reform.

In the next few years, his ideas gained considerable currency at the university, then the scene of a lively intellectual ferment. "The lectures on scholastic theology are deserted," he wrote to a friend, the Augustinian prior at Erfurt, on May 18, 1517, "and no one can be sure of an audience who does not teach our theology." Still, it is possible that Luther's reforms might have been confined to the theological curriculum had not his additional duties as a parish priest opened his eyes to certain abuses then current in the

Church, which actually imperiled the souls of his parishioners. Chief among these was the misuse of indulgences.

The particular case that touched off Luther's protest was the most flagrant abuse of indulgences in all the Middle Ages. Albert, of the House of Hohenzollern, though not of canonical age to be a bishop, was already bishop of Magdeburg and of Halberstadt. Now he aspired to be made archbishop of Mainz and primate of Germany. Were he to combine these dignities, the House of Hohenzollern would have an advantage over its rival, the House of Hapsburg. For the archbishop of Mainz was one of the seven electors of the Holy Roman Empire. But holding three such ecclesiastical offices was a violation of canon law. Further, the normal fee to the pope for installation to the see of Mainz was enormous; a previous incumbent, in his last illness, had apologized to his constituency that he would die so soon after his appointment and thus involve them in the expense of a successor. Albert would be the fourth archbishop in ten years, and Mainz was nearly bankrupt. Moreover, because of the canonical irregularities involved, he would have to pay more than the usual fee. A price of ten thousand ducats was agreed upon. Albert borrowed the money from the great banking house of Fugger in Augsburg and paid the pope in full.

To enable Albert to reimburse the Fuggers, the pope permitted an indulgence to be preached throughout his territories for eight years, half of the proceeds to go by way of Albert to the Fuggers and the other half to the pope, to build a mausoleum for the bones of Peter and Paul, the great Basilica of St.Peter. Albert made unprecedented claims for these indulgences; for example, that they would remit not only the penalties for sins but also the sins themselves and would give preferential treatment to one who sinned in the future. Those who secured indulgences on behalf of deceased relatives in purgatory need not themselves be contrite for their own sins. The Dominican Johann Tetzel, who hawked the indulgences, blithely proclaimed their power to ensure immediate release from purgatory, using the jingle:

As soon as the coin in the coffer rings,
The soul from purgatory springs.

This was too much for Martin Luther. On the eve of All Saints' Day, October 31, 1517, he posted on the door of the castle church at Wittenberg a series of propositions for debate; ever since known as the Ninety-five Theses, they were soon circulating everywhere in Germany. Luther did not know all the sordid details, but he had seen Albert's instructions to Tetzel, and these revealed quite enough. Among other points, he complained about the draining of so much money from Germany to Rome. If the pope knew of the poverty of the German people, he would prefer to see St.Peter's in ashes than that it should be built out of the blood and hide of his sheep. To this, all Germans would agree. Next, Luther claimed that the pope had no power over purgatory, but if he did, he should empty the place gratis. With this assertion many of the theologians would agree. But the final point was that the real treasury of the Church is the Gospel, which first of all brings conviction of sin, and they are damned who try to bargain with God to escape damnation. By implication, this statement denied the whole concept of the treasury of merits, for Luther had long since come to believe that no man can accumulate enough merit for himself, let alone anything extra. His critique decried not simply the abuses of indulgences, but the very idea itself.

He sent a copy of his theses to Albert of Mainz, who in turn forwarded it to Pope Leo X. That elegant dilettante at first dubbed Luther a drunken German who would soon be sober, but when his "inebriation" continued, Leo commissioned his censor of literature to draft a reply. This dignitary defended the claim of immediate release from purgatory and then moved to more fundamental assertions. The Church, said he, consists virtually in the pope and representatively in the cardinals, and he who goes counter to what the Church actually does is a heretic. Luther replied that the Church consists virtually in Christ and representatively in a Church council, but that not even a council, let alone a pope, is infallible. Now the ground had been shifted from indulgences to authority, which to this day constitutes the greatest line of division between Protestants and Roman Catholics. The latter commonly say that having rejected the authority of the Church, Luther was left only with private, subjective judgment. This Luther never admitted. For the authority of popes and councils he substituted the authority of the Scriptures, without perceiving that interpretation of the Scriptures must be to a degree individual and subjective.

Luther was a heretic according to the pope's spokesman, but to many the case did not appear so clear. There had been no definitive pronouncement about indulgences, nor—prior to the Vatican Council of 1870—were Catholics required to believe that the pope is infallible. One very crucial person in Germany was not satisfied. This was Frederick the Wise, senior member among the seven electors of the Holy Roman Empire, territorial prince of Saxony, and thus Luther's lord. He had founded the University of Wittenberg, and he was resolved that his professor should not be condemned without a proper hearing, particularly because he had the backing of the entire university. When the pope summoned Luther to Rome, Frederick intervened to secure a hearing on German soil.

This took place at Augsburg in 1518, before Cardinal Cajetan, an upright and learned theologian of the school of St. Thomas. He confronted Luther with the papal bull *Unigenitus*, issued 175 years earlier by Clement VI, which set forth the doctrine of the treasury of the merits of the saints and the power of the pope to issue indulgences drawn upon it. Luther hesitated to repudiate the bull, particularly because it had been incorporated into the canon law; but when pressed, he came out with a flat denial of the doctrine. Thereupon, the cardinal told him to leave and not return until he was ready to retract.

Luther had good reason to fear death at the stake and would have suffered it, had not the popes at the time been embroiled in politics. No better proof could be adduced for the justice of his strictures of the papacy than its slowness in disposing of him. A pope who took seriously the tenets of the Church should have given him a more summary treatment. Instead, the Church took almost four years to excommunicate the man who proved to be the most disruptive heretic in her history, because the popes were trying to manipulate the imperial election. Emperor Maximilian died early in 1519, and a successor had to be elected from among the reigning monarchs of Europe. The pope was loath to see any augmentation of power of a ruler already strong, that is, of either Francis I of France or Charles I of Spain. As a Hapsburg, Charles also controlled Austria, the Netherlands, and Naples; if in addition he were to have Bohemia and Germany, he could throw a ring around France and then put a vise on Rome. If Francis, on the other hand, were able to combine France with Germany and Bohemia, he would have such a bloc in the center of Europe that he might easily absorb the fringes, and he would dominate the papacy as France had done when the popes were at Avignon. Pope Leo X preferred a minor prince, and his choice was Frederick the Wise.

This was scarcely, then, the moment to pursue action against Frederick's protégé, although Luther's ideas were rapidly gaining adherents. In the summer of 1519, he was drawn into public debate at the great Catholic university at Leipzig with the distinguished doctor Johann Eck, professor of theology at Ingolstadt. The debate centered not on indulgences, but upon the antiquity, divine institution, and authority of the popes. Luther contended that the papacy, as it was in his day, was not over four hundred years old, that it was the creation not of God but of man, and therefore lacked authority, which resides solely in the Scriptures. Eck then drove him to admit his affinity with John Huss, the Bohemian burned for heresy by the Council of Constance. To endorse Huss was to impugn the authority of the council. One might have expected Luther's admission to have brought him also quickly to the stake. Instead, his stature increased, probably because Froben, the great publisher at Basel brought out at that very time Luther's collected Latin works. No other issue from this press was so speedily sold out, copies going not only all over Germany, but to England, France, Switzerland, and even to Spain and Rome. Luther was becoming an international figure. At home, in Germany, nationalists rallied to him as to the spokesman of their complaint against the pope for treating Germany as his "milch cow." The northern Humanists, on the other hand, saw in Luther another Johann Reuchlin, battling for freedom of scholarship. Erasmus insisted that Luther was a man of good life whose arguments should be met by reasoning rather than by brimstone.

Pope Leo delayed action against Luther for a whole year and only then issued from his hunting lodge the bull *Exsurge, Domine*, which begins: "Arise, O Lord, and judge thine own cause. . . . A wild boar has invaded thy vineyard." Luther was ordered to recant within sixty days after the bull was placed in his hands. So great was the obstruction, however, even from German bishops, that three months elapsed before the document was delivered to Luther, on the tenth day of October, 1520.

Luther himself took advantage of the delay in the prosecution to compose that summer several tracts, each more devastating than the preceding. The *Address to the Christian Nobility of the German Nation* was an appeal to the ruling class, including the emperor, of whom Luther did not yet despair, to take a hand in redressing primarily the financial and political abuses within the Church. Luther was reverting to the program of the reforming German emperors of the time before the Investiture controversy, and like them he believed that the temporal arm of Christendom had a responsibility to reform the spiritual. His claim, that temporal affairs should be handled by local churches, represented a resurgence of the particularism of the Middle Ages, against the universalism of the papacy. His graphic contrast between Christ— the poor and humble—and Antichrist—the pope, luxurious and lofty—savored of the style of Wycliffe and Huss.

But there was something in Luther's tract that went far beyond anything medieval. He proclaimed the priesthood of all believers. The medieval Church had held that the clergy, being alone priests with sacramental powers, might by giving or withholding the sacraments compel civil rulers to do the Church's bidding. Luther countered that Christian magistrates are also priests, as are all baptized Christians. Any Christian might administer the sacraments, though some are given this role as a vocation. The magistrate has another vocation, no less spiritual for all that, and should not be impeded by excommunication from administering the government, as Henry IV had been before Canossa; though, of course, a ruler, like any other Christian, might be excommunicated for immoral behavior. When Luther claimed that no one in a thousand years had so defended the secular power as he, his meaning was not that he was advocating political absolutism, but only that the state should be emancipated from clerical control.

An even more revolutionary tract written that same summer was called *The Babylonian Captivity*. It was a treatise on the sacraments—taken captive, according to Luther, by the false teaching of Rome. Luther spiritualized the sacraments by making their efficacy contingent upon the faith of the recipient, rather than operative in and of themselves (*ex opere operato*). The number of the sacraments was reduced to essentially two, baptism and the Eucharist (or three, if penance were to be included). A sacrament, he said, involves an outward sign of an invisible grace and must have been specifically instituted by Christ. On this basis, he rejected extreme unction, that is, the anointing with oil of one who is on the verge of death. He retained ordination and confirmation as rites of the Church, but not as sacraments: they had not, he claimed, been instituted by Christ. Marriage might be blessed by the Church, but it was essentially a civil matter; it was instituted by God in the Garden of Eden, not specifically for Christians, but for all peoples, including Jews and Turks, whereas a Christian sacrament must be exclusively Christian. The way was thus opened to make marriage a purely civil ceremony and to abolish the whole system of impediments based on spiritual and remote physical relationships. He reduced penance to voluntary confession of one's faults to any other Christian, even a layman. Strictly

speaking, he said, this is not the sacrament of penance. Baptism—
including that of infants—he retained as a sacrament. Finally,
there was the Eucharist, and at this point Luther touched the
keystone.

The Mass, he said, is not a repetition of the sacrifice of Christ,
which took place on Calvary once and for all. There should be no
Masses for the dead with no one present save the priest, because
the Mass is a communion of the faithful with each other; the
cup, therefore, he believed, as the Hussites before him, should be
given not only to the clergy but to the laity. The doctrine of
transubstantiation was rejected; bread and wine, said Luther, retain their substance. At the same time he believed in a real, physical presence because of the words of Christ, "This is my body."
How the elements could be Christ's body Luther did not try to
explain, other than to say that Christ is present with, in, and under
the elements. His presence is the result of no miracle worked by
the pronunciation of the words "Hoc est corpus meum" (This is
my body) at the consecration during the Mass, because Christ is
actually present everywhere, just as all matter is pervaded by the
spirit of God. What happens in the sacrament is that Christ's
presence is disclosed. This happens also in the preaching of the
Word, and the minister does no more at the altar than in the
pulpit.

When Erasmus read this tract, he said, "The breach is irreparable." Always conciliatory, undogmatic, and concerned for harmony, the great Humanist had been seeking to mediate, believing
that the doctrines of indulgences and papal infallibility were open
to discussion. But Luther's view on the Mass precluded mediation.
As a matter of fact, Erasmus did not discontinue his efforts at
mediation for another decade. He was himself torn, because he
spiritualized the Mass even more than Luther, but would not press
a private view to the point of disrupting the Church. Erasmus was
concerned for unity, Luther for truth.

When Luther's sixty-day period of grace expired, instead of
submitting to Rome, he burned the bull *Exsurge, Domine*, to-

gether with a copy of the canon law. The Church of Rome now desired that Luther be publicly excommunicated as a heretic and turned over to the secular authorities to be burned at the stake. The newly elected emperor, the Hapsburg Charles I of Spain—as emperor he became Charles V—could not act on his own authority except in his own hereditary domains. In the case of a subject of Frederick the Wise of Saxony, he required the consent of the Diet, which was to convene in January, 1521, in the city of Worms on the Rhine. The Diet was not disposed to act without giving Luther a hearing, especially since a bull of excommunication against him, signed by the pope in January, was withheld from publication until October. The delay was due to the discovery by Aleander, the papal representative at the Diet, that the bull excommunicated not only Luther but also others, including the leader of the German nationalists, Ulrich von Hutten, who was in a position to swoop upon the Diet with armed forces. In terror, Aleander sent the bull back to Rome with an urgent request for a substitute, naming Luther only. But the pope, with an eye to political repercussions, dallied. Now that a Hapsburg had been elected emperor, the pope foresaw the renewal of the old conflict between empire and papacy, and realized that Frederick the Wise might still be a useful ally. At any rate, Clement did not hasten to send a new bull with only Luther's name. The Diet thereupon declined to ban without trial one not publicly excommunicated by the Church, and Luther was summoned to come for a hearing.

The moderate Catholics of the party of Erasmus were aghast as they foresaw the tumults that would ensue if Luther were burned; they sought to avert schism and possibly war by persuading Luther to compromise on the question of the sacraments, in which case the other points in his attack might be negotiated. Before the Diet, Luther was confronted by a stack of his books and asked whether he had written them all. Had he disclaimed the tract on the sacraments, the Erasmians would have achieved their hope; but he acknowledged them all. Would he then stand by everything he had taught in his writings? Luther hesitated and asked for time to reflect. The next day, however, he came out with a ringing statement, centering not on the sacraments but on the principle of authority: "Since then Your Majesty and Your Lordships desire a simple reply, I will answer without horns and without teeth. Unless I am convicted by the Scriptures and plain reason—I do not accept the authority of popes and councils, for they have contradicted each other—my conscience is captive to the Word of God. I cannot and I will not recant anything, for to go against conscience is neither right nor safe. God help me. Amen."[3]

An attempt was then made to break Luther down in a committee meeting. He was asked whether he could not compromise on something. If he refused, there would be division, war, and insurrection. His reply was that truth is not open to negotiation. Luther, who was at that time still under a safe-conduct issued by the emperor, then left Worms.

Emperor Charles would have been willing to negotiate, for like Erasmus he treasured ancient unities and placed concord above dogmatic niceties. But, when confronted with intransigence, he could reply only with intransigence. A month later, Charles issued the Edict of Worms, placing Luther under the ban of the empire. Since the bull of excommunication was still withheld from publication, the Edict of Worms stressed the menace of his teaching to the state, asserting that his defiance of authority would be more subversive of the civil than of the ecclesiastical order. Luther replied by roundly asserting his political allegiance; in no sense did he mean, by doing this, to encourage political absolutism.

Meanwhile, Frederick the Wise, not yet convinced that Luther had been fairly heard and rightly condemned, secretly subverted the emperor's intentions by hiding Luther for nearly a year in the castle of the Wartburg. Luther took advantage of this enforced withdrawal to render one of the noblest of his contributions. In the space of three months, he translated the whole of the New Testament into a powerful German. There had been eighteen

---

[3] *Deutsche Reichstagsakten*, Jüngere Reihe (Gotha, 1893–), II, 555.

printed German Bibles before his time, but all were pedestrian. Luther's was off the press in September, 1522, and nothing did more to make the common man his own interpreter of the Scriptures.

During this time, two of Luther's colleagues at the University of Wittenberg took the lead in guiding the Reformation. The first was the twenty-five-year-old Philipp Melanchthon, a prodigy of classical learning, the grandnephew of Reuchlin. The other was Andreas Bodenstein, called (from his birthplace) Carlstadt, who had conferred on Luther the Doctor's degree. The less temperate among their followers at Wittenberg began intimidating the priests and monks with threats of violence; Melanchthon was too diffident and Carlstadt too impetuous to quell a tumult. The town council therefore asked Luther to return. The elector warned that he could not protect a man under the ban of Church and empire should he come out into the open. Luther sent word asking only that the elector not turn him over to the emperor; should the emperor come to take him, he advised Frederick not to resist. Luther came home and actually was able to live untouched for another twenty-five years, because Charles V was involved either in fighting the French or in resisting a confederation of smaller powers, which, if France were defeated, would rally to her side in order to restore the balance of power. At different times this confederation included England, Venice, the German Protestants, the Turks, and the popes.

With his return to Wittenberg in March, 1522, the second phase of Luther's career began. Hitherto, he had been the flaming prophet of rebellion. Hereafter, he was to be the harassed builder and administrator of a new Church. His first move was to calm the agitation. He pleaded that abuses, however appalling, should be corrected without violence and with discrimination. "Men can go wrong with wine and women," he said. "Shall we then prohibit wine and abolish women?" Catholic services continued in Wittenberg alongside the Lutheran until 1524, when the saying of the Catholic Mass was abolished in all the churches of the city.

At the same time, the new doctrines were spreading throughout Germany. In part they were carried by word of mouth, notably by graduates of the University of Wittenberg; but the most potent means of dissemination was the popular pamphlet—small, cheap, and pungent. More pamphlets were issued in Germany from the beginning of 1521 to the end of 1524 than in any other four years of her history, and the bulk of them dealt with the Reformation. The printers who issued these manifestoes were an intrepid breed, who risked not simply the confiscation of their pamphlets and the closing down of their presses, but also the danger of imprisonment.

Lutheranism was able to achieve the status of an established religion only in areas where it was favored by the government. In Germany, government meant either the municipal councils in the free, imperial cities; the bishops or abbots in the ecclesiastical territories; or the princes in the territorial states. The free cities took early a decisive stand for the reform, and Nuremberg, Ulm, and Strasbourg were the first among them. In the early 1520's the new teaching penetrated to the northern cities Danzig, Lübeck, and Stralsund. Sometimes the two forms of religion continued side by side longer than at Wittenberg. At Strasbourg, for some years Mass was said on the altar and Lutheranism preached from the pulpit. In the cities, laymen took a prominent lead in promoting the Reformation. At Nuremberg, the city secretary, Lazarus Spengler, published a tract favoring the reform, and Hans Sachs, a Meistersinger, celebrated Luther as "the nightingale of Wittenberg."

Among the lay princes, the first to espouse the new reforms was, of course, Frederick the Wise of Saxony; his successor, John, even more fervently, came out openly for Luther. The elector of Brandenburg, grand master of the Teutonic Knights in East Prussia, soon followed. The ecclesiastical princes held aloof from the new movement, with the exception of the archbishop of Cologne, who toyed with the prospect of changing over, only to reject it in the end. By 1529, the Protestant territories were Saxony, Hesse,

Brandenburg, Anhalt, and Lüneburg. The Palatinate and Württemberg came somewhat later. The princes in these areas did not
impose Lutheranism upon their subjects, but called in Lutheran
ministers to instruct the people. Where the government was hostile, the evangelical cause made slight headway, as in Bavaria.
But, if one branch of the government opposed another, Protestantism could be insinuated, as in the Netherlands, where the local
authorities resisted the Spanish overlords, and in Austria, where
the nobility opposed the crown. Among the national states, Denmark came first; Lutheran ministers were invited there in the early
1520's. Denmark and her dependency, Norway, were not officially
Protestant till 1536. Sweden moved slowly toward Protestantism,
and Finland and Livonia also became Lutheran.

But along with the gains in the cities and territorial states, there
were disappointments, particularly with the fact that, on the
whole, the liberal Catholic reformers did not join the Lutherans.
Between 1524 and 1526, Luther and Erasmus aired their differences in a series of pamphlets. While insisting all along that Luther, who accepted the Apostles' Creed, was no heretic, Erasmus
at the same time set forth fundamental disagreements. The most
basic concerned the question whether man can cooperate with
God in achieving his own salvation. Erasmus believed that man
can do a little something. God supplies the power, which man can
either neglect or utilize, and thereby cooperate with God.

Luther, on the other hand, felt that man can contribute nothing
toward his own salvation, for, although one deed is better than
another, none is good enough to establish a claim on God. Salvation depends solely on the acceptance of God's grace through
faith. As for authority in religion, Luther appealed to the Scriptures. Erasmus relied ultimately on the authority of the Church.
The Scriptures, he pointed out, are frequently obscure; how could
Luther be certain of his interpretation? Through inspiration of the
Spirit, Luther answered. Erasmus inquired how he received the
Spirit, and Luther said through the Scriptures. Erasmus called this
going round in a circle. Luther considered it a valid paradox.

Erasmus saw correctly that Luther's principle would lead to private interpretation, whereas Luther supposed that the Spirit would lead all responsive hearts to a common judgment. Yet, the difference between the two was even deeper than Erasmus perceived. Luther felt that Erasmus took religion too casually and was totally devoid of the sense of wonder. Erasmus felt that the cause of true piety could hardly be advanced by disrupting the Church.

The disapprobation of Erasmus infuriated Luther, though he congratulated his critic for penetrating to the core of the controversy with Rome: it was not primarily about morals or money but about man and his relation to God. Much more disquieting to Luther, as he took up the manifold tasks of building his new Church, was the development, within his own circle, of viewpoints more extreme than his own. No blow from the papacy, he said, ever hurt so much as this. To his dismay, he found himself in the middle between the Catholics to the right and the more extreme Protestant radicals to the left.

The first challenger was his old colleague Carlstadt, who interpreted the doctrine of the priesthood of all believers to mean that ministers should be laymen with no title of doctor—he himself desired to be called simply *Bruder Andreas*—without special dress and without a stipend, supporting themselves by manual labor. In addition to being a pastor, he took a farm. Such egalitarianism appeared to Luther to be an evasion of pastoral labors. "Good God," he ejaculated, "what would I not give to get away from the vexations of a parish and look on the marvelous faces of animals!"[4] Even more objectionable was Carlstadt's rejection of church music and of religious images (even those of Christ) as distractions, and his interpretation of the Lord's Supper as purely spiritual. A single concept unites these three points: disparagement of things physical as an aid to devotion. For Luther, spirit and flesh were never to be disjoined; his piety was aided by the sight of the crucifix, the sound of the anthems, and the partaking of the body of Christ upon the altar.

[4] Martin Luther, *Werke* (Weimar, 1883–1960), XLII, 158.

In consequence, Lutheranism retained the arts in the service of religion. But there was no innovation in architecture or in sculpture and painting within the churches, because the Catholic edifices were taken over. The minor arts became the expression of individual piety, as in the case of Rembrandt, rather than aids to public worship. The reform of the liturgy, however, gave abundant scope for creativity in music.

Meanwhile, as Luther was seeking to curb the excesses of some of his followers and laboring to give ecclesiastical form to the doctrines of the Reformation, all Germany was shaken by the revolution known to history as the Peasants' War. It was not, in its origins, a religious struggle, though the Reformation with its shaking of the existing order was contributory. Rather, the causes of the war were social and economic. Long before Luther broke with the Church of Rome, the peasants had been seeking to throw off the chains of feudalism. In opposing their demands, the princes had sought to introduce the principles of Roman law, which deprived the masses of access to communal woods, waters, and meadows. The resulting revolt, which began in the Black Forest in June, 1524, spread north, east, and west within a year and came to involve two-thirds of Germany.

Luther sanctioned many of the peasants' demands but did not approve of violence to achieve them. Like Augustine, he said that the common man must never take the sword, because the use of force by individuals on their own behalf results in anarchy and can never vindicate justice. Luther issued a tract excoriating the lords for their extortion but pleading with the peasants to exercise patience. Instead, they cut loose and began ravaging the land, pillaging, plundering, and guzzling down the wine of the monasteries. Frederick the Wise was of a mind to do nothing and leave the outcome to God. Luther told him that as a prince he was obligated to suppress disorder and came out with a second pamphlet in which he exhorted the rulers to "smite, slay, stab, and kill." Unfortunately, this tract appeared only after the peasants had been defeated and were being butchered. Thereupon, Luther came out with a third tract in which he declared that the devils, having left the peasants, had not returned to hell but, instead, had entered the nobles.

The claim has been made that the peasants, disgruntled by Luther's stand, forsook his Church, and that Lutheranism in consequence became a middle-class movement. This was certainly not true in Wittenberg, where to the end of Luther's day his congregation had manure on their boots. Lutheranism, where established, retained its hold on the populace until the defection of industrial workers in modern times. The chief effect of the peasant defeat was an increase in the power of the territorial princes in all areas, including the affairs of the Church.

In view of such disorders, the need was acutely felt for the introduction of some system into the church life of electoral Saxony. When Luther returned from the Wartburg in 1522, the town council was handling affairs in Wittenberg, but as the Reformation came to involve all Saxony, no one was in a position to stabilize the reform save the elector himself, now no longer Frederick the Wise who died in 1525, but his nephew, John Frederick, who was much more decisively committed to the innovations. Luther believed that the civil government, though it has no right to impede the Gospel, is nevertheless responsible for the maintenance of the true faith and, since the Elector was a devout believer, why should he not act as interim bishop in the emergency? John Frederick appointed "visitors," some of them laymen, some clerics, to investigate all the parishes in Saxony. Many priests, deplorably ignorant and immoral, were deposed; those who were reputable but still committed to the old Church were given instruction. Only gradually, therefore, did the territory become uniformly Protestant. Unfortunately, the system of state visitation became institutionalized; the appointment and removal of ministers became a government function, and the ministers became dependent on the state for their salaries, paid from the income of the confiscated properties of the Catholic Church. Under such circumstances, Luther's dictum that the minister should be the mentor of the magistrate became unrealistic.

For the newly constituted churches, Luther provided an immense body of aids for religious instruction and worship. There were two catechisms, one for children and one for adults, based on the Ten Commandments, the Apostles' Creed, and the Lord's Prayer. Luther issued two hymn books, writing the words for over half a dozen of the hymns himself and collaborating with the Wittenberg organist on the composition of the tunes. Luther is believed to have provided both the words and the music for the hymn "A Mighty Fortress is our God." He issued a body of sermons for the Christian year as models for the ministers and twice revised the liturgy, once in Latin and again in German. The latter version greatly amplified the time devoted to instructing the congregation as to the meaning of their worship.

One other great departure from Catholic teaching and practice was inaugurated by Luther after his return to Wittenberg: the abolition of monastic vows and obligatory clerical celibacy. While still at the Wartburg, he had persuaded himself from the Scriptures that monastic vows were not ordained by Christ and therefore were not binding. In the Middle Ages, the term vocation was applied only to the callings of priests, monks and nuns, but in Luther's view every occupation was a calling, since all Christians are priests. This view elevated not only the magistrate, but the family man, the wife and the mother as well as the maid. The discontinuance of mendicant monasticism made poverty either a misfortune or a crime, never a virtue, or a way of salvation. The ordinances of the Protestant towns forbade begging: those who could, should work, those who could not, should be supported by the community.

The monks and nuns who in consequence now began leaving their monasteries and convents in large numbers were, said Luther, free to marry, but he was of no mind to give them an example. "They'll never force a wife on me," he said, but in 1525 he was faced with a dilemma. A whole nunnery had escaped in a cart used to transport empty herring barrels and had come to Wittenberg. "A wagonload of vestal virgins has just come to town," a contemporary said, "God give them husbands lest worse befall."[5] Luther undertook to place them in homes, until only one remained unplaced, Katharina von Bora. She intimated that she would consider Luther. He reasoned that marriage would please his father and displease the pope; moreover, since Christ would come soon, there might never be another opportunity. He married and thereby established the archetype of the Protestant family parsonage, which has given so many eminent sons to Church, state, and school. Luther did not combine romance with matrimony—he married out of a sense of duty, but he became tenderly affectionate toward his *Herr Käthe* (Lord Katie).

By 1530, Lutheranism had taken on definitive shape and had achieved considerable territorial expansion, but for a long time its hold was precarious. The emperor demanded the enforcement of the Edict of Worms. But he was in Spain. The Diet of Nuremberg had decreed in 1524 that the Edict should be enforced, "in so far as might be possible." The Diet of Speyer, in 1526, left the question of enforcement to each ruler, "as he would have to answer to God and the emperor." But the Diet, assembled at Speyer in 1529, took stronger action. Until the meeting of a general council, Lutheranism might be tolerated where it could not be suppressed without tumult; but Catholic minorities must be allowed in Lutheran areas, whereas Lutheran minorities would not be tolerated in Catholic districts. The Lutheran princes protested and thereupon were called Protestants.

The next year, 1530, the emperor was able to come to Germany for the meeting of the Diet of Augsburg. He was resolved to try conciliation and then, if need be, coercion. The Lutherans presented as their statement of faith the Augsburg Confession, drafted by Melanchthon, who headed the theologians, since Lu-

[5] Beatus Rhenanus, *Briefwechsel*, eds. A. Horowitz and K. Hartfelder (Leipzig, 1886), p. 319.

ther, being under the ban, could not attend. The Confession was presented by the princes who stood to lose their titles, lands, and lives. It stressed the congruence of Lutheranism with Catholicism but yielded nothing on justification solely by faith and the denial of transubstantiation. The Confession was unacceptable to the Diet, and the emperor then gave the reformers until the following April to return to their old faith.

Several of the Lutheran princes and a number of the free cities thereupon organized at Schmalkalden a league for mutual defense. Faced by a new threat from the Turks, the emperor agreed to a truce with the league. In the years that followed, Lutheranism spread. By 1555, the Protestants were in a position to reach a settlement with the emperor, whereby territories adhering to the Augsburg Confession in 1552 were granted toleration. Catholic territories as such might not become Lutheran thereafter, but any of their subjects who embraced the new faith might emigrate without loss of goods, and of course the same *ius emigrandi* was enjoyed by Catholic minorities in Lutheran lands. By this arrangement, Lutheranism acquired a legal status within the framework of the empire.

Zwingli

Concurrent with the expansion of Lutheranism in Germany and to the north, another variety of Protestantism arose in German Switzerland. Ulrich Zwingli, its leader, was less indebted to Luther than to Erasmus, whose spiritualizing of the sacraments, the liturgy and the Church itself became more subversive of institutional Catholicism once the authority of the Church was rejected and its unity broken.

Zwingli was a Swiss Humanist. He became vicar of the cathedral at Zurich in 1519 and introduced there the Reformation by announcing that he would preach on the entire Gospel of Matthew, rather than on the excerpts designated in the liturgy of the ecclesiastical year; further, he would translate on the spot from the Greek. An auditor said he felt as if he were being pulled by the very hair of his head when he heard from the Word of God passages neglected for over a thousand years.

Zwingli was in some respects more bound to the text of the Scriptures than Luther. He regarded the Bible not simply as a proclamation of salvation, but also as a pattern for church organization, whereas for Luther polity and liturgy were nonessential and open to variety. Luther would also allow whatever the Bible did not prohibit, whereas Zwingli would reject whatever the Bible did not enjoin. This meant a much more drastic stripping away of all the remnants of Romanism. Luther would reject only that which conflicted directly or by implication with the gospel of Paul. Zwingli, even more than Erasmus, desired to restore the pattern and even the constitution of the primitive Church.

Strictly speaking, this should have entailed the separation of Church and state, which were obviously not united in the days of the apostles. But Zwingli argued that, after the state had become Christian, the Church was not obligated to behave as it had done in the first century, when the state was pagan. In a truly Christian community, Church and state could collaborate. At this point, Zwingli simply took over the pattern long prevalent in Swiss cities and elsewhere, whereby town councils exercised supervision over the morals and manners of cloisters and churches. To regard the state as an agency for registering the will of a Christian community was the more plausible in the Swiss city-republics, where important decisions in religious matters were taken only after a town meeting in which the populace could voice its opinions.

First of all, Zwingli desired to implement the reform of the Mass. Like Luther, he believed that there should be no private Masses for the dead and that the liturgy should include no adoration of the Host, no language of sacrifice, no withholding of the cup from the laity. Like Luther, he rejected also the authority of the pope, the invocation of saints, and clerical celibacy. Beyond that, Zwingli would also abolish fast days, remove images, and discontinue church music. At the cathedral in Zurich, the images were removed and the walls whitewashed. Happily, Zwingli did not feel called upon to smash the stained-glass windows. The organ was dismantled, not because Zwingli objected to music as such—he was in fact an accomplished musician—but because he felt God should be worshiped only in spirit and without sensory aids. He interpreted the sacrament of the Lord's Supper in particular as commemorative and spiritual. Luther, in his conflict with Carlstadt at Wittenberg, had already championed art, music, and the physical presence of Christ on the altar. It was Zwingli rather than Carlstadt who was to transmit the rejection of all three to English Puritanism.

But with regard to the concept of the Church, Luther and Zwingli were distinctly at odds. For Luther the true Church was so spiritual and intangible that it could not be identified with any particular organization. The Church, he said, consists of the elect, but the elect are known only to God. Zwingli, on the other hand, believed that for practical purposes the elect can be identified by their public adherence to the true faith, which is witnessed by their taking Communion in the presence of the congregation. The Lord's Supper thus symbolized the individual Christian's unity not only with God but with the whole Christian community. The children of those who made this public profession could be hopefully regarded as of the elect and might be baptized, because infant baptism in Christianity replaced circumcision, which in ancient Israel had designated a child as belonging to the community of the seed of Abraham.

For Zwingli, the reference to the Old Testament was more than an analogy, because he regarded the Christian Church as the new Israel of God, its people a holy people, the successors to the chosen people of old. Society was a theocracy in which Church, state, and all the people should submit to the will of God as set forth in the Bible—not only the New Testament but also the Old, in which the holy community should find the patterns for its social structure. The prophet should guide the king; the king should support the cultus and cast out the ungodly.

Zwingli's system was well suited to the city of Zurich, where, as already noted, the representative government directed the affairs of the Church. Since few non-adherents remained in the city, the populace might more plausibly be identified with the elect. Some of the other Swiss cantons soon followed her lead by embracing the evangelical faith, notably Bern, Basel, Schaffhausen, Glarus, and St.Gall. But the original cantons of the Swiss Confederation —Uri, Schwyz, and Zug, along with Lucerne and Unterwalden —were against the new ideas and remained loyal to the Catholic Church. Preparations were made for war, and political alliances were sought that might easily have disrupted the entire confederation, because Zwingli hoped for a military league, not only with France and Savoy, but also with the German Lutherans. This notion was absolutely abhorrent to Luther, who would use no force to defend the Gospel and who disagreed sharply with Zwingli on theological grounds, especially on the interpretation of the Eucharist. At the same time, the Catholic cantons looked to the traditional enemy, the House of Hapsburg, for help. The result was the Wars of Kappel in 1529 and 1531. In the second, Zwingli, no longer an Erasmian pacifist but a militant crusader, fell dead on the field of battle. Luther saw in his death the manifest evidence of the wrath of God against a minister wielding the sword.

The Second Peace of Kappel allowed Protestantism to remain where it was already established, but permitted no further expansion; Protestant minorities in Catholic cantons were not to be tolerated. This was in 1531, more than twenty years before the Peace of Augsburg. Switzerland was thus the first land after Bohemia to countenance religious pluralism. The basis, as later at Augsburg, was territorial.

Anabaptists

Within Zwingli's circle arose another type of radical reformation which in time came to be known as Anabaptism (that is, rebaptism). Its adherents called themselves simply Baptists, because in their eyes infant baptism was no baptism at all, but merely a "dipping in the Romish bath"; the only real baptism was adult baptism. But adult baptism was not at first the point of division, nor was it ever more than an outward sign of a new concept of Church, state, and society. These radicals believed that the Church is a voluntary society of convinced believers, separate from the state, and that where religion is concerned no man's assent should be won by force.

Although Anabaptism has sometimes been interpreted as the cult of the disinherited, the first leaders in the movement were men of substance, who were disinherited because they became Anabaptists. Conrad Grebel and Felix Manz were men of standing in Zurich. Grebel was a patrician, humanistically educated, exposed to the views of Erasmus, quite able to debate on equal terms with Zwingli. Others of similar stamp began to meet with Grebel to search the Scriptures and thereby recover the pattern of the primitive Church. They discovered that the early Christian churches were not financially supported by tithes collected by the state, but rather by the voluntary contributions of the believers. The demands of the peasants, then, for the abolition of tithes did have a biblical warrant as well as economic justification.

Next arose a more fundamental question: Should the reform of the Church wait for the consent of the magistrate? Zwingli wished to win all Zurich by persuasion and believed that the magistrate, though implementing reform, should await a mandate from the people. For two years Protestant and Catholic forms of worship continued in Zurich side by side. Zwingli was willing to be provisionally associated with such a half-and-half arrangement. But the radical Anabaptists objected that no such compromise was tolerable. Of course, the Mass was not to be forcibly suppressed, but those who did not believe in it should have no sort of affiliation with those who did and should in no way feel themselves bound to wait for the magistrate to register the mind of the community, but should set up a separate conventicle of true believers instead.

The radicals complained further that the conduct of those who confessed the reformed faith fell far short of New Testament standards. Neither Zwingli nor Luther denied this—Luther sometimes called his congregation "Wittenberg swine"—but neither of the two wished to use the ban so drastically as to reduce the Church to a handful of saints. This was precisely what the radicals demanded. The unworthy must be cast out, the tepid and doubting must never be forced to come in. Then came the point that focused the issue: The radicals insisted that the Church cannot admit infants, for to make baptism in infancy the mark of membership in a Christian society is to fill the Church with more tares than wheat. Infants should not be baptized. Nor should any adult be laved in the waters of baptism whose life is still bogged in the mire; first must come conversion and moral regeneration and only thereafter the sign of baptism. There is no sense, said one of the radicals, in washing cabbages while they are still in the dirt.

The little separatist congregation, which began to assume shape, grew even more radical in its rejection of the state as a non-Christian institution. Of course, the Apostle Paul had said that rulers are ordained by God to punish sinners, which means that if there were no sinners there would be no need for rulers. But, since there are sinners, let the sinners be the rulers and punish the other sinners. The saints should have no part in all this. Nor should they take up the sword, either in war or in the enforcement of civil justice.

Such were the views of the Anabaptists. They were for the most part pacifists, who took literally both the injunction of the Sermon on the Mount not to resist evil and the command to take no oath. Their position resembled that of the earlier Waldenses and appeared quite as subversive of the whole structure of society. Their first congregation was formed in the little town of Zollikon, a suburb of Zurich.

The first move of the Zurich authorities was to banish the Anabaptists, but this only spread the infection into the Grisons and beyond. Then a number of the sectaries were imprisoned. Grebel died of the plague. The other principal leader, Felix Manz, was drowned, in mockery of adult baptism, in January, 1527. The town council of Zurich justified the execution on the ground that Anabaptist beliefs were subversive of the state. Legal ground for the action was found in the Code of Justinian, which visited the penalty of death on the Donatists for rebaptizing the Catholics who joined their ranks.

The Zurichers would have done well to recall that the blood of the martyrs is seed. Anabaptist emissaries, both men and women, spread over the land, evangelizing the populace on the roads and in the homes. Conventicles sprang up in other cantons, and the movement shot its tendrils into northern Germany and down the Rhine into the Low Countries, where the local authorities obstructed the efforts of Spain to impose a pattern of rigid orthodoxy. The people of the Netherlands were hospitable to Anabaptism because its simple piety resembled in a measure that of the Brethern of the Common Life. The dissemination of Anabaptism was so broad that both Catholics and Lutherans feared displacement of the established churches.

Fear leads to repression. The Catholics burned, the Protestants drowned the Anabaptists. At the Diet of Speyer, in 1529, both Catholics and Lutherans agreed to subject them to the death penalty throughout the Holy Roman Empire. Luther was slower than others in giving his consent; but, by 1531, his fear of anarchy led him to agree to the death penalty, not for heresy, but for blasphemy and sedition. He considered pacifism to be sedition because it would destroy the police power of the state. The only Protestant ruler who refused to apply the penalty of death to the Anabaptists was Philip of Hesse. He took arms to defend Lutheranism, as

Luther would not, but would kill no man because of his faith.

For the first decade, the Anabaptists were sustained by a magnificent hope: the Lord Jesus was coming. The kingdom of Antichrist would fall, the new Jerusalem would descend, and the saints would reign. The more the pseudo-Christians raged, the more was their doom sure. Martyrdom was the way the Master had trod, and the saints must tread it too. As Christ had been exalted to the right hand of God, even so would the true Church inherit the kingdoms of the world. But, as more and more of the saner leaders were executed, the less balanced spirits came to the fore, announcing themselves as Elijahs, Enochs, or Davids returned to earth to usher in the speedy return of Christ. Some forsook their habitual pacifism and clamored for the slaughter of the ungodly. One group introduced polygamy in imitation of Abraham, Isaac, and Jacob.

The effects of the extravagances were twofold: increased persecution by their opponents and, on their own part, a recoil toward sobriety. Three groups emerged. The Swiss Anabaptists survived, as the Waldenses had done, by retreating to the mountains. From this group came the Amish, who established American colonies in Pennsylvania and the Midwest. In Holland, the great leader was Menno Simons, whose followers, the Mennonites, are to be found in Russia and in North and South America, as well as in Holland. Menno repudiated polygamy, revolution, private inspiration through dreams and visions, and the setting of dates for the coming of the Lord. His was the simple Christianity of the Sermon on the Mount, which laid minimal emphasis upon theology, stressed discipline in deportment, and insisted upon separation of the Church from the state.

A third branch of the Anabaptists was called Hutterite, after Jacob Hutter, whose followers established colonies of refugees in Moravia and Transylvania, where the old feudal lords provided an asylum against the encroachments of the emperor. Anabaptists have been able to survive for so long only by accommodating themselves to the surrounding culture—as the Dutch Mennonites have modified their pacifism—or by isolating themselves in more or less remote communities. They have had intrareligious difficulties; those who are superb in defying tyrants often find it hard to agree with one another. A German Anabaptist, visiting the Hutterite colonies in Moravia, found the temper so divisive that he said he could get along more easily with Turks and papists. Yet, the lesson of cohesion was finally learned, and these communities have displayed an amazing capacity to hold their children and preserve their identity to this day.

John Calvin

If Lutheranism, Zwinglianism, and Anabaptism are considered three varieties of Protestantism, then Calvinism may be accounted a fourth, though Zwinglianism and Calvinism are commonly grouped together and called the Reformed Churches. Calvinism emerged only after Lutheranism and Zwinglianism had grown rigid in the struggle with the radicals. John Calvin, a French theologian and reformer who left the Catholic Church in 1533 at the age of twenty-four, provided for Protestantism at this stage an integrated doctrinal system. His book, *The Institutes of the Christian Religion*, appeared in 1536 in Basel. Incipient Protestantism had been tolerated in his native France for a time. Marguerite of Navarre, sister of King Francis I, inclined to the new ideas, and her daughter, Jeanne d'Albret, was an avowed Protestant. Francis himself vacillated in his policy toward the innovators—depending on whether he desired an alliance with the pope, the Turks, or the German Protestants—but in 1534 he was deeply angered by the publication of the placards, vitriolic posters defaming the Mass. Even the Humanists were alienated by such an indecorous stab at the piety of the ages. The resulting repressions scattered the reformers, and precipitated Calvin's flight terminating in Basel.

Calvin's *Institutes* begin not with justification by faith, but with the knowledge of God. Calvin was in the tradition of those scholastics who declined to make faith and knowledge mutually exclusive, insisting rather that they are simply different modes of apprehension. Faith, Calvin said, may be described as conviction, assurance, certitude. His point was that the heathen philosophers, for all their genius, were blinder than bats and moles, whereas Christians relying on revelation could enjoy unshakable confidence. The God in whom they believe is the creator, sustainer, and sovereign ruler of the universe, seated in majesty, too high and too holy to share his divinity with man.

Calvin had no use for the view of the Christian Neoplatonists, or of any of the mystics, that man can be united with God. The chief end of man, according to Calvin, is not to be united with God, but to bow before his inscrutable decrees and to fulfill his evident commands. This, rather than man's own personal salvation, should be his concern. On that score, there is absolutely nothing that man can do, because God, out of time, has already decreed who should be saved and who damned. Calvin's theory of predestination was more sharply drawn than that of Luther or Zwingli, because Calvin confronted boldly not only election but also damnation. Since the fall of Adam, he said, all men have deserved damnation. God punishes the majority according to their deserts to illustrate his justice, but some he saves according to his good pleasure in order to manifest his grace. Calvin knew this decree to be frightful, but there it was.[6] How a good God can do this we do not understand, but we are not to complain or to worry about our salvation.

Yet, Calvin and his early followers felt reasonably sure of their salvation. He posited three tests: profession of the true faith, an upright life, and attendance upon the sacrament of the Lord's Supper. He who could meet these fairly tangible requirements could assume that he was one of the elect. Luther had denied that there were any such tests, and in consequence he could not form a community of the elect. For Zwingli, the elect could be identified

---

[6] LATIN: *Decretum quidem horribile, fateor.* FRENCH: *Je confesse que ce decret nous doit epouventer.* See J. Calvin, *Institutes*, III, xxiii, 7.

by their profession of faith, and the same was true for Calvin. The anabaptists added purity of life to the tests, as did Calvin also. He did not demand, as did the New England Puritans in later years, anything so thoroughly subjective as the rebirth of the spirit.[7] To the tests of Zwingli and the Anabaptists, he added a love of the sacrament of the Lord's Supper, his theory of this sacrament lying between the views of Luther and Zwingli. Calvin believed in the real, though not physical, presence of Christ at the celebration of the Lord's Supper; for him, the bread and the wine were signs in which Christ was present.

By these tests, a company of the elect could be recognized and assembled to constitute a holy commonwealth. For this society, God had a great work to be achieved on earth—the establishment of the kingdom of God, which, said Calvin, is the Church restored; God would allow time for its realization. When Calvin talked about man's destiny, commonly he had in mind the Last Judgment rather than he second coming of Christ. The apocalyptic hope, lively for Luther, and so cardinal for many of the Anabaptists, was attenuated by Calvin through an indefinite extension. Just as Augustine contributed to the realization of the churchly theocracy in the Middle Ages by dropping the primitive Christian hopes of a speedy denouement, so Calvin opened the way for a social gospel to redeem the fabric of society.

To this end, the Calvinists expended colossal energies in the ruling of cities, the converting of kingdoms, the beheading of a king, and the taming of wildernesses. Because they felt themselves to be the elect of God, they were fearless and indomitable. They worked with fury because they knew that, although history is long, life is short. For them, time became a precious commodity.

Calvinism has been credited with giving a great impetus to the spirit of capitalism because, more than Lutheranism, it induced men to work in their callings for the glory of God—not simply diligently, but relentlessly. Business was not disparaged but was regarded as one of the callings, legitimate alike for workers and

[7] Edmund Sears Morgan, Visible Saints (New York, 1963).

for entrepreneurs. Further, Calvinism had an ascetic aspect, which eschewed the use of profit for pleasure and could then make use of it only for philanthropy or so as to build up the business. Calvinism was certainly more hospitable to trade and investment than Lutheranism. Luther lived in a peasant community and had the economic outlook of a peasant. Geneva, the seat of Calvinism, was on the Rhone River and had close trade connections with southern France. Further, Calvin was confronted with the problem of finding maintenance for thousands of refugees with funds to invest. However, he imposed the same restrictions as Luther and Aquinas and disparaged the pursuit of gain. Yet, as in the case of medieval monasticism, the industry and thrift of his followers produced wealth and eventually made of Calvinists a prosperous middle class.

Calvin's program for a holy commonwealth found its realization in Geneva. At the moment, the city had just thrown off the authority of the bishop and the duke of Savoy with the help of Protestant Bern, but was not yet a member of the Swiss Confederation. Evangelical ministers came in from France, particularly William Farel, who had the populace on the verge of civil war when the magistrates recognized the reform. For all his forcefulness, Farel felt unequal to completing the reform of the city and, when young Calvin was passing through Geneva, impressed him into service by threats of hell if he declined. Calvin accepted.

His theory of the relations of Church and state soon led to friction. He believed in a Christian community where Church, state, and citizenry were equally dedicated to the glory of God. They should sustain each other, but their functions were not identical. The Church was to be independent and was to determine the forms of the liturgy and, above all else, should control excommunication. This demand was resisted by the magistrates, and Calvin, because of his insistence, was briefly banished from Geneva. He was recalled, and after another tussle in 1553 the point was definitely conceded that ecclesiastical discipline is the province of the Church. Thus, Calvinism became more independent of the state than Lutheranism or Zwinglianism. Jurisdiction over heresy, however, remained with the magistrates. Calvin won, partly because the constituency came to be almost as select as that of a monastery. The Catholics left the city. Thousands of refugees who came to Geneva because of their religious sympathies were made citizens and stoutly supported Calvin. Those banned from the Church, if not reconciled after a period, were banished from the city. Thus Calvin succeeded in uniting the idea of a Church as coterminous with the community and of a Church as a voluntary society of visible saints.

Calvin gave a great stimulus to education by treating teachers as members of the ministry. An academy was founded in Geneva. Calvin's views on arts and music were more moderate than Zwingli's. He would allow a cross but not a crucifix and permitted the singing of the Psalms in church, but no other music. Psalm-singing actually became a distinctive feature of Calvinist services in France, Scotland, and New England.

Calvinism was to become the most international form of Protestantism. The Calvinists refused to respect the previously established territorial principle in religion, and like the Anabaptists they insinuated themselves wherever they could, thus spreading into France, the Netherlands, England, Scotland, New England, Lithuania, Poland, and Hungary. In these countries, the Genevan pattern of Church, state, and community could not be reproduced, because Calvinism was at first a minority movement. Even later, when it became dominant, as in Scotland, there was never such a purging of the populace nor such a control over its behavior as there was at Geneva, where the Consistory governed with relentless rigor.

Henry VIII

Calvinism was ultimately to exert a great influence in England, where the Reformation began in 1534, two years prior to the appearance of the *Institutes*. The English Reformation is the supreme example of the fusion of nationalism and religious upheaval. It could never have happened if the Tudors had not terminated the wars of succession and established political absolutism. The quarrel with Rome was not over doctrine and not primarily over morality or finances, but over a point at which religion impinged upon politics, the matter of a royal marriage. As a sacrament of the Church, marriage was subject to ecclesiastical jurisdiction; but royal marriages were affairs of state, emphatically so because kings were expected to ensure the succession by producing progeny.

England required a male heir of King Henry VIII. But after sixteen years of marriage to his first wife, Queen Catherine, only one child survived—and a girl at that, the Princess Mary. The simplest solution would have been to annul the marriage and leave Henry free to marry another woman. There appeared to be good grounds for an annulment. Catherine had been first the wife of Henry's elder brother Arthur, and her subsequent marriage to Henry had violated the provision in Leviticus forbidding a union with a deceased husband's brother. Pope Julius II had given a dispensation to cover the irregularity. That dispensation could now be declared invalid as contravening the law of God, the marriage could be annulled, and Henry would be free to take another queen.

Henry took his case before the pope, Clement VII, without expectation of difficulties, since two of his sisters had been able to secure annulments. One may well suppose that the matter would have been speedily settled had there not been so many political angles. Catherine was a Spanish princess, the daughter of Ferdinand and Isabella and the aunt of the emperor, Charles V, who intervened on her behalf. However, Charles did not wish to push the case too strenuously, for trouble with England would provide France with advantages. The pope feared to offend the emperor, whose troops had sacked Rome in 1527 and captured the pope. On the other hand, if England were not obliged, she might renounce papal obedience. The pope instructed his representative to stall to the uttermost, and the case dragged on for four years. Catherine maintained that her marriage with Arthur had not been consummated and that there had never been any impediment to her marriage with Henry. If only she had been willing to concede Henry's point and retire on a pension, she might have saved the unity of the Catholic Church in England, but like Luther she would not compromise in the realm of truth.

Henry decided that what he could not get from the pope he could and would secure from the archbishop of Canterbury, Thomas Cranmer, who had been elevated to the primacy because he believed so unreservedly in the royal supremacy. Therefore, in 1534, Henry broke with the papacy and set up an independent national English Church, the *Ecclesia Anglicana*, with the king as the supreme head. The king did not become a priest, nor did he directly administer the church, but Cranmer declared that the king held the two keys, both temporal and spiritual, in a Christian society.

Significantly, Henry ordered the translation into English of the tract of Marsilius of Padua, which proposed that all the goods of the Church should be vested in the state. This doctrine, appropriated earlier by Wycliffe, had served to justify the confiscation of Church goods by John of Gaunt. It could serve equally well to justify the suppression of the monasteries by Henry VIII. Cardinal Thomas Wolsey, Henry's minister, had suppressed a number even earlier, in order to use their revenues to build colleges. Henry pursued this example piecemeal for five years until every monastic house in England had been dissolved. Whenever the time came to confiscate the glebes of a monastic house, its monks were charged with gross immorality and then were pensioned as if they had been altogether reputable. The monasteries were stripped and their goods sold at auction. Many a chalice turned up as a tankard in an ale house. Resentment was acute in the north, where feudal lords resisted interference in local affairs; a brief rebellion occurred there, but it was speedily quelled. However, there was amazingly little opposition to Henry's program on the part of the clergy, the monks, and the laity. A few, but only a very few, suffered death for their refusal to acknowledge Henry as the head of the Church of England: St.Thomas More, Bishop John Fisher, and several of the Carthusians.

A Catholic historian has said there never has been a major revolution carried through with so little bloodshed. One reason was that in the two hundred years prior to the Reformation, the English monasteries had been distinguished only for mediocrity. Another reason was undoubtedly the popularity of the Tudor monarchy, though another may have been the assumption that the changes would not last. In the Middle Ages, kings demanded of the pope more than they expected to get, weathered excommunication for a few years, and then submitted on terms which gave them most of that which they desired. The bishops who acknowledged Henry as the supreme head may have expected him to return before long to obedience to the papacy.

Under Henry, only one change affected the practice of religion: the Bible was introduced in an English translation into all the churches. In 1539, Henry commissioned Bishop Miles Coverdale to produce such a version. For the most part, he availed himself of an earlier translation, tinged with Protestantism, the work of William Tyndale; it had been printed on the Continent and for some time had been smuggled into England.

Toward the end of his reign, Henry pursued a religious policy midway between Catholicism and Protestantism. After his death in 1547, the duke of Somerset, regent for Henry's young son Edward VI, sought to introduce a more radical type of Protestantism, including the Mass in English. Somerset was unseated by Warwick, the future duke of Northumberland. The English Reformation moved toward Lutheranism, then toward Zwinglianism, and again toward Calvinism.

The great achievement of this period was the revision and translation of the liturgy into the English tongue, the work of Archbishop Cranmer, who was pre-eminently qualified for the task.

The stately cadences of the Book of Common Prayer, which he compiled, have for centuries carried the petitions of Englishmen to the throne of grace, and more than all else have endeared the Church of England to the people of England. Cranmer was assisted by a number of eminent Protestant refugees from the Continent with Zwinglian or Calvinist leanings. Their influence can be seen in the development from the first to the second Book of Common Prayer issued under Edward. The first, in the liturgy for the Eucharist, has the form: "The body of our Lord Jesus Christ which was given for thee, preserve thy body and soul unto everlasting life." This formula could be Lutheran or even Catholic. The second book read, instead: "Take this and eat, in remembrance that Christ died for thee, and feed on him in thy heart by faith and by thanksgiving." This savors of Zwinglianism. So also does the frequent substitution in the second book of the word "minister" for priest and "God's board" for altar.

When Edward died in 1553, the succession went to his half-sister Mary Tudor, the daughter of Catherine of Aragon, who all along had refused to give up the Mass. In July, 1554, she was married to her cousin Philip of Spain, the son of Emperor Charles. They had minted a coin in 1555 with the faces closely adjacent, giving rise to the jingle,

> Amorous, fond, and billing,
> Like Philip and Mary on a shilling.[8]

Mary brought England into conformity with Rome. One marvels that the English, if they loved Rome, should have permitted the Protestant Reformation, and if they loved the Protestant Reformation, should have been willing to return to Rome. Evidently they did not care greatly what happened to monks, whether priests were married or celibate, and whether the Mass was in Latin or in English. Rather than incur civil disorder, they were ready to return to the old ways.

[8] Samuel Butler, *Hudibras*, ed. A. R. Waller (Cambridge, Eng., 1905), Part II, Canto I, p. 215.

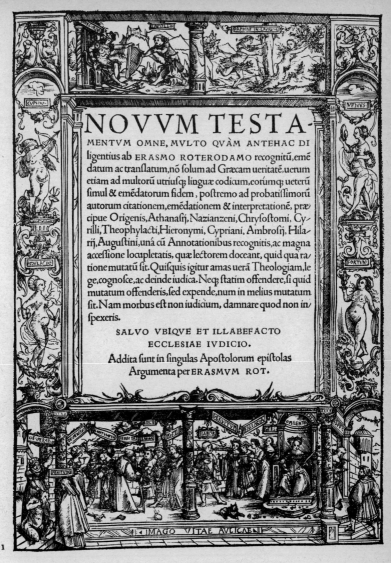

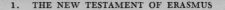

The second edition of the New Testament of Erasmus has title pages for each section. This one is amazing for its use of classical mythology. Above are Apollo and Mercury and Daphne fleeing through the woods; on the sides are blind Cupid with his bow and Venus, Adulation and the goddess Fortuna, and below an odd assortment of personified virtues, vices, and qualities. Erasmus was not responsible for the illustration which the printer Froben had in stock and in later life criticized the lush use of pagan mythology characteristic of the Humanists.

Louvre, photo by Giraudon

From a drawing by Albrecht Dürer.

Nationalmuseum, Stockholm

This portrait is attributed to Lucas Cranach the Elder, often referred to as the "painter of the Reformation." It was painted in 1526, after Luther's marriage to Katharina von Bora, a former nun.

The first page of the book of Genesis in Ximenes' Complutensian Polyglot. The Vulgate is in the center, flanked by the Greek Septuagint (with an interlinear Latin translation) on the left and by the Hebrew on the right. Below is an Aramaic version and a Latin translation of the Aramaic. This page was photographed from the copy in the Beinecke Library of Yale University.

Biblia cũ pleno apparatu
summariorum/cõcordantiarũ et quadru
plici repertorij siue indicij numericz folio
rum distinctiõe Basilee nuper impressa.

Matthie Sambucelli pro libri cõmendatione hexastichon.

Emendata magis scaturit nunc biblia tota;
  Que fuit in nullo tempore visa prius.
Qua loca canonici concordant singula iuris:
  In summa casus que tenet et capitum.
Qua legum veterisqz noui argumenta vident;
  Omine felici quam Basilea premit. 1518

5

The title page of Luther's copy of the Vulgate, printed at Basel with the city's coat of arms. The notes are in Luther's hand, dated 1542 and 1543. His signature is at the bottom.

6

Museum Plantin-Moretus, Antwerp

Woodcut by Christophe Jegher after his own drawing. From *Icones imperatorum Romanorum*, Vol. V of *Opera omnia Huberti Goltzii* (1645).

· CHRISTO · SACRVM ·

· ILLE · DEI VERBO · MAGNA PIETATE · FAVEBAT ·
· PERPETVA · DIGNVS · POSTERITATE · COLI ·

· D · FRIDR · DVCI · SAXON · S · R · IMP ·
· ARCHIM · ELECTORI ·
· ALBERTVS · DVRER · NVR · FACIEBAT ·
· B · M · F · V · V ·
· M · D · XXIIII ·

7

Elector of Saxony and Luther's protector. The engraving is by
Albrecht Dürer.

8

Uffizi; Scala

Raphael's portrait of Leo shows the pope flanked by two cardinals, Lodonio di Rossi and Giulio de' Medici (left), who became Pope Clement VII. Leo remained blind to the full import of Luther's revolt and failed to act decisively against him before Luther won Saxony to his cause.

Ain anzaigung wie D.

Martinus Luther zů Worms auf
dem Reichs tag eingefaren durch K. M. In
aygner person verhört vnd mit jm da
rauff gehandelt

9

The title page of a tract recounting Luther's appearance at the Diet of Worms, published at Strassburg in 1521, the year of the diet.

10

Luther went into hiding here after the Diet of Worms and, in the course of about nine months, translated the entire New Testament from Greek into German, and in addition wrote the tract "On Monastic Vows."

11

The title page is thoroughly medieval in its themes, in sharp contrast to the title page in Erasmus' edition of the Greek New Testament. Above left we see Moses receiving the Ten Commandments. On the other side, a cherub with a cross appears to the Virgin Mary. In the middle, on the left, are Adam and Eve and, below them, a skeleton signifying death, which came into the world because of their sin. On the right is Christ the Redeemer on the cross and, underneath, Christ arising from the grave and trampling death underfoot. Beside the tree, at the bottom center, a man seeking his salvation is being directed to the Redeemer by two pointing men. Underneath the branches of the tree are the brazen serpent lifted up in the wilderness on the left and the angel proclaiming the birth of Christ to the shepherds on the right. This edition in Low German was published at Lübeck in 1533.

12

Luther's lifelong associate at the University of Wittenberg, author of the Augsburg Confession, Melanchthon is portrayed here in his old age by Lucas Cranach. The woodcut was published after Melanchthon's death.

13

Shortly after the death of Julius II in 1513, there appeared an anonymous tract, *Julius Exclusus*, describing the pope's arrival in full armor at the gate of heaven. He himself had led his troops in the capture of Bologna and is bearded here because he had allowed his beard to grow after that victory. On his chest appear the letters P. M. St. Peter, peering through the gate of heaven, asks who he is. "Can't you read?" demands the pope, "P. M., Pontifex Maximus." "Pestis Maxima," retorts Peter and asks to know why he should be admitted. Julius responds with a glowing picture of the power and magnificence of the papacy. It was not like that in his day, says Peter, and refuses to let him in.

It was widely believed that the author of this tract was Erasmus, and his responsibility is well-nigh proved by a manuscript copy in his own hand. The significance of the tract is that a liberal Catholic of that era could indulge in a virulent, albeit anonymous, satire on a pope, and at the same time be utterly resolved not to leave the Church.

The woodcut is taken from a German edition of the tract published in 1523.

14a

The reformer of Nuremberg, Andreas Osiander, converted a bit of medieval reformatory iconography into a weapon of the Protestant Reformation. He came upon a copy of the prophecies of Joachim of Fiore, abbot of Corazzo in Calabria in the late twelfth century, who predicted the advent of a new age of the Holy Spirit, to be preceded by the coming of the Anti-christ who would be cut down by a monk. Posthumous editions of Joachim's prophecies added predictions of events up to the time of publication. These predictions were grouped around the pontificates of the popes. The one for John XXIII, deposed at Constance, (Fig. 14a), shows not the pope but the monk with the sickle to cut him down like the rose. John's original name was Baldassare Cossa. The B stands for his Christian name. The thigh is called *coscia* in Italian, close in sound to his last name, Cossa.

14b

Osiander, innocent of the original meaning, identified the monk with Luther, converted the *B* into a branding iron, and interpreted the thigh and the rose as signifying equally that all flesh is grass. Luther bears the sickle to cut down the papacy (Fig. 14b). The Counter Reformation reissued the prophecies (Fig. 14c), precluding Osiander's interpretation by turning the monk into a pope with the tiara. See my article "Eyn Wunderliche Weyssagung, Osiander-Sachs-Luther," *Germanic Review* XXI, 3 (October, 1946), pp. 161-164.

14c

15a

A striking demonstration of the effect of the Reformation on a
great artist is afforded by a comparison of two treatments of the Last

15b

Supper by Albrecht Dürer, the first done when he was experimenting with the techniques of the Italian Renaissance, the second after he had experienced the impact of Luther's teaching. In the first, one's attention is drawn to the artist's skill in depicting arches and vault in perspective and also to the marvelous craftsmanship in delineating the ringlets of the apostles and the folds in their robes. Theologically, Christ is haloed by a broad aureole; He is abstracted from the group. On the table is the paschal lamb, signifying his body. In the second treatment, the craftsmanship is no whit inferior, but it is not obtruding. Jesus has a much smaller halo. He converses with his disciples. On the table is the chalice which the Lutherans gave to the laity.

16

This was no organized campaign, but a series of uprisings with skirmishes in field, farm, and town. Above is depicted the struggle in the streets of a city.

ANNO AETATIS EIVS XLVIII.

17

The reformer of German Switzerland, from the woodcut that appeared 1539 in the tract *In evangelicam historiam annotationes.*

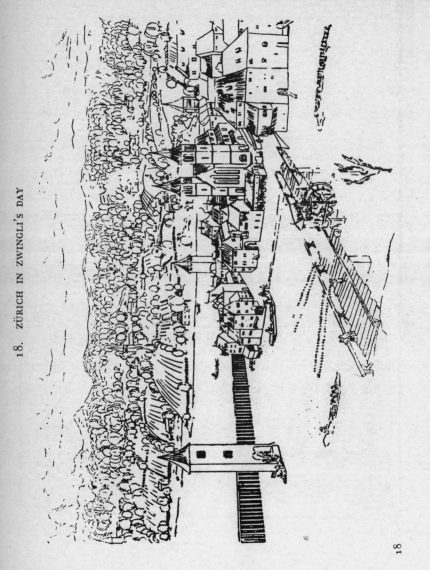

The church in the center is the Münster, where he preached.

Silberisen Collection, Kantonsbibliothek, Aarau

In 1529, Zwingli urged the Protestants to fight the assembled Catholic cantons. Instead, a truce was signed. The Catholics then enlarged their army and returned to defeat Zürich in 1531. The encounter, known as the second Battle of Kappel, is depicted in the drawing above. At the close of battle, Zwingli's body, found on the field, was burned as that of a heretic.

Examination before the Inquisition.

Death by water.

Death by fire.

The mercy of a quick death through the explosion of a bag of gunpowder.
From Tileman van Braght, *Het bloedig Tooneel*, American, 1685.

IOANNES·CALVINVS·

Museum Boymans–van Beuningen, Rotterdam

As a young man Calvin had a luxuriant beard. This portrait is by
an unknown master, about 1550.

The annulment of their marriage hinged on the status of Catherine's previous marriage (depicted in Fig. 22a, from *The Traduction of Marriage of the Princesse* [*Katereyne*], Pynson, 1501) with Henry's brother Arthur. If, as she claimed, the marriage had never been consummated, there was no impediment to her second marriage. But, if it had been, then the dispensation which Pope Julius II had given allowing the second marriage was not valid. Fig. 22b shows the papal bull against the dissolution of Henry's marriage.

23

From a portrait by Hans Holbein the Younger.

The shop of the Romish Church.

Shippe over your trinkets and be packing ye Papistes.

Burning of images.

The Temple well purged.

The Papistes packyng away their paultrye.

According to Foxe, this iconoclasm occurred in the reign of Edward VI. The captions read: Burning of Images, The Ship of the Romish Church, The Temple well purged, Shippe over your trinkets and be packing ye Papists, The Papists packing away their paultrye. The picture is from p. 1483 in John Foxe's *Book of Martyrs* (London, John Day, 1570) and applies to the year 1547.

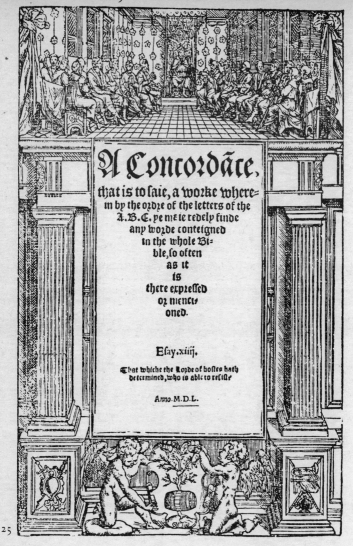

A Concordāce,

that is to saie, a worke where=
in by the ordre of the letters of the
A.B.C. ye mete redely finde
any worde conteigned
in the whole Bi=
ble, so often
as it
is
there expressed
or menci=
oned.

Esay.xiiij.

That whiche the Lorde of hostes hath
determined, who is able to resist?

Anno.M.D.L.

25

Printed in the reign of Edward VI (who is shown above at the head of the page, seated on a throne and surrounded by his counsellors). The title reads: A Concordance, that is to say, a work wherein by the order of the letters of the A. B. C. you may readily find any word contained in the whole Bible, so often as it is there expressed or mentioned. Isaiah XIIII. That which the Lord of Hosts hath determined, who is able to resist?

26

Hugh Latimer (1485?–1555), bishop of Worcester, champion of English Reformation, famous for his impassioned and persuasive preaching. Burned at the stake as a heretic, together with Ridley and Cranmer, at Oxford, in 1555. (From John Foxe's *Book of Martyrs* [1563], p. 1353.)

Although Mary Tudor came to be known as Bloody Mary because of the burnings at Smithfield, one does well to remember that the execution at Smithfield depicted above took place in 1546, the last year of the reign of her father, Henry VIII. From John Foxe's *Book of Martyrs* (1570), p. 1420.

❧ The description of D. Cranmer, standing on the stage in S. Maries church, in the time of Coles Sermon, where he gaue the last confession of his faith, and was plucked downe therefore by the Fryers and other.

28

From John Foxe's *Actes and Monuments* (London, 1563), p. 1502. The caption reads: The description of D. Cranmer, standing on the stage in S. Mary's church, in the time of Cole's sermon, where he gave the last confession of his faith, and was plucked down therefore by the friars and others.

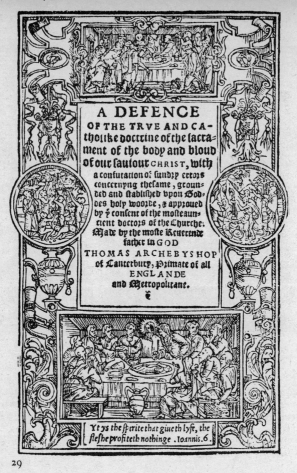

The title page is entitled: *A Defense of the True and Catholike doctrine of the body and bloud of our saviour Christ*, etc. The vignettes on the sides are: left, the giving of the manna, signifying the body and, on the right, Moses striking water from the rock, signifying the blood. The course of Cranmer's eucharistic doctrine has been subject to much discussion. The latest treatment, based on new evidence, is Peter Brooks's *Thomas Crammer's Doctrine of the Eucharist* (Seabury Press, 1965). Brooks finds three phases that do not precisely reproduce continental views but show affinities with, first, Rome, then Wittenberg, and finally Zürich and Geneva.

But Mary actually could not restore all the old ways. The monastic lands had been alienated beyond recovery. Cardinal Reginald Pole, son of the martyred duchess of Salisbury, came back from Italy to assist in the restoration of Catholicism, and Cardinal Bartolomé de Carranza came from Spain. The chief Protestant clergy went to the stake, among them Archbishop Cranmer. He went through a frightful ordeal of conscience, because he had been the most forward in asserting the right of the king to be the head of the Church. If the authority of the sovereign were absolute and the sovereign decided to return to Rome, should not the subject submit to Roman authority? But, thus to submit was to deny the absolute sovereignty of the king. Cranmer repeatedly recanted and abjured his recantations. He was condemned to be burned, nevertheless. Before the execution, he was called upon to read his final recantation in St. Mary's Church at Oxford. In a pillar of that Church to this day one sees an iron ring inserted in the stone to support the platform on which Cranmer stood. The audience had come to see a reed shaken by the wind, but Cranmer startled them by confessing his shame in having renounced his Protestant faith and then strode smiling to the stake. Over two hundred Protestant leaders shared his fate. The burnings at Smithfield account in a measure for the intense anti-Romanism of England in the period to follow. Well has it been said that "Englishmen never got the smell of Smithfield out of their nostrils."

X

The Confessional Age

C HARLES V, in view of the spread of Protestantism, made repeated efforts to induce the popes to convene a council to reform the Church and reunite Christendom. The popes, fearing a resurgence of Conciliarism, long obstructed, but, in the face of the increasing menace of Lutheranism, eventually yielded and a great council was convened at Trent in 1545 and sat intermittently until 1563, with the dual purpose of instituting moral and administrative reforms and of defining Church doctrine.

Toleration and Recognition

The council did not reduce tensions between Protestants and Catholics; rather, it confirmed Erasmus' statement that the breach was irreparable. But it had other impressive results. In spite of earlier doubts, the council remained under papal control, thus assuring the centralization of the Church. And it ended by stating the Catholic position in matters of dogma and doctrine with admirable lucidity. The doctrine of justification by faith was so defined that a Christian could still cooperate in his salvation through the accumulation of merits, contrary to the Protestant belief in justification by faith alone. The belief in purgatory was maintained, and tradition was placed on a par with the Scriptures as authority for the teachings of the Church. The Vulgate version of the scriptures was declared to be the only authentic translation to be used in all disputations and not to be called into question (a position no longer held by the Catholic Church today).

The council insisted that the rules of the Church regarding clerical celibacy were to be enforced. The clergy were to be in residence in their parishes, with only one parish to a man; plural holdings were forbidden. Provisions were made for better education of the clergy, and bishops were given greater control of their own dioceses. The doctrine of indulgences was upheld while the attendant financial abuses were corrected. Specifically, Protestant doctrines were rejected and Humanist scholarship excluded from the field of biblical translation. The condemnation of certain works of Erasmus excluded the liberal type of Catholicism prevalent earlier in the century. Pope Paul IV went beyond the council and, in 1559, on his own authority, placed on the index everything Erasmus had ever written, even that which had nothing to do with religion. Later in the century, censorship became more discriminating. Catholicism thus became entrenched against liberal and later against scientific and democratic tendencies, until the latter part of the nineteenth century. To exclude Protestant teaching, the council reaffirmed the seven sacraments and the doctrine of transubstantiation.

The Council of Trent manifestly accentuated the breach with the Protestants, and attempts on the part of the emperor to achieve a compromise were abortive. The alternative to a war of extermination was toleration, and it came about in Germany with the Peace of Augsburg in 1555, which granted Lutheranism recognition in those areas where it had been established up to 1552. By this agreement, the Catholics admitted the end of the system of one empire and one religion. Charles V would not accept responsibility for such an admission; he left the onus of promulgating the Peace to his brother. Ferdinand of Austria stipulated that its terms would not apply to his hereditary domains in the Netherlands and abdicated. The Lutherans, for their part, had to relinquish the ideal of a Protestant Germany, especially because the Peace required that the ecclesiastical states should never embrace the reform. The Lutherans had to give up also their initial attempt to include the other Reformed Churches in the Peace. This exclusion of the Calvinists intensified confessional strife among the Protestants.

The conflict between Catholics and Protestants led each to purge its own moderates. In Spain, the earlier reforms of Ximénez had fortified the Church against intrusions of Protestantism and imposed a zealous orthodoxy. All the machinery of the Inquisition was brought into action not only against any traces of Lutheranism but against Erasmians and mystics as well. To celebrate the return from the Netherlands of Philip II, son of Charles V, a great *auto-da-fé* was held in 1559, in which large numbers of heretics were strangled and burned. In that same year, Bartolomé de Carranza, archbishop of Toledo and primate of the Spanish Church, returning from his position as confessor to Mary Tudor in England, was imprisoned by the Inquisition because of his Erasmian leanings and remained incarcerated for the last seventeen years of his life.

Reform in Spain and in the New World

The Spanish spirit of reform had been spread beyond the Pyrenees through the founding of the Society of Jesus by Ignatius Loyola, a Spaniard of noble birth, nurtured on romances of chivalry and dedicated as a knight to the service of the queen. As an officer defending a castle against a superior force of the French, he refused to surrender like a feudal knight, until his leg was shattered by a ball from a cannon of modern warfare. During his long convalescence, he called for romances but was given, instead, lives of the saints and, when all efforts failed to restore his leg to its former grace and power by sawing and stretching, this knight of the Queen of Spain resolved to become a knight of the Queen of Heaven.

In her warfare the pen is mightier than the sword and Loyola, therefore, though a grown man, went to school with boys until able to enter the university. At school he engaged in pastoral work among fellow students and their mistresses and was several times investigated and twice imprisoned by the Inquisition for this unauthorized activity. From Spain, he repaired to the University of Paris for further study. There, he gathered a band of fellow students, including Francis Xavier, who vowed to devote their lives to Church and pope. In 1540, Pope Paul III approved the formation of this group as the Society of Jesus, with an autocratic constitution under an elected general with absolute authority, subject only to the pope. The Jesuits became the new militia of the papacy for the recovery of Europe from heresy and for the conversion of the New World. Like the Calvinists, they were to justify revolution and even tyrannicide in the interests of religion. The high standards of Jesuit scholarship and learning, as was witnessed at the Council of Trent, made them invaluable advocates of papal authority.

One of the greatest expressions of the new, reforming zeal of Catholicism was to be found in the spread of missionary work around the globe, a work in which the Jesuits, Franciscans, and other orders played an extraordinary role. In 1541, obeying the command of Loyola, Francis Xavier left on a day's notice for a decade of heroic Christian labor in India and Japan; others who followed penetrated to China. But the major fields of expansion were in the New World. Franciscans and Dominicans followed hard on the heels of the conquistadors, and after them came Jesuits, who were very active in Paraguay. Conversions by the thousands were made among the native Indians. The Jesuits and others advanced also by way of Quebec into the wild heartland of North America. The published records of their intrepidity in the face of great perils constituted the most exciting reading at the French court.

Under missionary auspices, the culture of Mexico in the sixteenth century was remarkably advanced. The first university in the Western Hemisphere was founded there and books were printed far surpassing anything published in New England in the seventeenth century. The missionaries to America were confronted with the old problem that converts who are received into Christianity *en masse*, with little prior preparation, tend to carry their paganism into their Christian worship. The cult of the Virgin of Guadalupe began in this fashion. An Indian painted an image of the Virgin in the garb of the Mexican goddess Toxantzin, and miracles were attributed to the portrait. The Franciscan bishop, Zumarraga, an Erasmian, disparaged the popular enthusiasm, saying, "Seek not miracles. The greatest miracle on earth is a Christian life." But miracles multiplied. The legend grew, and popular piety at last received ecclesiastical recognition.

The method of teaching the Indians centered on the system of the *encomienda*, a large estate with a central village clustering around a school and a church. The missionaries practiced segregation in order to preserve the Indians from the corruption of the whites. The Jesuit colony in Paraguay became so renowned for kindly treatment of the Indians that escapees from other areas flocked in. The resentment of Spaniards and Portuguese against this asylum led to its suppression.

Reform and Purges in Italy

Meanwhile, in Italy, the Humanistic approach to reform gave way to sterner procedures. The Inquisition was re-established in Rome in 1542 by Giampietro Caraffa as a special tribunal to deal with heresy. Many of the liberal reformers went to prison or to the stake. After Caraffa became Pope Paul IV in 1555, the liberal cardinal Giovanni Morone was immured in the chambers of the Inquisition until Paul died in 1559. When Paul's inquisitor general, Michele Ghislieri, became Pope Pius V in 1566, the turn came for Pietro Carnesecchi, a Humanist and one-time secretary of Clement VII. Carnesecchi was a man of singular attractiveness, engaging incaution, and grand illusions about the possibilities of reform by liberal means. For some time he was saved from the Inquisition by the protection of the Medici, but when this failed he was incarcerated and tried. Under torture, he would neither incriminate the dead nor accuse the living. He was ambiguous about his own views until he was given the choice of recanting or going to the block. Then he did not waver. The pope required the whole body of cardinals to attend the public reading of the long indictment of Carnesecchi and the pronouncement of the death sentence. Next morning, as the cardinals came from a conclave, they saw on the Ponte di Sant'Angelo the charred remains of the reformer.

Some of the liberal Italian reformers escaped into exile. They were small in number, but they were a colorful, highly stimulating group who disquieted the Lutherans and especially the Calvinists because of their inability to accomodate themselves to the increasing rigidities of Protestant orthodoxy. One group of such Italian exiles, the so-called Socinians found a haven in Transylvania and in Poland, where they converted some of the feudal magnates. The Socinians questioned the propitiatory death of Christ and, because they subordinated God the Son to God the Father, were known as anti-Trinitarians.

Protestant Purges

At the same time, the Protestants ruthlessly conducted their own purges. They did not burn Catholics, but they drowned Anabaptists and they beheaded and burned anti-Trinitarians, whose beliefs were repugnant to most Protestants as well as to Catholics. One victim was the Spaniard Michael Servetus, who attacked the dogma of the Trinity by rejecting the orthodox view that the second person in the Trinity, the Son, was eternal. Rather, Servetus maintained, the Son came into being when the pre-existent Christ was united by God with the man Jesus. Christ the Word, the Light of the World, was eternal, but the Son was not.

For his heresy, Servetus was burned in effigy in Catholic France and de facto in Protestant Geneva. While he was passing through the Swiss city in 1553, he was recognized and indicted by John Calvin, with whom he had earlier corresponded but who had repudiated the Spaniard's anti-Trinitarianism. The town council of Geneva conducted a trial and pronounced the sentence that, because of his errors, Michael Servetus should be burned at the stake, "in the name of the Father, the Son, and the Holy Ghost."

The execution of Servetus touched off a controversy over toleration within Protestantism. In 1554, Sebastian Castellio, a Protestant Humanist and a professor of Greek at the University of Basel, issued a treatise with the title *De Haereticis* (*Concerning Heretics*). In it, he claimed that Christians do not know enough to persecute. The tenets for which men are burned are still being disputed and, as Erasmus had observed, are by that very token uncertain. In any case the sincerity of a conviction matters more to God than the correctness of an opinion; Castellio defined conscience as loyalty to that which one believes to be right, whatever the objective truth.

An Italian, Jacobus Acontius by name, insisted in the same period that there should be persecution only over points declared in the Scriptures to be necessary for salvation. Of these, he said, there are only two: belief in justification by faith and belief in the Lord Jesus Christ. The failure to accept the first might be taken to exclude Catholics, and the second to debar the Socinians. But, even in dealing with these, Acontius advocated only persuasion; and the way to persuade, he said, is to treat the dissenter with respect and make plain that not victory in debate but verity is the issue. In their own day, Castellio and Acontius were voices crying in the wilderness, but the issues they raised and the arguments they provoked resulted in an agitation running in a direct line to the English Act of Toleration more than a century later.

As the sixteenth century advanced, resurgent Catholicism and militant Protestantism confronted each other, each purged and girt for the conflict. In April, 1559, Spain and France foreswore their long rivalry and by the Treaty of Cateau-Cambrésis cemented an alliance, including a mutual commitment to extirpate heresy in their respective domains. Spain had already largely done so by the great *auto-da-fé* already mentioned (there would be others), although heresy was still rife in her dependency, the Netherlands.

Huguenots

In France, the Protestants—Huguenots, as they were there called—were a strong minority. In the year the Treaty of Cateau-Cambrésis was signed they formed a national organization, Calvinist in persuasion, at the meeting of a synod in Paris. The execution of the Treaty meant civil war.

The religious struggle in France was made more intense because the issue also involved political and social divisions within the realm. In its efforts to centralize authority, the crown was impeded by rivalry on the part of the nobility and disaffection in the towns. The ruling house of Valois was dominated, after the middle of the century, by the queen mother, Catherine de Médicis, who, although she was a Catholic, was too politically minded to put the interests of the Church above those of her house and her country. The Bourbons, the family next in line to the throne, were partly Protestant. Their ablest member was the Prince de Condé, who adopted Protestantism for political reasons. The powerful House of Guise, represented by Duke Francis, his brother, the cardinal of Lorraine, and their sister Mary, queen regent of Scotland, was intransigently Catholic. The House of Châtillon, whose most distinguished member was Gaspard de Coligny, the admiral of France, was intensely Protestant and ready on religious grounds to oppose the crown. The Huguenots were primarily urban artisans who had economic as well as religious grievances. Quite possibly, there would have been civil war, even if the religious issue had not been injected.

In 1562, by the so-called Edict of January, Catherine had, in the interest of tranquility, granted to the Huguenots the right to worship in certain localities. When in March of that year the duc de Guise attacked a congregation of Huguenots at Vassy, claiming it was beyond the bounds stipulated by the Edict, war broke out. In the course of the next nine years, three conflicts followed, each ending inconclusively.

By 1572, the people were sick of carnage, and Catherine thought the time propitious to try again for pacification of the warring elements. Peace between the religions might be cemented by the marriage of her daughter Margaret to Henry of Navarre of the House of Bourbon, a Huguenot and heir to the crown, after the Valois. Leaders of all parties came to Paris for the wedding, among them Coligny, a Calvinist. Catherine considered his influence over her son, King Charles IX, dangerously strong. Further distressed, because Coligny was meditating an alliance with Elizabeth of England, Catherine appears to have plotted with the duc de Guise to have him murdered. Coligny was wounded, but not killed. Panicking at the thought of the religious strife certain to ensue, Catherine and her son Charles connived to murder all the Huguenots gathered for the wedding. On the day of St. Bartholomew, thousands of Huguenots were slaughtered in Paris and other large French cities.

When the last male of the Valois died without issue, the Protestant Henry of Navarre became heir to the throne. To pacify the land, he joined the Catholic Church and also, in 1598, issued the Edict of Nantes, which allowed the Huguenots freedom of worship in certain cities to be garrisoned with troops at state expense as a guarantee of this freedom. The Huguenots were to have full rights to public office.

Spanish Inquisition in the Netherlands

In the Netherlands, the Protestant struggle for religious freedom was joined with a revolt against Spanish domination. Emperor

Charles V had always favored the Netherlands, where he had been reared. But in 1555, when he abdicated to spend his last days rehearsing his funeral in a monastery, his son and successor Philip II subjected the Low Countries to the Spanish Inquisition. The central figure in the resistance was William of Orange, once a favorite of Charles, now the implacable enemy of Philip. William passed from Catholicism to Lutheranism and from Lutheranism to Calvinism; toward all he counseled tolerance, particularly since a religious war would wreck the economic prosperity of the Netherlands.

William's resources were small. When told that he must seek the aid of a foreign potentate he replied, "We are aided by the greatest of all potentates, the Lord of Hosts." Nevertheless, he did not disdain clandestine help from Queen Elizabeth and was looking for aid from the Huguenots under Coligny when word came that the French admiral had been slain in the massacre of St. Bartholomew. In the end, however, William's forces were able to secure the northern provinces of the Low Countries, which declared their independence in 1581, with religious liberty assured for Catholics, Lutherans, Calvinists, and even Mennonites.

Reformation in Scotland

The struggle of Protestantism in Scotland was also complicated by political relations with France and England. Mary, the queen regent and widow of James V, was of the rabidly Catholic House of Guise. Her daughter Mary was the queen of France until 1561, when, following the death of her mother and her husband, she became Mary, Queen of Scots. Herself a Catholic, she arrived to confront a sternly Protestant country.

Shortly before, the impassioned reformer John Knox had returned to Scotland. Knox was an extreme Calvinist who had earlier lived in exile at Geneva, which he considered to be "the most perfect school of Christ since the days of the apostles." There were in Scotland those who were rabidly anti-Roman and, among the nobility, those who were staunchly anti-French and pro-English. Knox was able to unite the two factions and, in 1560, to obtain the acceptance of Calvinism by the Scottish Parliament. He had arrived enflamed with the conviction that a celebration of the Mass was more deadly than a draught of poison, and Parliament issued a decree prescribing the death penalty for anyone who attended Mass more than twice.

Mary blatantly defied the decree herself, although she did nothing to interfere wth the Protestant settlement. She even made several attempts to soften Knox, but he continued to berate the young queen because her conscience was tied to "that harlot, the kirk of Rome." He was quite right in that Mary, if she could, would have imposed on Scotland obedience to the Roman Church.

Had Mary been discreet and upright, she might have detached the moderates from the intransigent Knox, but her indiscretions and crimes played into his hands. Knox inveighed against the saying of Mass in her private chapel and railed against the prospect of her remarriage with a Catholic. She summoned him to her presence and argued with him as if he represented Scotland, which indeed he did more than any lord of the realm. She was sufficiently politic not to marry a Spanish or a French Catholic, but she did marry Darnley, a Scottish Catholic, whose claim to the throne of England she hoped would strengthen her own. When, after a series of sordid intrigues, she was accused of having Darnley murdered, Protestants and Catholics alike turned against her and she was forced to seek asylum in England. Conspiracies with Catholic plotters to dispose of Elizabeth and take over the crown of England led to her execution.

In the meantime, under the leadership of Knox and his followers, Presbyterianism became the established religion in Scotland, with an emergent church polity, which in its final form consisted of a series of representative assemblies, from presbyteries through synods to the General Assembly.

Elizabeth I

England was the country least affected by religious strife in the late sixteenth century. Her turn was to come in the Puritan period. In 1559, the year of the Treaty of Cateau-Cambrésis, Queen Elizabeth reverted to the policy of her father and severed relations with Rome, but suffered herself to be proclaimed by Act of Parliament not as the supreme head, but only as the supreme governor of the Church of England. The queen was not personally interested in doctrinal differences. On the other hand, she was not indifferent to religion or to Protestantism. With a Catholic coalition on the Continent and, at the time of her accession, a Catholic Scotland to the north, she was involved in risks that made her stand seem one of strong conviction. However, her settlement was definitely not belligerently Protestant. A reference to the "detestable enormities" of the bishop of Rome in an earlier draft of the Act of Supremacy was deleted. The doctrinal position of the Anglican Church was set forth in the Thirty-nine Articles and was broad enough in its doctrines and definitions to have proved acceptable to all but the confirmed Catholics and the rigorous Calvinists. The Book of Common Prayer removed the Zwinglian implications of the Second Prayer Book of Edward and combined the words from the first and the second version to be used in the giving of the bread in the Eucharist, thus: "The body of our Lord Jesus Christ, which was given for thee, preserve thy body and soul unto everlasting life. Take and eat this in remembrance that Christ died for thee, and feed on him in thy heart by faith, with thanksgiving."

Though the temper of the Anglican settlement was not inquisitorial, on one point no room was left for individual predilections. Englishmen might believe as they would, but must worship as Parliament required, which meant that they must accept episcopacy, the royal supremacy, and the Book of Common Prayer. Richard Hooker set forth the rationale in his *Treatise on the Laws of Ecclesiastical Polity.* Hooker contended therein that the attempt of the Calvinists to make the outward forms of the Church conform to the Scriptures is, in view of scriptural ambiguity, to "torment weak consciences with infinite perplexities." Better to regulate such matters by "the light of nature and common discretion." Most English Protestants were satisfied to have it so during the reign of Elizabeth, though a Puritan party was in the making that would convulse the land in the next century.

The Catholics, of course, could not acquiesce, and their position was rendered frightfully difficult when the pope excommunicated the queen in 1570 and absolved her subjects of allegiance. Thus, Catholics loyal to the pope were traitors to the crown. Jesuit missionaries entered England, and the situation was further complicated by the plots against the crown on the part of Mary, Queen of Scots, and Philip II of Spain. To protect her government, Elizabeth undertook the persecution of Catholics. Although executions were relatively few, the hostility of both France and Spain was aroused. By diplomacy, Elizabeth averted war with France, but not with Spain. The dramatic sequel, culminating in the defeat of the Spanish Armada, dispatched by Philip II to restore England to the Catholic faith, is well known. England remained Protestant.

Thirty Years' War

By the close of the sixteenth century, the religious confessions had become fairly stabilized in Europe. Several different religions were tolerated on a territorial basis in Switzerland, Germany, and Poland. Catholicism, Lutheranism, Calvinism, and Anabaptism were all permitted in Holland, while in France Catholicism and Calvinism coexisted in separate areas. Religious liberty for individuals was not yet envisaged. Catholicism was proscribed in Scotland and England. In Spain and Italy, Protestantism was banned. Catholicism largely prevailed in the south and Protestantism in the north. Nevertheless, the simplification is untenable according to which Catholicism is Latin and Protestantism Nordic because of a difference in temperament. After all, Ireland is Catholic but not Latin and Calvinism at Geneva and in France is Protestant but not Nordic. Besides, in all lands the division would not have been so clear-cut if minorities had not been sent into exile.

The seventeenth century had hardly begun when a war broke out in 1618, destined to embroil all Europe for thirty years. The issues were complex, for never have religion, economics, and politics been more closely interwoven. Yet, the Thirty Years' War was at the outset a religious war; the behavior of many of the participants frequently makes no sense unless one realizes that military considerations were overriden by religious convictions. The war dragged on as long as it did because neither the Catholics nor the Protestants presented a united front.

The struggle was so complicated that only the barest outline can be offered here. It began in Bohemia, essentially because the Peace of Augsburg no longer corresponded to the facts. That settlement had granted toleration only to the Lutherans among the Protestants and had excluded Calvinists, who subsequently declined to accept this territorial solution and who continued their propaganda at the expense of both Catholics and Lutherans. Many areas covered by the settlement had become Calvinist, including Brandenburg and particularly the Palatinate. There were Calvinist penetrations also into Württemberg and Hesse. Hungary was strongly Calvinist, and Bohemia had, in addition to the various Hussite groups, both Lutherans and Calvinists.

Shortly before he was elected Holy Roman emperor, Ferdinand II, a Hapsburg Catholic, was made king of Bohemia. By rigidly applying the principle of the Augsburg settlement, he attempted to root out Protestantism from his domain and to impose Catholicism. Thus the long conflict was precipitated. The Bohemians would not submit and, in a revival of medieval particularism, challenged the very constitution of the empire. Claiming the right to choose their own king, they invited the elector of the Palatinate, an ardent Calvinist, to serve as sovereign, and he accepted. Such flagrant disregard for the structure of the empire, coupled with the establishment in Bohemia of a form of Protestantism not countenanced by the Peace of Augsburg, caused Bavaria to line up with the Austrian Hapsburg, whereas Lutheran Saxony maintained neutrality. The Bohemians were crushed, and most estates of the insurgents were confiscated. Thereupon Lutheran Denmark, appalled by this Catholic advance, imprudently intervened. The Danes were repulsed and retreated within their own borders.

The Catholic forces swept up to the Baltic. Then the Swedes intervened under their great king Gustavus Adolphus, a brilliant administrator and tactician who had built up a centralized government and created a professional army. Like William of Orange, he was a man of profound but not narrow religious convictions and, though Lutheran, he did not scruple to assist Calvinists. Catholic France, abetted by the pope, actually gave support to the Swedes in order to curb the Spanish Hapsburg imperialists. Electoral Saxony still held aloof from an alliance with Sweden to the north and Calvinists to the south, until the Catholic coalition had the indiscretion to sack Magdeburg in Saxony. Then Saxons, Swedes, German Lutherans, and Calvinists, assisted by the French and the pope, confronted the Catholics, and Gustavus Adolphus gained a smashing victory. However, the Catholic forces rallied and, at the Battle of Lützen in 1632, the valor of Gustavus outran his prudence. He rode into a band of the foe and was cut down.

Had Gustavus lived, he might have been able to form a great northern, Protestant confederation, consisting of Sweden, Germany, Denmark, Holland, and probably England and Scotland. After his death, however, religious issues were displaced by secular concerns. For another sixteen years, a desultory conflict dragged on, largely as a struggle between France and Spain for the control of the Rhineland. Faced by the opposition of France, Bavaria, and the pope, the empire was unable to unify Europe under the dynasty of the Hapsburgs. At the same time, a deep attachment to the idea of the empire held back the German states from the realization of national unity. Their lands were left ravaged.

Though religious questions played a diminishing role in the further course of the war, the issues that had precipitated the conflict could not be disregarded. When the struggle finally ceased, the Treaty of Westphalia in 1648 provided a religious settlement, albeit an unimaginative one. The territorial principle still prevailed, but the lines were more realistically drawn. Calvinism was accorded the same status as Lutheranism and Catholicism; the territorial status was stabilized according to the prevailing conditions of January 1, 1624. (After that date there had actually been little change.) The Treaty precluded interference from the Church of Rome in religious matters in Germany, and it was therefore condemned by Innocent X, which only highlighted the point that thereafter the Church was no longer regarded either as an overlord or even as a partner in the arranging of political settlements.

Absolutism in France

The period following the war saw the growth of political absolutism on the Continent. France was the most notable example, but Spain, though diminished in prestige abroad, became even more absolutist at home. And the German states, although they were incapable of political unification, built up despotic regimes within their own territories.

France emerged from the Thirty Years' War as the most brilliant, most powerful, and most absolutist of the European states. Late in the previous century, the Edict of Nantes had solved the problem of religious duality by a kind of territorialism within the state. The Huguenots, to be sure, were not separated from the Catholics in the schools, the markets, or the courts, but their temples—they were not called churches—were restricted to fortified and garrisoned citadels. Thus the guarantee of religious freedom entailed political decentralization; Huguenot cities corresponded to the baronial castles of the Middle Ages.

This system, of course, conflicted with monarchical absolutism. Cardinal Richelieu, who became actual ruler of France early in the course of the Thirty Years' War, saw very plainly that the Huguenots constituted a state within the state and a menace to the authority of the crown. He resolved therefore to take away from them their fortified cities. The strongest of these was La Rochelle, since it was open to the sea and to succor by allies, who at that moment were the English. Richelieu determined to reduce the city. After a year of incredible effort, he succeeded in blocking its harbor with sunken ships, thus cutting off help from the English, and the city was called upon to surrender. The mayor, one Jean Guiton, placed his dagger on the table, declaring that he would stab anyone who entertained the thought of yielding, and reminded the people that it was better to die than suffer the ravages of the soldiery. As hunger and disease took over, the city might nonetheless have surrendered several times had not the white sails of the English fleet appeared beyond the harbor bar. But each time the would-be rescuers were halted by the barricade, and the people on shore watched the sails disappear beyond the horizon.

When La Rochelle at last surrendered, after heroic resistance, Richelieu and the king rode into the city at the head of perfectly disciplined troops, followed by food trains for the famished. The cardinal allowed a meeting of the Protestant assembly. The religious clauses of the Edict of Nantes were confirmed, but all the Protestant fortresses were to be razed. Tolerance for the Huguenots was to depend henceforth on the good will of the crown, and there was every reason why the crown should have continued to extend that good will, because the Huguenots, when their religion was confirmed, became utterly loyal. Later, when there were insurrections against the crown on political grounds—the Fronde in the time of Louis XIV was an attempt by the nobles to recover their independence—the Huguenots would have nothing to do with them. Mazarin, the successor of Richelieu, expressed to them the gratitude of the throne.

Nevertheless, before the century had ended, the Edict of Nantes was revoked. To understand why, one must consider Louis XIV's concept of monarchy and the trends of thought within the French Church in the seventeenth century.

Descartes

In this period, French Catholicism produced great minds and great spirits, profoundly exercised for the faith. There was the philosopher René Descartes. His philosophical problem was at the same time a religious problem. How can a man be sure of the existence of God? Let man start, Descartes counseled, by stripping his knowledge down to the bare assumption of his own existence. This he may assume because he cannot even doubt unless he exists. Thus the departure is to be made from the capacity for logical thought: "I think; therefore, I am."

But how do I move now from myself to God? asked Descartes. The passage from my mind to God is really easier, he answered himself, than from my mind to matter because mind and matter are different, but God is mind. There is still a difficulty, because God has characteristics that cannot be predicated of man. God is eternal, omniscient, omnipotent, immutable. Man, in order to perceive that he lacks these characteristics, must be able to conceive of them. But how can he conceive of them if they do not exist? The idea of a being more perfect than man could have proceeded only from the existence of a being more perfect than man. Here we have again an ontological demonstration. Whether or not this reasoning is convincing, the significant point is that it preoccupied a French philosopher of the seventeenth century as urgently as it did St. Anselm in the twelfth.

Pascal

The argument was, however, not at all convincing to another great philosopher of the period, Blaise Pascal, who devoted much of his time to problems of religion. He was the great proponent of the Jansenists, who might be called Calvinist Catholics, because of the rigor of their deportment and their acceptance of the doctrine of predestination. Pascal held that man arrives at his belief in God by no processes of ratiocination, but only by seeing God disclosed in Jesus Christ. Pascal wrote:

> The God of the Christians is not a God who is simply the theory of geometric truths. This is the God of the pagans. He is not a God who crowns with blessings those who serve him. This is the God of the Jews. The God of the Christians is a God of love and consecration, a God who makes them feel their utter misery and his infinite mercy, who unites himself with the ground of their being and fills them with humility, joy, confidence, and love. He makes the soul feel that its peace lies wholly in him, and that it has no joy save to love him. To know God after this fashion one must know first one's own misery and worthlessness and the need of a mediator in order to approach God and be united with him. The knowledge of God without the recognition of our misery engenders pride. The recognition of our misery without the knowledge of Jesus Christ produces despair. But the knowledge of Christ frees us alike from pride and despair, because here we find conjoined God and our misery and the only way in which it can be repaired.[1]

Religious Absolutism in France

To these philosophers, preoccupied with religion, one must add as exemplars of a revived Catholicism the great mystic François de la Mothe Fénelon and the eloquent preacher Jacques Bénigne

[1] Blaise Pascal, *Pensées*, chap. xxii, abridged, tr. R. H. Bainton.

Bossuet. One may not imply that these men directly instigated the revocation of the Edict of Nantes, though Bossuet did approve. Primarily, however, he used his great talents and prestige as court preacher to persuade rather than coerce. Yet, it was the revived Catholic consciousness that resuscitated the ever latent conviction that to tolerate error is to betray truth. And the old conviction was still very much alive that the state can prosper only if supported by the true religion and the true religion can be but one.

These ideas were pressed upon King Louis XIV by a most remarkable woman. She was the granddaughter of an ardent Protestant from the days of Henry IV. In her early years she had been reared as a Huguenot, and to the end she practiced their austere deportment. A convert to Catholicism, she combined the strictest Catholic orthodoxy with Protestant or Jansenist mores. A widow, she was brought to the court as a governess to the illegitimate children of the king. By her winsome piety, she came soon so to influence the king that he dismissed his mistresses and was reconciled to the queen. When she died, the king married the governess, making her his wife, though not his queen. She continued to be known as Madame de Maintenon. She pressed upon him the ancient ideal of the one true Catholic faith for all France and the suppression of the reformed religion.

The Edict of Nantes was abolished by degrees, in mounting brutality. Prior to the Revocation, troops were quartered on the Huguenots with license to pillage, violate, and bludgeon. Thousands of conversions were reported as a consequence. Yet, when the edict was revoked in 1685 and the Huguenots were confronted with submission or banishment, some of those who had previously submitted now elected to share in exile. The unification of religion and the establishment of a homogeneous state were achieved by the expulsion of some two hundred and fifty thousand persons. A contemporary estimated that the king thereby lost nine thousand sailors, twelve thousand veteran soldiers, and six hundred of his best officers, not to mention thousands of the finest artisans in France. The refugees were welcomed in Switzerland, in Prussia,—

the greatness of Berlin as a city dates from their arrival—in England and Holland, in the English colonies in North America, and in the Dutch colonies in South Africa.[2] France was again the land of *un roi, une loi, une foi*. After the Huguenots had been cast out, French Catholicism was confronted in the next century by that most unreasonable of all deities, the goddess of Reason.

Religious Currents in England

The course in England was very different. While France moved toward absolutism, England moved toward constitutionalism. England had had her chaos in the Wars of the Roses in the fifteenth century. The despotism that restored order came with the Tudors in the sixteenth century. With order restored, the cry for emancipation from despotism came during Stuart rule, in the seventeenth century.

There were particular circumstances that enabled England to stage a moderate revolution. One was her isolation from the Continent and her comparative non-involvement in the Thirty Years' War. Another was the union with Scotland, which occurred in 1603 when James VI of Scotland—the son of Mary, Queen of Scots, and Darnley—became James I of England. This union was, to be sure, a decisive factor in the outbreak of the civil war, but still the conflict was not primarily between the two kingdoms but between parties in both; and those parties were all Protestant, less bitterly opposed to each other than all of them were to Rome. Another important consideration was the convergence of economic, political, and religious interests in resistance to the crown and the established Church.

The first Stuarts, James I and his successor Charles I, were in dire need of funds. They were loath to appeal for Parliamentary grants, for this would have subjected them to Parliamentary control. Instead, they had recourse to levies by royal decree. Two

[2] A. J. Grant, *The Huguenots* (London, 1934).

sources that could be tapped were land and trade. But, to touch them, involved the religious issue indirectly, since many of the landed gentry and the London merchants, from whom such revenues might be raised, were of the Puritan party. These interests were also all well represented in Parliament, where economic, political, and religious opposition to the crown was centered.

The Puritans, who were essentially Calvinists in their doctrine, had deep grievances against the established Church. For them, the Elizabethan settlement had not gone far enough. They wished to abolish all religious ceremonies not expressly called for by the Scriptures. They attacked the Anglican Church for its "popery," preferring a simplified service with emphasis on the sermon. A petition enumerating the changes they desired was presented to James I in 1603, but none of their requests was granted, except that for the revision of the Bible. In 1611, the "authorized" or King James version made its appearance. James aggravated the grievances of the Puritans by a number of measures, especially by recommending sports and games as Sunday pastimes, in violation of their own emphasis on a strict observance of the Sabbath. The Puritans were further alienated by James's restoration of episcopacy in Scotland and by his forcing on the Scottish Parliament the Articles of Perth, which legally instituted such Anglican practices as kneeling for Communion and the observance of Easter and Christmas.

The widespread fear of a Catholic restoration, should the king's party prevail, accentuated the conflict. The slogan "No Popery" gathered up memories of the persecutions under Mary, of the plots to assassinate Elizabeth, of the Armada, and of the Guy Fawkes's plot of 1605 to blow up the Houses of Parliament. James's negotiations to marry his son Charles to a Spanish Catholic princess and his failure to aid the German Protestants in the opening years of the Thirty Years' War were resented not only by Puritans but by all those with anti-Catholic sentiments.

Under Charles, who succeeded to the throne in 1625, the monarchy became increasingly associated with the Catholic cause in the minds of many Englishmen. Charles's marriage to the Catholic princess, Henrietta Maria, sister of Louis XIII of France, was unpopular, as was his refusal to help his own sister's husband, the Calvinist elector of the Palatinate, now the exiled king of Bohemia. The uneasiness was great when Charles's deputy in Ireland, Thomas Wentworth (the later Earl of Strafford), by efficient and upright administration increased the prosperity of Ireland and built up an army consisting mainly of Roman Catholics.

The figure on whom Puritan disaffection focused was William Laud, whom Charles appointed archbishop of Canterbury in 1633. Laud was himself a reformer. He lamented the low quality of the clergy, but perceived that its roots lay partly in their extreme poverty. The Tudors had not turned over the confiscated monastic lands to the Church of England. For the sake of ready cash, the Church had leased her own lands for long terms on condition that the lessee collect the tithes and support the clergy on these estates. But the lessee pocketed the bulk and left the starveling curate to eke out a living by tending his own glebe, or by taking several charges to the inevitable neglect of all. Laud wanted direct grants from Parliament to relieve the need of the clergy, but these were never conferred.

Laud's program differed fundamentally from that of the Puritans. Following the theory of the Elizabethan settlement, Laud believed there should be latitude in doctrine but uniformity in polity and liturgy. The liturgy was set forth in the Book of Common Prayer, which required that the Communion table should always be at the east end of the church and not in the nave as if, said Laud, the church were a tavern. He also believed that the clergy should be attired in the vestments prescribed by the changing seasons of the Christian year. Laud cared more that every Englishman should eat the same kind of wafer at the Lord's Supper than that all should have the same theory as to the real Presence.

Laud punished non-compliance with his measures by mutilation and imprisonment. The Star Chamber, which had been instituted to force obedience to the state, and the Court of High Commission, which since Elizabeth's day had been employed against nonconformists to the established Church, were both called into use against the Puritans. An individual might suffer at the hands of both. Alexander Leighton, for example, who had issued *Sions Plea Against the Prelacie*, was defrocked by the Court of High Commission and then was sentenced by the Star Chamber to be whipped, his ears cropped, his nose slit, and his forehead branded, and, in addition, to be fined and imprisoned. The like treatment of other Puritans, such as William Prynne, John Bastwick, and Henry Burton, provoked intense resentment. Despite the outcry against barbarous penalties, Laud would grant no concessions and no relief. In 1640, an oath was imposed on all members of the learned professions, "Never to consent to alter the government of this Church by archbishops, bishops, deans, and archdeacons, etc., as it stands now established." That "etc." was derided as a cover behind which might lurk the Mass, the pope, and the Church of Rome.

The opposition to the king and to Laud was not united in its own programs, save in antagonism to the government and the established Church. Religious pluralism, combined with religious intensity, threatened to nullify not only Laud's program but any other. After a century of placidity in England, the fire of religious enthusiasm had leaped across the Channel. Englishmen, who under King Hal and Queen Bess had accepted religious changes with docility, had become dogmatic about their own increasingly various religious beliefs and practices.

Sects in England

England had become a welter of sects: there were Presbyterians, Independents (Congregationalists), Baptists, and Unitarians, to name those that have survived; and, besides, there were a number of others now extinct: Familists, Ranters, Seekers, Fifth

Monarchy Men, not to mention political parties with a strong religious cast, such as the Levelers. In the near future still others, such as the Quakers, the Muggletonians, and the Diggers, would be added to the list. The very existence of these different groups enormously complicated the problem of religious settlement.

Of the main groups, one of the most important was that of the Presbyterians, which included the English and the Scottish Calvinists, who both objected to the imposition of episcopacy and of the Book of Common Prayer by the Stuarts. Politically, they favored constitutional monarchy. Their great proponent, Samuel Rutherford, wrote a book called *Lex Rex*, which means "the law is king," as opposed to *rex lex*, "the king is law."

The Independents had for their central idea the concept of the gathered Church, espoused a century earlier by the Anabaptists. Attempts have been made to trace a direct connection between the Independent conventicles and the few Anabaptist nuclei known to have been in England during the preceding century, but the search has proved elusive thus far. There may well have been no connection, because like ideas in like circumstances may recur independently. The Church, they said, consists not of those baptized in infancy. Still, they did baptize their children, probably because their actual tradition had been strongly influenced by Zwingli. But children, although under the aegis of the Church, were not members, since the Church must consist only of visible saints, those who, in reasonable charity, may be adjudged to be saints. Precisely what the marks of identification were among the English Independents at that time is not altogether clear. For Calvin, as we noted, there had been three tests: profession of faith, uprightness of life, and attendance upon the sacraments. New England Puritanism was to drop the third and substitute for it a heartfelt experience of regeneration. This was the most crucial mark of election, and the necessary condition for membership in the Church and for admission to the sacraments. There is no evidence, however, that the English Independents had set up this condition in any formal way, although they surely sympathized with the stipulations of their American cousins, that to be accounted members of a gathered Church, folk must give evidence that "they have been wounded in their hearts for their original sin and actual transgressions and can pitch upon some promise of free grace in the Scripture for the ground of their faith, and that they find their hearts drawn to believe in Jesus Christ for their justification and salvation." Those who could thus testify made a covenant with God and with each other, namely "a solemn and public promise before the Lord, whereby a company of Christians, called by the power and mercy of God and fellowship with Christ, and by His providence to live together and by His grace to cleave together in the unity of faith, and brotherly love . . . do bind themselves to the Lord and to one another, to walk together . . . in all such ways of holy worship in Him and of edification one towards another, as the Gospel of Christ requireth."[3]

Once again, the doctrine of election cut athwart all other distinctions in society. Social station was no mark of election and, although the Puritan party included men of substance among the gentry and the merchants, soon enough they were reproached with being but a concourse of "Glovers, Boxe-Makers, Button-Makers, Coach-men, Felt-makers, Bottle Ale sellers, and Mechaniks."[4] The polity of the Independents was congregational. Above the local congregation stood neither a bishop, nor a general assembly, nor a synod, nor a presbytery. There was disagreement as to whether church discipline within the congregation should be exercised by elders or by the congregation as a whole. On one point there was agreement: that discipline should be rigorously exercised and the unworthy disowned.

Whether such a constitution for the Church influenced the constitution of the state is open to question. Opponents argued at the time that the congregationalism of the sectaries would of necessity

---

[3] Richard Mather, *Church-Government and Church-Covenant Discussed, in an Answer of the Elders. . . . Together with an Apologie . . . in the yeare 1639 . . .* (N. p., 1643), p. 3.

[4] William Haller, *The Rise of Puritanism* (New York, 1957), p. 263.

lead to democracy in the state, and that they were, therefore, "blowing the bellows of sedition." The Independents rejected the aspersion by asserting that what was true for the Church was not true for the state. Yet their opponents may well have been right.

The Baptists sprang from a group of Independents living in exile in Holland. Contact with Mennonites convinced them that infant baptism was incompatible with their views of the Church. There is a connection here with the Anabaptists, but the concept of the gathered Church had already been formed before this contact occurred. Thomas Helwys, having reached this conclusion, came also to feel that to remain in exile conflicted with the command of the Lord to bear witness before kings. Therefore, he returned to England and founded the Baptist Church.

The Quakers, called by preference The Society of Friends, had their origin in the north of England. George Fox, their founder, had a profound experience of religion, "Now I was come up through the flaming sword into the Paradise of God. All things were made new, and all the creation gave another smell unto me than before, beyond what words can utter."[5] Fox began traveling about like a medieval friar, gathering an elect people. His message sounds sometimes like ultimate Puritan reductionism with regard to the remnants of Romanism, with no ministers, no liturgy, no sacraments, no music, and no sanctuary. There was a number of contributory motives. The appalling state of the parish churches in the north of England is enough to explain why Fox should talk of hireling priests, steeple houses, and money changers. His objection to music and sacraments goes only one step beyond Zwingli in decrying all external aids to religion. The exclusive reliance on the Bible was common to all Puritan groups. But Fox would appeal to the Bible in support of a position adopted on other grounds. For example, he argued that since in the King James Bible all the characters addressed each other as thee and thou, so also should all Englishmen. The real point was to rebuke

[5] *The Journal of George Fox*, ed. John L. Nickalls (Cambridge, Eng., 1952), p. 27.

the pride of social station because, in his day, English had two modes of address like the continental languages at present. The polite form was "you," and the familiar form "thou," used for intimates or for inferiors. Fox insisted on the practice, then highly offensive, of addressing even the king in the same term as a servant. The effect, of course, was social equalitarianism and, curiously, Fox won his point in reverse. Today, English is the only European tongue that does not have the two modes of address. The polite "you" has become universal, whereas the familiar "thou," except in prayer, survives only as a sign of intimacy among the Society of Friends.

In some respects, Fox's program was a reaction against Puritanism. All the bitter contention over the wafer, the communion table, vestments, liturgy, episcopacy, and presbyteries he ended by the simple expedient of abolishing them all. But, despite his ability to cite the Scripture, his emphasis was upon the Spirit, which transcends the letter. Every meeting was led by the Spirit with silence until someone, whether man or woman, was driven to utterance. The Quaker testimony against war emerged gradually. At first, some Quakers were in Cromwell's army, but General Monck expelled them because the army cannot tolerate communications from the Holy Ghost to any below the rank of general. Fox took a stand against war as such, saying that he lived in the spirit that "takes away the occasion of all wars."[6] The Quaker rejection of war and of the oath is reminiscent of the Anabaptist position. Yet, there was a significant difference. The Quakers did not withdraw from the framework of society, probably because they were not subject to the penalties of death and banishment. They retained the hope for a Christian world and addressed their pleas not simply to Friends but to all England.

The Unitarians in this period were few and may have derived their theology from books imported from Holland, where the Socinians had taken refuge after their expulsion from Poland. The

[6] George Fox, Cambridge Journal, i, 11–12, as quoted in M. E. Hirst, Quakers in Peace and War (London, 1923), p. 43.

Unitarians gained greater strength in England in the eighteenth century and in New England in the late eighteenth and early nineteenth, in each case by deviation from Calvinism, which by its emphasis upon the monarchical absolutism of God, tends to exclude the concept of pluralism within deity. The unity can be achieved either by identifying Christ completely with God or by subordinating Christ to God.. This was the Unitarian solution. For England, the importance of this group at that time consisted primarily in lending emphasis to the problem of religious liberty. Even one Unitarian was enough to pose that problem, because the denial of the Trinity was the offense for which the last heretic in England had been burned.

The existence of all these groups—Presbyterians, Independents, Baptists, Quakers, and Unitarians, not to mention all the smaller ones—confronted any ruler in England with a grave dilemma. Although the disagreement among the sects was in one respect a boon to Charles, who hoped to conquer by dividing them, he was unable to solve the problem of dealing with increasing religious pluralism. Corporal punishment and imprisonment were proving of benefit to the nonconformists by advertising their claims, as in the case of John Lilburne, leader of the Levelers, who made a career of going to jail as a protest against unconstitutional procedures on the part of every government. On the other hand, if the government were to remove all restrictions on religious dissent, what would the sects then do to each other?

That depended upon their views of Church, state, and liberty. The Presbyterians would not have been more tolerant than the Anglicans. They were actually more illiberal than Laud, because their insistence upon uniformity applied not only to liturgy and polity, but also to doctrine. Among the so-called Separatists, the Baptists and the Quakers, with their demand for a complete separation of Church and state, were most unequivocally in favor of religious liberty. The Independents were not altogether of one mind. Some among them believed in a thoroughgoing separation of Church and state with full religious freedom. But others were willing to continue the union of Church and state, provided both were fashioned according to their model. That policy was followed in early New England, but at home, in England, the Independents were never other than Dissenters. Until quite recent years they have continued to agitate for the disestablishment of the Church of England, and indeed of any Church in any country.

Religious Liberty

In championing freedom in religion, some of the Independents and many Baptists frankly repudiated the ideal of uniformity. They declared that variety is the law of creation, and that competition is the lifeblood not only of trade but also of religion, because truth emerges only in the battle of free minds. The effect of constraint, they claimed, is to make martyrs of the stalwart and hypocrites of the weak. They redefined conscience as loyalty to what one believes to be true, even though it may actually be false, because only by the path of sincerity can truth be attained. So said John Milton, fully confident that truth would vindicate itself. "Let truth and falsehood grapple; whoever knew truth put to the worst in free and open encounter? . . . For who knows not that truth is strong next to the Almighty. She needs no policies nor stratagems nor licensings to make her victorious. . . . Give her but room, and do not bind her when she sleeps."[7] Such a position left Christendom intact only as a state of mind, rather than as a corporate structure.

Such divergent viewpoints may have encouraged the pursuit of truth but they certainly did not help the cause of the Dissenters. There was good reason to doubt whether the sects could hold together long enough to deal with Charles and Laud. Their strategy allowed for only two possibilities. Either they would have to leave England or dominate England. They could emigrate sepa-

[7] *The Works of John Milton* (New York, Columbia University Press, 1931–38), IV, 347–48.

rately, but if they were to dominate, they would have to hold together. They tried everything. Emigration and agitation with a view to domination went on concurrently. The fortunes of the émigrés will engage us later. Suffice it to point out here that they continued to participate in the English struggle by printing tracts in Holland for English consumption and by constant comings and goings between England and America.

Neither the inquisitorial procedures of the High Commission, nor the brutal sentences of the Star Chamber, nor Wentworth's Catholic army in Ireland, nor Charles's demands for money and monopolies precipitated civil war in England. It remained for Laud's handling of the religious controversies in Scotland to accomplish that. He believed, as most men still commonly believed, that one kingdom should have one religion, or at any rate, one Church. England and Scotland were now united under one king and should have a uniform religion. Each wished to impose its form of Protestantism upon the other. Laud took the initiative. There was no need to enforce episcopacy on the Scots, for James had already done that, without provoking rebellion. Laud was not interested in requiring subscription to the Thirty-nine Articles; he was willing to let the Scots believe as they would. But he insisted that they conduct their services from the Book of Common Prayer.

To the Presbyterians, the Book of Common Prayer was anathema, despite its stately cadences and noble piety, because it was "an unperfect book, culled and picked out of that popish dunghill, the Mass book, full of abominations."[8] It called for the use of a wafer instead of ordinary bread in the Lord's Supper and for kneeling at Communion, which might be taken to imply belief in the physical presence of Christ. It called for a ring in the marriage ceremony as the visible sign of a sacrament, whereas the Presbyterians, like Luther, did not include marriage among the

[8] "An Admonition to Parliament" in *Puritan Manifestoes*, ed. W. H. Frere (London, 1954).

sacraments. The Prayer Book, furthermore, was built around the Christian year, which the Presbyterians and Puritans as a whole rejected. Christmas, they said, is "Christ-Mass, the devil with the sting in his tail." Away with Ash Wednesday, Lent, and Easter and all the holy days of Rome, which withdraw men from their godly callings! The Sabbath only, they insisted, was instituted by God and should be scrupulously observed, on penalty of divine displeasure. When, then, Archbishop Laud, in 1637, issued the order to the clergy of Scotland that they must use the Book of Common Prayer, a riot broke out in Edinburgh.

In 1638, the Scots drafted the National Covenant, which read: "From the knowledge and conscience of our duty to God, to our king and country, without any worldly respect or inducement, we promise and swear by the great name of the Lord our God to continue in the profession and obedience of the aforesaid religion [referring to the Confession of 1580]; that we shall defend the same and resist all those contrary errors and corruptions according to our vocation, and to the utmost of that power which God has put into our hands, all the days of our life."[9]

Through hamlet and kirk all over the lowlands—there were still Catholics in the highlands—men set their hands to the marriage contract of this nation with God. The reference in the Covenant to the "utmost of that power" meant war. The clans were mustered to the singing of Psalms. The good wives of Edinburgh sacrificed three thousand sheets to make tents for the soldiers.

Charles called out his troops, but in the face of the Scots' strength he could not risk a battle. A treaty was signed before any fighting took place. The king then summoned Wentworth from Ireland, making him Earl of Strafford, to raise an effective fighting force. To pay for troops, money was necessary. In order to raise it, Charles had to convene Parliament, which was soon to be dubbed the Short Parliament. But he could not count on a united England. The Puritans in England would not fight the Presby-

<hr>

[9] C. V. Wedgewood, *The King's Peace* (New York, 1956), p. 198.

terians of Scotland. Instead of granting funds for an army, Parliament began discussing its political and religious grievances, and Charles was soon obliged to dissolve it.

That summer, the king's forces were defeated by the Scots, who crossed the Tweed, and Charles had to negotiate again. As the Scots refused to quit England until Charles paid their troops, the king, now desperately in need of money, again convened Parliament. This, the so-called Long Parliament, consisted principally of Puritans. It was ready neither to fight the Scots nor to allow the king money to pay them. It imprisoned Laud, who was later executed, and brought the Earl of Strafford to trial for treason. A letter had been discovered written by Strafford to the king, stating, "You have an army in Ireland you may employ here to reduce this kingdom."[10] The word "this" was taken by John Pym, the Puritan leader in the Parliament, to refer to England. Strafford averred that "*this* kingdom" meant Scotland. Both sides were right. When he wrote, Strafford surely was thinking only of Scotland, but had Scotland been reduced, the royal will would certainly have been imposed upon England. Yet, since the charge could not be proved, Pym dropped the accusation of treason and introduced a bill of attainder, by which a man could be put to death "for the safety of the state." The vote carried. Its execution required the signature of the king. Charles protested and wept, but when he was told that he must distinguish between his duty as a man and his duty as a king, he signed. Subsequently, he looked upon this as the greatest sin of his life. He did not see that it was also a blunder, since he conceded thereby that the king is a constitutional monarch whose function it is to implement the will of Parliament.

Parliament carried through the Root and Branch Bill for the abolition of bishops in May 1641. Meanwhile, the removal of the strong hand of Stafford led to an uprising in Ireland in October and November, 1641. Rumor reported that thousands of Protestants were massacred in Ulster. The disgruntled Parliament presented Charles with the Grand Remonstrance, enumerating all

[10] *Ibid.,* p. 328.

grievances of his reign. Charles replied with an attempt to arrest the five leading members of Parliament. They escaped, the king left London, the five returned, the war was on.

In general, the north and west aligned themselves with the king, the south and east with Parliament. The first battles were indecisive, largely because there were many in Parliament itself— notably the Presbyterians—who had grave misgivings about fighting the Lord's anointed. As one of them said, "If we beate the King 99 times he would be King still . . . but if he beate us but once we should be hang'd."[11] The answer to that was not let the king win once. In order to secure the aid of the Scots, Parliament signed with Scotland the Solemn League and Covenant, promising to work toward uniformity of religion in the British Isles and toward the abolition in England of both "popery" and episcopacy. Scottish commissioners joined the Westminster Assembly, whose duty it was to reform the Anglican Church. The Westminster Confession, a confession of faith for the British Isles issued by the Assembly, was an exposition of Calvinist doctrine. It was accepted by Parliament in slightly modified form in 1648.

Cromwell

Meanwhile, the increasing successes of the Parliamentary forces were largely due to the extraordinary abilities of Oliver Cromwell, who had risen to leadership of the Parliamentary armies. He was resolved to have an army of saints, "men of spirit." Only such could stand against the sons of gentlemen, who fought for the king. Social station was not to be regarded. "I had rather have a plain russet-coated captain that knows what he fights for, and loves what he knows, than that which you call a gentleman and is nothing else. I honor a gentleman that is so indeed."[12] Nor did religious affiliation matter within the general framework of Puritan

[11] Robert S. Paul, *The Lord Protector* (London, 1955), p. 88.
[12] *Ibid.*, p. 63.

Protestantism. The charge was leveled against Cromwell that his men were "a company of Brownists, Anabaptists, factious inferior persons, etc." However, when a Presbyterian officer wished to discharge a fellow officer as an Anabaptist, Cromwell rejoined: "Sir, the State, in choosing men to serve It, takes no notice of their opinions, if they be willing faithfully to serve It, that suffices."[13] Cromwell was an Independent imbued with Milton's ideal of variety. Cromwell compared the several sects to the trees mentioned by the prophet Isaiah, the myrrh and the olive, the cypress and the plantains of Israel, all different and all alike affording shade.

Cromwell was not fatuous in looking upon the regiments thus recruited as Congregational churches; their chaplains were Congregational ministers. A meeting of officers was conducted alternately as a debate and a prayer meeting. Cromwell would sum up the sense of the meeting as if he were the clerk of the Society of Friends. When he was not in accord with the general will, he would offer to resign. Colonel William Goffe, one of Cromwell's commanders, would then remonstrate that, although Moses was not permitted by God to cross over into the Land of Promise, nevertheless he did not resign. The reference to the Old Testament was not lost on Cromwell, for the whole concept of the Holy Commonwealth was deeply rooted in the pattern of ancient Israel. The Old Testament supplied the ethics for the holy war. *The Souldiers Pocket Bible* disposed of the Sermon on the Mount by setting up texts in this manner:

Matthew 5:44 I say unto you, love your enemies.

II Chronicles 19:2 Wouldst thou help the wicked and love them that hate the Lord?

Psalm 139:21–22 Do not I hate them, O Lord, that hate thee? . . . I hate them with an unfeigned hatred.

All Cromwell's victories were ascribed to the Lord. God gave the enemy "as stubble to our swords." The Battle of Dunbar, occurring late in the war, when Cromwell was fighting the Scottish

13 *Ibid.*, p. 65.

royalists, might well have been considered a miracle, for Cromwell had been outgeneraled and outnumbered. He called his officers to a day of prayer. The leaders in the other camp, against the counsel of their general, forsook advantageous ground. Cromwell, singing the 68th Psalm, drove them into a wedge. Three thousand Scots fell, ten thousand were captured, and Cromwell lost less than thirty men. His army started in pursuit, but he halted them to sing the 117th Psalm. It has only two verses, but these were enough to praise the Lord and hold the ranks. To Parliament, Cromwell wrote, "We that serve you beg you not to own us, but God alone"; and to his wife, "The Lord has showed us an exceeding mercy; who can tell how great it is? My weak faith has been upheld. I have been in my inward man marvelously supported."[14] The victories were described by Cromwell as providences, and providences were the proof of divine favor. "My dear friend," he wrote, "let us look unto providences; surely they mean somewhat. They hang so together; have been so constant, so clear and unclouded. . . . What think you of Providence disposing the hearts of so many of God's people this way, especially in this poor army, wherein the great God has vouchsafed to appear? . . . We [desire] only to fear our great God, that we do nothing against his will."[15]

Three years before that battle, the king had surrendered to the Scots. Unable to come to terms with him, the Scots turned Charles over to the English. The king continued to negotiate with the Presbyterians, who controlled Parliament. He intrigued against the Independents, who largely made up the army, but also with the Independents against the Presbyterians, and separately with Scotland and France. Cromwell favored the king's restoration until his deviousness came to light. The king's courier was intercepted and his saddlebag rifled. It contained correspondence with the queen in which the king made it plain that he had no intention of keeping promises after he should have the power to break them. The king and Cromwell could not fathom each other. The king could not

[14] *Ibid.*, p. 408.
[15] *Ibid.*, p. 409.

understand a man with no ambition and no point of corruptibility. Cromwell could not comprehend a man of undeviating intent but devious strategy. The king was of no other mind than to restore absolute monarchy and the Church of England. Had he said so flatly, he might still have gone the way of Laud, but he would not have been left to atone for a record of duplicity by the dignity of his dying.

Cromwell's party had come to feel that if the king could not be trusted his life would have to be forfeit. Since the Presbyterians would not lift their hands against the Lord's anointed, the army, full of Cromwell's Independents, purged the Presbyterians from Parliament. That body was now declared to be a Supreme Court of Judicature, with authority to sit upon the king's life. Constitutionalists pointed out that it had never been anything of the sort, but Cromwell was impatient of all such "fleshly reasonings," for providences had declared the mind of the Lord. The charge against the king was really war guilt. He was responsible "for unnaturall Warres" by which "much Innocent bloud of the Free-people of this Nation hath been spilt."[16] The King refused to recognize the jurisdiction of the court, saying that "a King cannot be Tryed by any Superiour Jurisdiction upon Earth" and to violate this principle was to violate the "Freedome and Liberties of the People of England." Cromwell replied that the king had been guilty "of a breach of trust," which, "in a king ought to be punished more than any crime whatsoever."[17] Arbitrary power was being terminated by an exercise of arbitrary power, which could be justified, if at all, only by a sincere intent to terminate itself.

That was not easy, because the war did not end with the execution. Charles II was crowned by the Scots, who, never having approved of extremities, now undertook to place him upon the throne of his father. Cromwell's last battles were with the Scottish Presbyterians. The ultimate victory posed all the problems of a

[16] *Ibid.*, p. 187.
[17] *Ibid.*, p. 192[3].

settlement. The treatment of Ireland was brutal. Cromwell was persuaded that eight years previously the Irish "unprovoked had put the English to the most unheard of and most barbarous massacre (without respect of sex) that ever the sun beheld."[18] When, then, Drogheda fell, the whole garrison was massacred. Cromwell's justification was that this bitterness will save much "effusion of blood,"[19] the current justification of those who extenuate the incineration of cities to shorten war. Even greater resentment was occasioned in Ireland by the deportation of priests, the confiscation of estates, and the prohibition of the public exercise of Catholicism. The settlement in Scotland was generous. Presbyterianism became established, and the union between the two kingdoms was not disrupted.

And now came the question of England. The suggestion was offered that Cromwell be made king, but he declined the bauble of a crown and wisely so, for he would have been a pretender pitted against the legitimate aspirant. He chose rather the title used by the duke of Somerset during the minority of Edward VI, and was called the Lord Protector. He was a constitutional ruler, operating under an Instrument of Government. But Cromwell had as hard a time trying to be constitutional as Charles I had trying not to be. Three Parliaments were dismissed. The reason was their internal dissensions. The conservative element wished to retain property qualifications for the franchise. The more radical Levelers pointed out that not a few had lost their property through supporting the parliamentary cause and ought not on that account lose their votes. Some even asserted that "the poorest he that is in England hath a life to live, as the greatest he."[20] That was too much for Cromwell, who believed in the reign of the saints.

But who were the saints, and what was to be done with regard to the whole question of Church, state, and freedom of con-

[18] *Ibid.*, p. 215.

[19] *Ibid.*, p. 210.

[20] Rainborough in the Putney Debates, *Puritanism and Liberty*, ed. A. S. P. Woodhouse (London, 1938), p. 53.

science? What Cromwell actually did was to abandon a state church in favor of a national religion resting on three pillars: Presbyterian, Independent, and Baptist. They enjoyed full liberty, and to them he looked for full support. His second Parliament consisted of nominees from the Independent congregations. It was called Barebones Parliament, from the name of one of its members. At its first session, Cromwell delivered a commission that sounded like a sermon of ordination. As for the other groups, he applied Milton's theory of variety restricted by Acontius' theory of the two essentials. The Catholics and the Unitarians were not to be tolerated. The Quakers were to enjoy freedom of worship, and Cromwell had great respect for George Fox, saying to him, "If thou & I were butt an houre a day togeather wee should bee nearer one another."[21] But the Quakers were imprisoned for refusal to pay tithes, which Cromwell had not abolished. Whether to allow the Anglicans to make public use of the prayer book was a question that divided Cromwell and the House. He favored liberty, but could ensure it only by flouting democracy. Rather than override his own Parliament, he suffered the Book of Common Prayer to be suppressed.

Two notorious cases of blasphemy came up during the Protectorate. Blasphemy was deemed more serious than heresy because a public affront to the faith of the community. Biddle, the Unitarian, because of a heated public defense of his position, was arrested under the Blasphemy Act. He was not put to death, but banished to the Scilly Isles, where Cromwell saw to it that he should receive an allowance.[22] More exasperating was the case of James Nayler, the Quaker, who, distraught by long imprisonment, had not the gumption on his release to silence some enthusiastic women who, as he was riding into Bristol, marched alongside singing, "Hosanna, Hosanna, blessed is he that cometh in the name of the Lord." Nayler was arrested on the charge that he had staged a triumphal entry in imitation of Christ. This was deemed

[21] R. S. Paul, op. cit., p. 329, note 5.
[22] Ibid., p. 330, note 4.

manifest blasphemy. His case was tried before Parliament, which spent a whole session wrangling over this, instead of getting on with the business of government. The upshot was that Nayler was subjected to the barbarous penalties in vogue under Laud, but his life was spared. This was one of the great gains of the Protectorate. Neither heresy nor even blasphemy was any longer subject to the penalty of death.

The reign of the saints was little more successful at many points than that of the Stuarts. In the sphere of public finance, more church lands and crown lands were sold and the estates of Royalists confiscated. Direct taxation caused resentment among the saints. Another difficulty was that the revolution had been the work of the army, and the army was loath now to surrender in favor of Parliament. The army took over, and England was organized into districts under Major Generals. This meant the centralization of administration, even more than under the Stuarts. Attacks on the government became so irritating that censorship had to be introduced, and John Milton, proponent of free speech, became the licenser of books. He had never meant that the warfare for truth should include scurrility. A tone of disillusionment is heard in the prayer ascribed to the dying Lord Protector:

> Lord, though I am a miserable and wretched creature, I am in Covenant with Thee through grace. . . . Teach those who look too much on Thy instruments, to depend more upon Thyself. Pardon such as desire to trample upon the dust of a poor worm, for they are Thy People too. And pardon the folly of this short Prayer,— even for Jesus Christ's sake. And give us a good night, if it be Thy pleasure. Amen.[23]

After the brief interlude of Richard Cromwell, Charles II was summoned to England with the approval of Cromwell's General Monck and even of that rabid Puritan, William Prynne, and the reason was primarily that the Restoration did not undo the Protectorate. Charles II came to London as the constitutional monarch,

[23] *Ibid.*, p. 379.

taking office under an agreement and paid as a civil servant by Parliament. Furthermore, he came promising to extend "a liberty to tender consciences and that no man shall be disquieted or called into question for differences of opinion in matters of religion which do not disturb the peace of the kingdom."

Resurgence of Intolerance

Yet the reigns of Charles II and James II were marked by the last important resurgence of persecution. Curiously, the reason was in large part a fear of persecution. Englishmen would not tolerate Catholics because they did not trust Catholics to be tolerant of Protestants.

For that reason, every move on the part of Charles II to fulfill his promise of indulgence, if it included any relaxation for Catholics, was looked upon askance by Parliament, lest the glove should prove to hold the whip. And, again, such misgivings were not without warrant, for Charles did entertain a vast plan whereby England should be made Catholic in religion and absolutist in government. Charles did not avow his plan, but his brother James, the Duke of York, openly declared himself to be a Catholic and he was the heir to the throne. Protestant England responded by passing the Test Act of 1673, which excluded from public office any who did not disclaim the doctrine of transubstantiation. Yet the succession to the throne was not altered.

But, if the hostility against Rome was motivated by distrust and fear of Roman intolerance, one might suppose that the attitude toward the sectaries would have been indulgent. It was not so, however. The basic reasons were fear of disorder and the refusal to relinquish the ideal of one state and one Church, embracing one people, born and baptized into a commonwealth both of earth and of heaven.

The actual measures against the nonconformists were enacted under Charles II in the Clarendon Code, including the Conventicle Act, forbidding unauthorized meetings of as many as five persons at a time, and the Five-Mile Act which forbade ministers of the sects to come within five miles of cities. The most drastic stroke was the Uniformity Act of 1662, which required all the clergy to give unfeigned assent to *The Book of Common Prayer*, newly revised. They must also renounce the Solemn League and Covenant and profess the unlawfulness of taking up arms against the king. Those who refused to comply by the feast of St.Bartholomew should be deposed from the ministry of the Church of England. The number of evictions approximated two thousand. Greater were the sufferings of those members of clergy and laity who, for disobedience to the Conventicle Act and the Five-Mile Act, suffered distraint of goods and prolonged imprisonments. In the course of twenty years, eight ministers died in prison. The last persecution, which kept John Bunyan in Bedford jail, there to write *Pilgrim's Progress*, and so many Quakers in durance, is not by any means to be minimized. Neither is it to be exaggerated, for the treatment of dissent had been greatly modified since the days of Torquemada or John Calvin.

When James II succeeded his brother Charles II in 1685, he felt that the time had come for toleration; he therefore issued, in 1687, a Declaration of Indulgence, in which he candidly avowed his own adherence to the Church of Rome and his wish that all his subjects might be members of this communion:

> . . . Yet we humbly thank Almighty God, it is and has of long time been our constant sense and opinion . . . that conscience ought not to be constrained nor people forced in matters of mere religion. It has ever been contrary to our inclination, as we think it is to the interest of government, which it destroys by spoiling trade, depopulating countries, and discouraging strangers, and finally, that it never obtained the end for which it was employed.[24]

The king's behavior, however, rendered dubious his sincerity,

[24] Henry Gee and William John Hardy, *Documents Illustrative of English Church History* (London, 1914), pp. 641–42.

since in Scotland he demanded of the estates a sanguinary law against Protestants. England had had enough. The king must be a Protestant. An invitation was therefore issued to the king's son-in-law, William, Prince of Orange, to come over from Holland to England and assume the government. Thus came to pass the Glorious Revolution of 1688.

Act of Toleration

The religious question had now to be settled. William would have been glad to make the Church of England more comprehensive by reducing its demands, and would have granted toleration to those who still would not adhere, and he would exact no religious test for public office. But Parliament was not willing and, instead of comprehension, enacted toleration of those who would not conform. The Act of Toleration of 1689 is commonly regarded as one of the milestones in the struggle for religious liberty. As over against the past, it marked a great gain, though the liberty it accorded was distinctly limited. The Presbyterians and Independents, in order to be tolerated, had to subscribe to all of the Thirty-nine Articles, save those bearing on polity and liturgy. The Baptists were excused from the article on infant baptism. The Quakers received a special exemption from the obligation to take an oath. But Catholics and Unitarians were left still entirely without the pale, and disabilities as to public office and university degrees continued to apply to all nonconformists.

The significance of the Act of Toleration is less to be found in its actual enactments than in its position on the boundary between two eras. Behind lay the Inquisition, the wars of religion, the dragonnades, imprisonments, and exiles. The sixteenth century had been marked by extensive use of the death penalty for heresy, and the seventeenth, in England, by incarceration or exile, plus many social distraints. The eighteenth century was the age of Enlightenment, with its war upon superstition, fanaticism, and bigotry, even to the point of extinguishing all enthusiasm. The Act of Toleration stands at the threshold of this change. Its ambiguity lies in the effort to combine religious liberty with a national Establishment, to bring together a union of Church and state and freedom of religion. The concept of a Christian society, if only on a national scale, was still not abandoned, though its outward structure was relinquished when the sects were conceded an existence alongside of the Church.

Puritan Settlements in the New World

In the meantime, Puritanism had made an attempt to realize more perfectly its objectives in the New World than had been possible to do in the old: The erection of God's Holy Commonwealth. The migrations had not begun with so lofty a plan, but simply with the intent to escape persecution, and the first asylum, early in the seventeenth century, was found in Holland. At first, the refugees had difficulty in getting away and had to elude the officers of the Crown. One company surreptitiously rowed in small boats several miles offshore to a rendezvous with a Dutch vessel. On arrival, the fugitives were seasick. The men boarded the ship, leaving the women and children in the rowboats in the calm waters of an estuary till they were better recovered. The king's officers being in sight, the Dutch captain set sail, leaving the women and children behind. They contrived to join their husbands only a year later. During the Cromwellian period emigration was unimpeded, of course, and Puritan trading companies financed the ventures.

Holland proved to be only a temporary haven, because the arm of Archbishop Laud reached across the channel to inform the Dutch government that, unless surveillance were exercised over the refugees in Amsterdam and Leyden, whose nefarious notions were printed there and smuggled into England, he would curtail the religious freedom of Dutch merchants in London. This threat appears to have been the prime cause for the move to the New World, though Governor Bradford, in his *History of the Plymouth Plantation,* said that the Pilgrims left not out of "new-fangledness or giddy humor," but lest their children be seduced by the licentiousness of evil company and lest they be absorbed into the Dutch community and cease to be Englishmen.

Those who traversed the deep insisted they had not abandoned "deare England." They still regarded themselves as participants in the struggle in the homeland and believed that their "hazardous and voluntary banishment into this remote wilderness" would light a candle whose rays would span the ocean and enlighten old England. There was constant going back and forth between the old land and the new, and those in the old home watched in high hopes the rearing of the model of that godly commonwealth to which they aspired.[25]

The oddest and most troublesome feature of this venture was that, at the outset, the constituency was not homogeneous. The "Mayflower" carried fewer saints than strangers, "profane men, who being but seeming Christians, have made Christ and Christianity stinke in the nostrils of the poore Infidels"[26] (the Indians). The saints brought servants, craftsmen and, moreover, representatives of the merchant company which financed the expedition and expected to be repaid out of the labors of the next seven years. There were "sundry elder and younger persons who came over hither not out of respect to conscience or spirituall ends, but out of respect to friends or outward inlargements."[27] There was near mutiny on the "Mayflower" when the strangers announced that upon landing they would have their liberty. The saints then assembled the strangers and by "wisdom, patience, and a just and

[25] Sources cited in R. H. Bainton, "The Puritan Theocracy and the Cambridge Platform," *Collected Papers* (Boston, 1964), Vol. III.

[26] E. Winslow, *Good Newes from New England* (London, 1624), end of Dedication.

[27] John Cotton, *The Way of Congregational Churches Cleared* (London, 1648), p. 102.

equal carriage" quelled their mutinous speeches and induced them to drop this talk of liberty and submit to the reign of the saints in a Civil Body Politic. The Mayflower Compact was both a Church covenant and a civil contract. After all, the critics of Puritanism were right, that there was a connection between the theory of the Church and the constitution of the state. But it was no democracy, save within the coterie of the saints. Church and state were one, but not identical with the community. Only those who had tasted the sweetness of the Lord were qualified to come to Communion, and only those qualified could be members of the Church. Only members of the Church could hold office or vote for the highest offices. Only saints were full citizens. Others were inhabitants. This system instituted in Massachusetts in the 1630's was unlike anything in the old world.

Yet the spirit was not narrow, and there was regard for the scruples of a divergent conscience. On Christmas Day, for instance, Bradford, in order to show contempt for this Romish festival, summoned the men to work in the woods. Some protested a scruple and he excused them. Again, when a Jesuit visited the colony to discuss Indian affairs, Bradford was at pains to serve him only fish on Friday.

But positive schism could not be tolerated in the colony. There was an ex-Anglican clergyman, Lyford by name, who, having been received with his family, complained that the Pilgrims did not observe the Lord's Supper. The reason was that their ordained pastor, John Robinson, had been left behind in Holland. Lyford, on the strength of his previous Anglican ordination, set up a dissenting group and proceeded to administer the rite. The Pilgrims protested that they had carved this colony from the wilderness with incredible labors. Was it meet that this man, whom they had harbored with his family, should create a schism in their midst like a hedgehog who, in a storm, receives hospitality in the burrow of a rabbit, and then prickles the rabbit out?

The Pilgrims, and a little later the Bay Colony, were operating on the territorial principle. They had staked out an area for their holy experiment. Let those who joined, conform. If they would not conform, let them stake out another claim for themselves. There was room in such abundance that John Cotton could actually say, "Banishment in this countrey is not counted so much a confinement as an enlargement." Thus, the principle of territorialism was vastly more liberal in the New World than in the old, because here there was somewhere to go. This situation explains why Massachusetts fell later far behind England, by reverting to the death penalty in the hanging of four Quakers on Boston Commons. They were hanged because they refused to stay out of Massachusetts. They had been repeatedly expelled and had repeatedly returned. They were offered their lives if they would leave and promise not to come back; in Pennsylvania, or Rhode Island, they would be unmolested. But they would not promise and died for their rejection of territorialism in religion.

Puritan Economics

The confessional era, like every other, made its contributions to the relations between religion and culture. In the economic sphere, Puritanism, like the earlier Calvinism, has been credited with accelerating the rise of capitalism. Certainly the industry, diligence, thrift, and integrity of the Puritans tended to make them prosperous, and they contributed one essential ingredient to the capitalist system, a sense of honor in keeping their word, for capitalism is possible only if contracts are made with the intent of being kept rather than evaded.

The generosity of the Puritan laity during the seventeenth century was amazing. Poverty in this period was acute. One reason was the increase in population, which went up forty per cent during the sixteenth century and thirty per cent between 1600 and 1640. A larger agricultural production was needed. For that reason forests were cut back, and farms were "enclosed," not to raise wool as formerly, but to improve agriculture. But tenants were displaced thereby, and not readily relocated in developing industries. The Crown had no answer other than to resist all change and relieve poverty by enactments never fulfilled. Of the huge sums contributed for relief between 1480 and 1660 only seven per cent came from taxation. The Church could not exercise her ancient role because "her wings had been clipped and some quite cut away—feather, flesh, and bone." Then it was that the laity stepped in, not to dispense alms, but to relieve, educate, and rehabilitate. During the above eighteen decades, the total contributions amounted to £3,102,696, a sum equal to the royal revenue from lands. The men who gave all this were from among the gentry and the merchants, that is, those who were the mainstay of the Puritan party.[28]

Puritan Social Life

In the area of love the Puritans were far from frigid, but had no use for the cult of romantic love, for adoration should be directed only to God. When Cromwell's wife chided him for not being duly mindful of her and the little ones in the midst of his campaigns, he answered, "My Dearest: Thou art dearer to me than any creature: let that suffice."[29] Mutual commitment to God made of marriage a partnership in the service of an ideal, a companionship enhanced by God's love of variety, evidenced, as Milton said, in "a resembling unlikeness and an unlike resemblance"[30] of the sexes. *Paradise Lost* is a love story. Eve comes to Adam proposing that in the interests of efficiency they divide their labors, he tending the woodbine and the ivy, she the myrtle and the rose. He protests that he would rather have her company than increased

[28] Wilbur Kitchener Jordan, *Philanthropy in England 1480–1660* (London, 1950).

[29] R. S. Paul, *op. cit.*, p. 229.

[30] *The Works of John Milton* (New York, Columbia University Press, 1931–38), IV, 85–86.

production, but he will not constrain her, and Eve trips blithely into the bushes. Adam prepares for her return a garland to adorn her tresses. She comes back holding the already tasted fruit from the forbidden tree. Adam turns pale, for he knows that now she must surely die. Rather than continue without her, he, too, eats, that he may share her doom. Adam fell through chivalry. But chivalry may also make the marriage bond more unstable, and Milton it was who advocated divorce for incompatibility. Since marriage is of the spirit, the bond does not exist if there be no union other than that of the flesh. As for the relations of the sexes within some of the religious societies, notably the Quakers, women came to exercise a full equality with men.

Baroque Art

In the field of arts and literature, this is the period of the Baroque, characterized by the ornate and extravagant, the passionate and dramatic, delighting in the portrayal of conflicts whose only resolution can be death. Some feel that this style belongs peculiarly to the Catholic Counter-Reformation and to Spain. It is claimed that every Spaniard is both a Don Quixote and a Sancho Panza, and the conflict of the two in the one is the secret of the Spanish soul. There are, indeed, Spaniards who fit the picture, for example, St. Theresa with her rapturous visions and her eminent common sense. For, when her companion began to weep over the thought of what would happen were she to die and leave Theresa alone, the saint answered, "If you die I will face it then. Now, let's go to sleep." Giovanni Bernini conveys the joy and the torment of her ecstatic trance in his sculpture: she floats on clouds of stone, an angel over her, and above, colored windows suffuse the carved stone with golden light. But, is all this spiritual tension more Spanish or Italian than the state of the Puritan with "a civil war in his bowels"?

Protestant art found in painting its master in Rembrandt, but in

30

Convened for the purpose of dealing with the widespread dissension within the Roman Catholic Church in the wake of the Protestant Reformation, it defined the position of the Church, precluding reconciliation with the Protestants and, at the same time, furthered the Catholic Reformation. Illustration from Martin Chemnitz, *Examinis Concilii Tridentini . . . opus.* Frankfort am Main, 1585.

31

A woodcut of Erasmus in the *Cosmographia* of Sebastian Münster, 1554. This picture in a copy of the book found in Spain was defaced by the Inquisition.

32

Among the Protestants church music was revised by Luther to meet the needs of congregational participation, though not to the exclusion of the choir. From his powerful hymns the line runs to Bach and Handel. The Catholic Reformation was marked by an effort to achieve austere simplicity. The Council of Trent in 1562 severely criticized elaborate embellishments in the settings of the Mass. Palestrina, however, saved church music from a too-stark simplicity. Before the subject grew controversial he had already presented his *First Book of the Mass* to Pope Julius III in 1554, as is shown above. In 1557, his second Mass (dedicated to Philip II of Spain, although it was called the *Mass of Pope Marcellus*) satisfied the reductionists without going to the length of unaccompanied plain song in unison. Pope Pius IV compared the music of this Mass to that heard by St. John during his vision of the New Jerusalem.

33a

Fig. 33a shows the Virgin of Guadalupe above symbols derived from the Aztecs: the eagle with the serpent standing on the cactus. The black crescent under the feet of the Virgin is probably the moon, since the Virgin is shown with stars on her robe as the Queen of Heaven. The appearance of the crescent, however, suggests rather the horns of an ox.

33b

33c

Fig. 33b shows Francisco Pareja teaching Chrisianity to the Indians in Mexico.

Fig. 33c is from a native account, unfriendly to the missionaries in Peru, expressing resentment against their efforts to have the natives marry.

The massacre precipitated the wars of religion in France. The Duke Francis of Guise, who had instigated it, claimed that the Protestants were overstepping the boundaries on worship assigned to them by the Edict of January 1562. A key identifies characters and scenes; it is easier to follow by the order on the page. On the left, leaning on the wall and marked *E*, is the Cardinal of Lorraine, the duke's brother. Below the cardinal, marked *K*, is the trumpeter; on the bottom to the left, marked *D*, is the minister whose life was saved because the

sword of his assailant broke. At the bottom, a little left of center, marked *B*, is the duke. To the right is the pulpit, marked *C*, with a praying minister. On the far right, marked *G*, are persons trying to escape over the wall. At the top, *F* indicates a hole broken through the tiles, and *H* is used twice to designate those seeking to escape over the roof while being "arquebussed." The illustration is from *Scènes Historiques* par J. Torotel et L. Perrissin, ed. Alfred Franklin (Paris, 1886), p. 130.

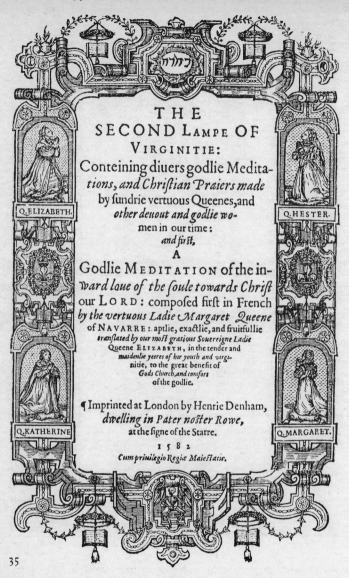

THE
SECOND Lampe OF
VIRGINITIE:
Conteining diuers godlie Meditations, and Christian Praiers made
by sundrie vertuous Queenes, and
other deuout and godlie women in our time:
and first,
A
Godlie MEDITATION of the inward loue of the soule towards Christ
our LORD: composed first in French
by the vertuous Ladie Margaret Queene
of NAVARRE: aptlie, exactlie, and fruitfullie
translated by our most gratious Souereigne Ladie
Queene ELIZABETH, in the tender and
maidenlie yeeres of hir youth and virginitie, to the great benefit of
Gods Church, and comfort
of the godlie.

¶ Imprinted at London by Henric Denham,
dwelling in Pater noster Rowe,
at the signe of the Starre.
1582
Cum priuilegio Regiæ Maiestatis.

Q.ELIZABETH.   Q.HESTER.
Q.KATHERINE   Q.MARGARET.

35

The title page of this tract published in 1582 reads: "The Second
Lampe of Virginitie: Conteining diuers godlie Meditations, and
Christian Praiers made by sundrie vertuous Queenes, and other
deuout and godlie women in our time . . . aptlie, exactlie, and fruitfullie translated by our most gratious Sovereigne Ladie Queene Elizabeth, in the tender and maidenlie yeeres of her youth and virginitie,
to the great benefit of Gods Church, and comfort of the godlie." The

figures around the margin are Elizabeth herself, Catherine Parr, Henry VIII's widow, Hester (Esther) and Margaret of Navarre, the sister of Francis I and the grandmother of Henry IV, respectively.

Elizabeth was not averse to having her piety heralded and herself composed prayers for public consumption in which "with bowed heart and bended knees" she rendered "humblest acknowledgments and lowliest thanks; and not the least for that the weakest sex hath been so fortified by Thy strongest help that neither my people might find lack by my weakness nor foreigners triumph at my ruin. . . ."

36. TRACTS ANENT MARY TUDOR

36

Mary Tudor's persecution of the Protestants, which gave her the name "Bloody Mary," resulted in several tracts defending the rightness of popular revolution against a sovereign suppressing the True Religion. The print above appeared in a Catholic satire by Peter Frarin, *An Oration against the Unlawful Insurrections of the Protestants of our time* (1566) and refers to two Protestant tracts that appeared in 1559. That by Christopher Goodman, who appears on the left blowing his blast, was entitled *How Superior Powers Ought to be Obeyed.* The other was by John Knox, who appears on the right also blowing his blast, and was entitled *The First Blast Against the Monstrous Regiment of Women.* (The word regiment meant rule.) Knox was inveighing against Catherine de Médici and Mary of Guise, the regent in Scotland and mother of Mary, Queen of Scots, as well as against Mary Tudor. The queen in the print above is probably Mary Tudor.

37a

Fig. 37a shows Gustavus Adolphus, king of Sweden, at the Battle of Leipzig in September, 1631. (Engraving from G. Winter, *Geschichte des dreissigjährigen Krieges* [Berlin, 1893].)

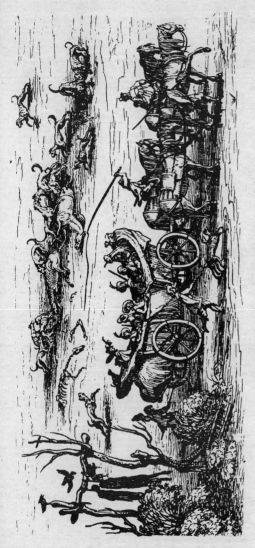

37b

Reisewagen während des dreißigjährigen Krieges.

Facsimile aus Jacques Callots (1594–1635) Radirung „Belagerung von Breda'', 1624.

Fig. 37b is a detail from an engraving "The Siege of Breda, 1624" by the French artist Jacques Callot (1594–1635). Breda, a city in the Netherlands, was then besieged by the Spaniards. The inscription reads "Travel Coach during the Thirty Years' War", and shows packs of wild dogs feasting on carcasses of horses, travelers in the stage-coach armed with arquebuses, and two hanged men on a makeshift gallows. The picture typifies conditions of hunger, terror, and anarchy in large parts of central Europe. The Thirty Years' War was to last for another twenty-four years. (Facsimile from G. Winter, *Geschichte des dreissigjährigen Krieges* [Berlin, 1893].)

René Descartes (Cartesius), 1596–1650, French philosopher and mathematician, founder of the philosophical system known as Cartesianism. It created the basis for modern philosophical thought. The best-known saying of Descartes is *Cogito, ergo sum* ("I think, therefore I am"). The inscription under the picture reads *Bene qui latuit, bene vixit*, which may be freely rendered "A life well hid is a life well spent." (Engraving by Gérard Edelinck [1640–1707], from a portrait by Frans Hals [1580?–1666].)

38

Rijksmuseum, Amsterdam

39. LAUD'S PROGRAM

Archbishop Laud announces that there shall be only canonical prayers and no afternoon sermons. The bishops say they so desire it. The citizens relpy, "Then no bishops." (From a contemporary cartoon.)

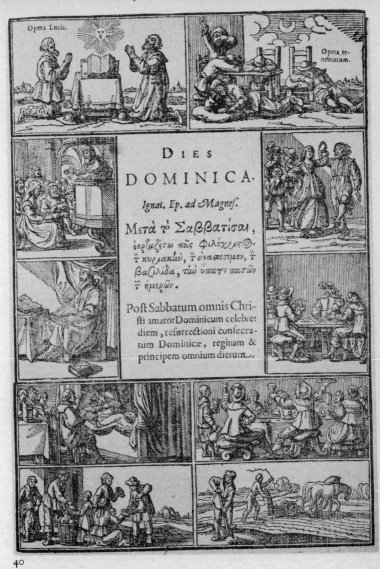

The observance of the Sabbath, i.e., of Sunday, is contrasted here with non-observance. The *Opera lucis*, "the deeds of light," on the left, are shown opposite the *Opera tenebrarum*, "the deeds of darkness," on the right. (Title page of a Puritan tract by Thomas Young, published 1639.)

41a

10 of Maÿ the Boocke of Sportes vpon the Lords day was burnt by the Hangman in the place where the Crosse stoode, & at Exhange

41b

Charles I aroused the ire of the Puritans by issuing a *Book of Sports* lawful to engage in on the Sabbath. Puritans objected to *any* sports on the Sabbath, and objected to the sport of bear baiting on *any* day of the week.

Fig. 41a shows the traditional pastime of bear baiting as depicted already in the Luttrell Psalter (1325). The rules of the game had probably not changed very much in the succeeding centuries.

Fig. 41b depicts the burning of the *Book of Sports* in 1644 by the Puritans, evidently a symbolic and solemn ceremony. The inscription reads: "10 of Maÿ the Boocke of Sportes upon the Lords day was burnt by the Hangman in the place where the Crosse stoode, & at Exchange".

The Anabaptist. The Brownist.

The Familist. The Papist.

42

The Anglicans claimed that the sectaries as much as the Catholics tossed the Bible up in a blanket. The Anabaptists were really not a live problem in the England of the seventeenth century, though there had been some of them in the previous century. In the Puritan period they were merely characters in old books, whose names men still feared. The Brownists were named after Robert Browne, who first promulgated congregational principles, but whom the Congregationalists did not claim as their spiritual father because after many imprisonments he returned to the Anglican Church. The Familists were the followers of Hendrik Niclaes, a sixteenth-century Dutch prophet who claimed that his initials signified Homo Novus (the "new man"). His "Family of Love" sect gained a considerable following in England. The above illustration dates from 1641. Across the picture a hand has written "All Independants."

The Puritans were called "Roundheads" because they wore their hair short. The Cavaliers allowed theirs to fall in what their opponents called "lovelocks." In the above illustration (from "A Dialogue or Parley between Prince Rupert's Dog Puddle and Tobie's Dog Pepper," 1642), we see the two parties railing at each other with the aid on the Cavalier side of a long-haired poodle, and on the Roundhead side of a short-haired mongrel.

A contemporary cartoon against Archbishop Laud and the High Commission, with a particular dig at the *Et cetera* oath. (From Th. Sterry, *A Rot Amongst the Bishops*, London, 1641.)

44

45. ICONOCLASM IN THE PURITAN REVOLUTION

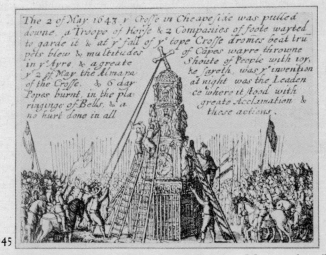

45

Pulling down the Cheapside Cross in London, May 2, 1643. (From a contemporary engraving by W. Hollar.)

46

For the first time in the history of Christendom in the West, women were allowed to raise their voices in the public meeting-houses of the Quakers. This was done in apparent disregard of the injunction of St. Paul in his first letter to the Corinthians, 14:34–35: "Let your women keep silence in the churches: for it is not permitted unto them to speak; but they are commanded to be under obedience, as also saith the law. And if they will learn any thing, let them ask their husbands at home: for it is a shame for women to speak in the church." From then on, women have gradually achieved complete equality of rights among most Protestant denominations, at least in theory if not in fact. In the seventeenth century, however, the Quakers made themselves conspicuous by this revolutionary innovation, and the motif of a preaching woman served as a subject for various painters and engravers. This engraving, now in the British Museum, is by Carolus Allard, a Dutchman, early eighteenth century.

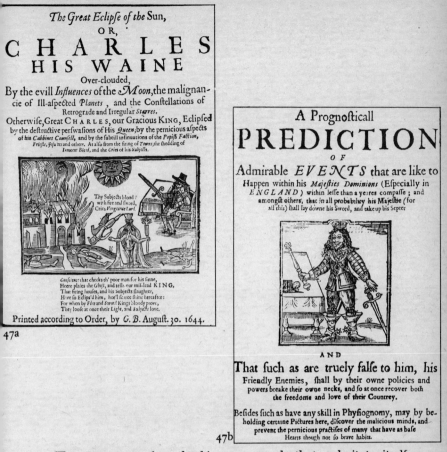

The Great Eclipse of the Sun,
OR,
CHARLES
HIS WAINE
Over-clouded,
By the evill *Influences* of the *Moon*, the malignan-
cie of Ill-aspected *Planets* , and the Constellations of
Retrograde and Irregular *Starres.*
Otherwise, Great CHARLES, our Gracious KING, Eclipsed
by the destructive perswasions of His *Queen*, by the pernicious aspects
of his *Cabinet Counsell*, and by the subtill insinuations of the *Popish Faction,*
Priests, Jesuites and others. As also from the firing of *Towns*, the shedding of
Innocent Blood, and the *Cries* of his *Subjects.*

Thy Subjects blood!
with fire and sword,
Cries *Vengeance Lord.*

Conscience that checks th' poor man for his sinne,
Heere plaies she *Ghost*, and tells our mis-lead KING,
That firing houses, and his Subjects slaughter,
H've so Eclips'd him, hee'l scarce shine hereafter:
For when by *Fire* and *Sword* Kings bloody prove,
They loose at once their Light, and Subjects love.

Printed according to Order, by *G. B.* August. 30. 1644.

47a

A Prognosticall
PREDICTION
OF
Admirable *EVENTS* that are like to
Happen within his *Majesties Dominions* (Especially in
ENGLAND) within lesse than a yeares compasse ; and
amongst others, that in all probability his Majestie (for
all this) shall lay downe his Sword, and take up his Scepter

AND
That such as are truely false to him, his
Friendly Enemies, shall by their owne policies and
powers breake their owne necks, and so at once recover both
the freedome and love of their Countrey.

Besides such as have any skill in Physiognomy, may by be-
holding certaine Pictures here, discover the malicious minds, and
prevent the pernicious practises of many that have as base
Hearts though not so brave habits.

47b

The party opposed to the king was very loath to admit to itself
that it was rebelling against his sacred person. At first the claim was
made that the struggle was designed to liberate the king from his
evil counsellors, "the Malignants," among whom his wife was the
worst inasmuch as she was a French Catholic who attended Mass and
had priests in her entourage. In this tract (Fig. 47a), she is portrayed
as the moon whose shadow is eclipsing the Sun, her husband the king.

King Charles declared himself to be voluntarily on the side of those
who were alleged to be holding him in captivity by their evil counsel.
When, then, he grasped the sword to resist his would-be liberators
(Fig. 47b), they warned him that if he would retain the scepter he
must drop the sword.

48

The Rump Parliament brought King Charles I to trial on January 20, 1649. After thirty-two witnesses were examined, Charles was condemned to death on the fifth day of the trial, as a "tyrant, traitor, murderer, and enemy of his country." The execution was carried out on a scaffolding erected outside the Banqueting Hall at Whitehall, on January 30, 1649. Much of England and most of Europe were horrified at the news. (Engraving from A. D. Innes, *A History of the British Nation* [London, 1912].)

49. THE RUMP PARLIAMENT DISMISSED

49

In 1653 Cromwell dissolved the Rump Parliament. This cut depicting the dismissal was printed in Holland and is obviously satirical. Note the owl with the candle on the right. Cromwell and his men are inaccurately shown on the left with the hats and long hair of the Cavaliers. The caption on the wall (upper right) reads: "This House is to let." Beneath Cromwell's cane we read: "Be gone you rogues. You have sete (sat) long enough."

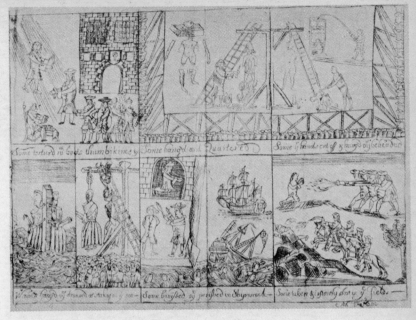

Some tortur'd to bate thumbikines. Some hang'd and Quartered. Some if heads cut of & hung'd & beheaded.

Who's hang'd & drown'd at Stake & set. Some banished or perished in Shipwrack. Some taken & instantly shot in ye field.

The Scots abhorred the measures of Charles I to subject the Church of Scotland to the Church of England. The "Covenant with God," first drawn up and sworn to when Mary was plotting against Protestantism, was now renewed, in 1638. The National Covenant, as it came to be known, found enthusiastic support throughout Scotland. It provided the spark that touched off the civil war, as a result of which Charles I lost his crown and his head.

The acts of persecution of the Covenanters depicted here are most likely those committed by the troops of the Duke of Monmouth, bastard son of Charles II, in 1679, following the defeat of the Covenanters at Bothwell Brigg, on June 22. (Facsimile of the frontispiece to *A Cloud of Witnesses*, 1720, from Th. B. Macauley, *History of England*, ed. Firth [1913], I, 496.)

James Naylor Quaker set 2 howers on the Pillory at Westminster whiped by the Hangman to the old Exchainge London, Som dayes after Stood two howers more on the Pillory & at the Exchainge and there had his Tongue Bored throug with a hot Iron, & Stygmatized in the Forehead with the Letter B: Decemr. 17: anno Dom: 1656:

51   A contemporary engraving attributed to W. Hollar, showing the penalties inflicted on James Naylor, the Quaker, who was charged with blasphemy.

The Manifeſtation of Joy, Or, The Loyal Subjeƈts grateful acknowledgment.

Occaſionally Written upon the Publication of His Majeſties moſt Gracious Declaration,

Allowing *LIBERTY* of

CONSCIENCE.

Tune of , The Country Farmer.

This may be Printed, R. P.

52

James II issued a Declaration of Indulgence which was hailed with enthusiasm in the ballad "The Manifestation of Joy," the illustration for which appears above. However, this Declaration was regarded by most Englishmen actually as a device to secure toleration for Catholics, who would deny it to Protestants when they themselves were in power.

53. THE GLORIOUS REVOLUTION

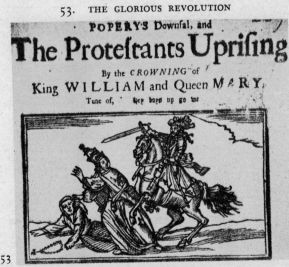

POPERY'S Downfal, and

The Proteſtants Upriſing

By the *CROWNING* of

King WILLIAM and Queen MARY.

Tune of, hey boys up go we

53

Rejoicing was widespread in England when William of Orange expelled the Catholic James II and when the Protestant succession was secured through William and Mary.

54a

In the art of Rembrandt one observes a personal development away from the extravagances of the Baroque to a more subdued and deeper piety, as is shown here in the comparison of an earlier with a later treatment of the self-disclosure of the risen Christ to his disciples at Emmaus. In the first (Fig. 54a), Christ is seated at a table, blocking the light of the candle, so that one sees little more than his silhouette. On the other side of the table the light falls fully

54b

on the face of an astounded disciple who with dramatic gestures expresses his utter astonishment. In the second (Fig. 54b), the Master and the disciples sit in a subdued light. There is nothing dramatic or even attractive about the figure of Jesus. He is "without form and comeliness and when we see him, there is no beauty that we should desire him." In the moment of recognition the disciples are too awed for gesture or speech and one beholds only their wonder.

55

As seen in an old woodcut reproduced from a pamphlet, *The Covenant in the Wilderness*, by Roland H. Bainton (printed by the Printing-Office of the Yale University Press, presented by the New Haven Association of Churches and Ministers to our friends attending the General Council of the Congregational Christian Churches, June 23–30, 1954).

"On the twenty-fifth day of April, it being the Sabbath, in the year 1638, a band of immigrant Puritans gathered for the worship of God under a great oak on the shore of Quinnipiac Bay. The spot was near the present corner of College and George Streets in New Haven, Connecticut, and is commemorated by a plaque. There were two ministers in the company. The first, John Davenport, preached in the morning on the text, 'Then Jesus was led up of the Spirit into the wilderness.' The second, Peter Prudden, spoke in the afternoon on 'The voice of one crying in the wilderness.' Evidently they were agreed as to where they were! . . . Pictorial representation of the event was delayed for over a century, and first appeared in the quaint cut reproduced above from a broadside entitled 'Some Poetical Thoughts on the Difficulties Our Forefathers Endured in Planting Religious and Civil Liberty in This Western World' (New Haven? ca. 1770). Observe that the sexes are segregated like Adams and Eves on either side of the Tree of the Knowledge of Good and Evil. The practice of separate seating in churches was thus projected backwards into the wilderness."

56. SKYLINE OF BOSTON SHOWING THE CHURCHES IN 1774

Print by James Turner.

56

57a

The earliest New England churches are more properly called meeting houses. The structure was square with a four-sided hip roof culminating in a point. Fig. 57a, built in West Springfield (Mass.) in 1702, is a little more elaborate, having four dormers and a belfry. The Christopher Wren style became dominant from 1710 to 1800. Frequently the door would be placed in the middle of one of the long sides of the rectangle that comprised the church instead of in the middle of one of the short sides. We see this in Fig 57c, built in Farmington (Conn.) in 1771. The purpose behind this was to depart as fully as possible from the liturgical type of church which conventionally had the altar in

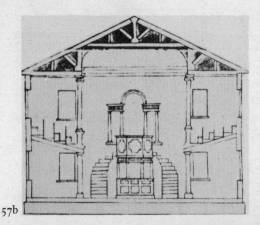

57b

the apse at one of the short sides, and the door at the other. Also, in the Puritan churches the pulpit was opposite the door. During the first quarter of the nineteenth century, however, the pulpit was moved back to the end of the church, as seen in the architect's plan of Asher Benjamin (Fig. 57b). The pulpit was elevated by stairs on either side. Below it was the communion table. Pews were banked in front, with aisles on the sides. The Greek revival style commencing around 1825 (Fig. 57d) gave the building an appearance approximating more nearly that of an ancient temple. (Fig. 57c and Fig. 57d are from *Meetinghouse and Church in Early New England* by Edmund W. Sinnott, copyright © 1963 by Edmund W. Sinnott, and are used by permission of McGraw-Hill Book Company.)

57c

57d

58a

58b

58c

what respect was his painting Protestant? Perhaps only in the sense that it is the expression of personal piety manifest in the delineation of biblical figures with a new intensity and sensitivity. Witness his treatment of the "Prodigal Son" or of the "Flight into Egypt."

In church architecture, the seventeenth century affords a notable new departure in the smaller churches, especially in those of Christopher Wren. The need to replace the edifices destroyed by the Great Fire of London in 1666, and to build virgin sanctuaries in the New World, provided an opportunity for creativity lacking wherever the older buildings were simply taken over. The newness is less evident in St. Paul's Cathedral, which employs the Renaissance dome, as it is in the smaller churches which are essentially Greek temples surmounted by Gothic spires. The interior has the proportions of a temple. The orientation is Protestant, with attention focused on the pulpit rather than upon the altar. In New England, where new sites could be chosen, the church was usually built on an eminence, as Andrea Palladio (1518–80) had recommended, so that the ascent to the threshold might convey the sense of elevation. The interior was plain, without stained glass windows. At one point, however, decoration was permissible; in the carvings of the pulpit chairs, the communion table, and the pulpit itself, commonly of the swallow's nest type, elevated and reached by gracefully winding staircases, after the manner so dear to the Baroque in the palaces of princes. The disparate elements were brought together by Wren into a unified whole, at once simple, chaste, dignified, and reverent.

XI

Enlightenment and Revival

Enlightenment in the eighteenth century was in revolt against confessionalism. There was an intense revulsion against the religious fanaticism of the preceding era, euphemistically referred to as enthusiasm. According to John Locke, enthusiasm arises from "the conceits of a warmed and over-weening brain."[1] Samuel Butler in his *Hudibras* berated "The petulant capricious sects, the maggots of corrupted texts," "Those spider-saints, that hang by threads spun out of the entrails of their heads." They are contentious: "The Ghibellines, for want of Guelphs, divert their rage upon themselves."[2] Butler mocked that the Quakers kept their hats on to conceal the cracks in their skulls. The virulence of such jibes discloses that, in inveighing against enthusiasm, men can themselves fall prey to enthusiasm.

Religious Peace

A measure of truth in these strictures cannot, of course, be denied. One finds it strange and sad to discover two such religious leaders as Roger Williams and George Fox writing tracts against

---

[1] John Locke, *On Enthusiasm*, appended after 1700 to the *Essay concerning Humane Understanding*, Book IV, chap. xix, excerpts in John M. Creed and John S. B. Smith, *Religious Thought in the Eighteenth Century* (Cambridge, Eng., 1934), pp. 10–16, especially p. 13.

[2] Samuel Butler, *Hudibras*, ed. A. R. Waller (Cambridge, Eng., 1905), Part III, Canto I, p. 234; Part III, Canto II, p. 239, 257.

each other. That of Williams was entitled, *George Fox digg'd out of his burrowes*, and the reply of Fox, *A New-England fire-brand quenched*. At the same time, one is not to forget that such sectaries had been chiefly responsible for creating that toleration so prized by the eighteenth century. Comparatively speaking, this century was, indeed, an age of toleration. In England, the Dissenters suffered only from disabilities. They were excluded from public life, but could obviate the rule by the compromise of taking Communion once in their lives in the Anglican Church. This was called "occasional conformity." They could not take degrees at the universities, but founded the Dissenting Academies which so excelled the universities that the Anglicans sent their sons to the Dissenters. In the German lands, the Treaty of Westphalia was based on the territorial principle and, under its terms, the archbishop of Salzburg banished fifteen thousand Protestants, but such actions were very rare. In Prussia, Frederick the Great tolerated all religions because he believed in none. In Austria, Joseph II, a Catholic sovereign whom Frederick contemptuously called "my brother, the sacristan," asserted that the state is not a cloister and that coercion of conscience is an arrogant flouting of the patience of God. In France, despite the revocation of the Edict of Nantes, there were still Protestants. In the Cevennes, they had rebelled rather than go into exile. The insurrection was suppressed, but survivors enjoyed thereafter the tolerance of indifference.

Pope Benedict XIV was ready to let rest the thunders of the Vatican, for Christ had refused to call down fire from heaven. The Inquisition, to be sure, continued in Spain and in South America until the early decades of the nineteenth century, but the Jesuits, the puissant arm of the Counter-Reformation, were expelled from Portugal, Spain, and France, and in 1773 Pope Clement XIV dissolved the order. (It was reconstituted in 1814.) By comparison, at least with previous centuries, the eighteenth was an age of religious liberty.

Likewise, the century was relatively a peaceful one. War is commonly followed by revulsion against war, and the literature against war flourishes in the first flush of peace. "Sweet is war to him who has had no taste of it," wrote Pindar and, after him, Erasmus. Equally true was the converse, and Erasmus' *Complaint of Peace* was more frequently reprinted in the eighteenth century than in the sixteenth, and its themes developed with renewed poignancy by satirists and pundits. Voltaire, in *Candide*, had his hero pass from a village of the Avars, fired by the Bulgars, to a village of the Bulgars, fired by the Avars. And Jonathan Swift, in *Gulliver's Travels*, explained to repulsive horselike Houyhnhnms, how human beings called Yahoos fought over such questions as "whether flesh be bread or bread be flesh, and whether the juice of a berry be blood or wine." The Houyhnhnms were not greatly disturbed because the Yahoos could do each other little damage, having no claws on their feet. Then Gulliver, to set forth the valor of his own countrymen, described their weapons of carnage and told how he had seen them blow up a hundred enemies at once in a siege and as many in a ship, and had seen the dead bodies come down in pieces from the clouds to the great diversion of the spectators. The Enlightenment revived the old Stoic theme that animals of the same species are not so deadly to each other as men to men. Voltaire concluded his history with the query, "Is this history which I have finished the history of serpents or tigers? No, serpents and tigers would never treat their fellows so."

But satire is born of hope, and the men of this generation were profoundly hopeful that they could achieve permanent peace not by conquest but by a federation of the world. This was the age of peace plans. They were advanced by William Penn in England; by Abbé Charles-Irénée de Saint-Pierre, Eymeric Crucé, and Jean-Jacques Rousseau in France; by Immanuel Kant in Germany; and by Johann Comenius in Moravia. Their hopes did not appear fatuous because a relative degree of peace had been achieved. The reason was in part that the national states were marked by a balance of power and a community of culture in which none desired the extermination of any other. Accessory factors were the centralization of government and the regulation of finance, so that monarchs could pay their mercenaries and restrain them from living by pillage. Again, mercenaries were not crusaders and preferred to serve their paymasters by wearing down the enemy through maneuvers rather than by shedding of blood. Defoe said that in his day it was customary for armies of fifty thousand men to spend the whole campaign in dodging each other. The art of war, said another, consists less in knowing how to defend a fortress than in knowing how to surrender it honorably. The enlightened commanders, moreover, revived the code of honor of the age of chivalry. The French commander would say to the English, "You shoot first," and the English would reply, "Oh, no. You have the honor." If battles did occur, they were costly. But when hostilities ended, the peace would be magnanimous.[3]

Search for Natural Ethics

One observes in this development a blending of circumstance and codes of conduct, but more significant than the anachronism of chivalry was the philosophy of life, Christian in impulse, but Stoic in form. The doctrine of natural law had long enabled Christians to believe that they could deal with Jews and Turks on the basis of a common moral code. In the early sixteenth century, the Spanish theologian Francisco de Vitoria had extended the doctrine to include the American Indians. But, could natural law provide a common morality for Christians if they were split into warring confessional groups? To insure that it should, Hugo Grotius, a devout Dutchman of the seventeenth century, dechristianized natural law by treating it as an ethic, valid "even if there were no God (which God forbid)."[4] This secularized view of natural law was further developed in the late sixteenth and the seventeenth century by the German jurists Johannes Althusius (1557–1638)

[3] Denis de Rougemont, *Love in the Western World* (New York, 1940), p. 239.

[4] Hugo Grotius, *De Ivre Belli ac Pacis* (Amsterdam, 1642), Prolog, xx.

and Samuel Pufendorf (1632–94), and in the eighteenth it became commonplace. Such natural law is not anti-Christian but sub-
Christian, an ethic of justice interpreted in that age in conservative
rather than revolutionary terms. But, if political morality rests on
a base broader than Christianity, then there is no ground for
churchly direction of governmental affairs. Such a conclusion was
already implicit in the view of Aquinas, according to which political principles are discernible by reason without revelation. The
Enlightenment went still further in disclaiming the need for divine
guidance in reaching political decisions. That was why Franklin's
proposal of recourse to prayer to resolve a deadlock in the Constitutional Convention was rejected.[5] Cromwell's officers would have
taken a day out to seek the mind of the Lord, but the American
Founding Fathers felt that politics lie within the domain of man's
natural reason, which should not be abdicated. Prayer begins
where reason ends. This does not mean that the state is emancipated from the will of God, but that in matters of state man need
seek no special illumination. This whole point of view, widely
prevalent in the age of Enlightenment, allowed for diversity in
religion and unity in ethics. Thereby, a new garb was tailored for
Christendom.

Spirit of Inquiry

In an atmosphere of tolerance and peace, the spirit of inquiry
revived. Men began to grapple afresh with the perennial difficulties
of religious faith. In their aversion to all the bickering of the
preceding age, they reverted to the cardinal tenets of Erasmus:
charity, modesty, and minimal belief couched in terms of simplicity and universality. They spoke much of reason, and reason
meant simply common sense; as Jonathan Swift unkindly said,
"that which any fool can get through his noddle." But, as a matter

[5] Max Farrand, *The Records of the Federal Convention* (New Haven,
1911), I, 451–52.

of fact, the credo of these rationalists was not so simple. They were men of learning. The Puritan elect had become the enlightened elite, who were no longer content like Erasmus with the simple faith of the penitent thief that Christ would take him to Paradise. The men of the Enlightenment commended rather the inquiring spirit of the Virgin Mary when she said to the Angel Gabriel, "How can these things be?" The enlightened were engaged in a new war of the Lord against superstition on the one hand and against skepticism on the other. Against the first, they could be vitriolic; confronted by the second, they were wistfully and earnestly seeking grounds for assurance. Their religious problem cut deeper than Luther's who had asked, "How can I get right with God?" Their question was, "How do I know there is a God to get right with?"

Deism

The type of religion by means of which they found their answer is called Deism and is to be distinguished from Theism and Atheism. The Atheists, and there were a few, like Paul-Henri Holbach in France, were scornful of the Deists, saying that they were neither weak enough to be Christians nor strong enough to be Atheists. But the Deists did consider themselves to be Christians. Their God was not the personal God of the Theists, a God who manifested himself through history and was concerned continually with the affairs of men. Their God was the great artificer of the universe who, with a thrust of his almighty hand, sent rolling the myriad spheres, preserving their courses without collision, in accord with celestial harmony. The mighty architect had done his work so well that he could withdraw into the vast silence, and leave men to order rightly their own affairs, guided by reason, that "candle of the Lord." In all this scheme, there is little need for Christ, save that in him as in a single shaft of light man's ignorance of the Ultimate was once relieved.

Deism became a universal phenomenon throughout Europe and in the English colonies. It developed territorial varieties and was no more able to achieve a universal concord than the sects. The Deists, to be sure, did not start wars of opinion, though one is not to forget that in the end the goddess of reason became a Fury. There were national varieties.

English Deism was mild and comparatively timorous and able, therefore, to find a place among the divines of the establishment. Nicholas Tindal, in his *Christianity as Old as Creation* (1736), penned these lines:

> The Builder of this universe was wise. He planned all souls,
>   all systems, planets, particles:
> The plan he shaped all worlds and aeons by was—heavens—
>   was thy small nine and thirty articles!

But, to say that the articles had not been God's blueprint in the creation of the universe was not to impugn any one of them within its own domain. John Toland, in his *Christianity Not Mysterious* (1696), after an imposing proclamation of the supremacy of reason, denied no more of the traditional faith than transubstantiation and consubstantiation. As an English Protestant, he naturally criticized Catholic superstitions. He became really radical only when he denied the fall of Adam and impugned the character of Old Testament worthies. David Hume, the Scottish philosopher, was, of course, much more skeptical, but he put his manuscript back into his drawer lest he be too disconcerting.

The French Deists had no such inhibitions, because they were avowedly assaulting the Catholic church. The *philosophes*, as they were called—not philosophers, actually, but literati—were infuriated men, akin in their temper to the Jansenists and the Puritans. Voltaire, for all his persiflage, was "also among the prophets." It was he who made the Calas affair into the Dreyfus case of his generation. Calas' son committed suicide. The father and the family were Huguenot, but the son had been going sometimes to Mass. The charge was made that his relatives had done away with him to prevent his conversion to Catholicism. Calas, the father, was tortured, executed, and his goods confiscated. Voltaire pursued the case until he secured a vindication and indemnification of the family.

In the English colonies of North America, Deism had the French complexion. Tom Paine scoffed that if the devil had taken Jesus to the top of a mountain from which he could see all the kingdoms of the earth, he ought to have discovered America. Benjamin Franklin and Thomas Jefferson took over from France also the slogans of nature and equality, and that reasonableness of temper which preferred to acquire Louisiana by purchase rather than by war.[6] In Germany, "Old Fritz" (Frederick the Great) had the flippancy of the French, but Gotthold Ephraim Lessing started a course of rigorous historical investigation of Christian documents. Russia's first major contact with the West came precisely at the time when Deism was regnant. Peter the Great took his cue from the English Deists, whereas Catherine the Great looked to the French *philosophes*.

Within this framework, all varieties of Deism were engaged in the mighty quest, first of all to demolish superstition and then to replace it by a rational religion, lest man be left a creature in the void. Is there any God at all? was the question. Descartes' revival of the ontological argument carried no conviction. If one may infer the existence of God from the idea of God, why might one not infer the existence of a hippogriff from the idea of a hippogriff? jibed one of the scoffers. A similar question had been addressed to Anselm who had answered that the argument was valid only as to God. But the Enlightenment distrusted the entire reasoning which proceeds from what is within to what is without. God is without; nature is without. Man must study nature and thence proceed to nature's God. Such was the view of John Locke,

[6] The purchase, though due to a fluke, realized a philosophy. See Gertrud Phillipi, "Imperialistische und pazifistische Strömungen in der Politik der Vereinigten Staaten von Amerika 1776–1815," *Heidelberger Abhandlungen zur mittleren und neueren Geschichte*, XLV (1914).

who insisted that we are not to start from our own existence but
from our own experience, resulting from the impressions made
upon us by that which is without, namely sensations. Without
sense perceptions we get nowhere, because the mind is at birth a
clean slate. There are no innate ideas. But, given sense experience,
the reasoning faculty of man is competent to deduce the unknown
from the known.

Science and Philosophy

During the eighteenth century, the range of these sensations had
come to be enormously enlarged. This is the period when the new
natural sciences first began to influence general thinking. When
Galileo Galilei trained his "optic glass" upon the moon's "spotty
globe," a friend of his refused to look, lest his presuppositions be
shattered. But no one hesitated any longer now, and after Galileo
came Newton. Alexander Pope wrote,

> Nature and Nature's laws lay hid in night:
> God said, 'Let Newton be!' and all was light.[7]

The Milky Way now proved to be a galaxy of stars, all held in
their respective courses by that principle of attraction known as
gravitation.

The vast universe, which thus swam before the eye, filled some
with dismay, like Pascal, who recoiled before "the terrifying ex-
panses which engulf us as a fleeting atom," but the prevailing
mood was that of Joseph Addison, who sang:

> The spacious firmament on high
> With all the blue ethereal sky
> And spangled heavens, a shining frame,
> Their great Original proclaim.

Kant was awed by the starry heavens and Voltaire was moved
to write:

[7] Alexander Pope, Works, Twickenham Edition (London, 1939–61), Vol.
VI, "Minor Poems," eds. Norman Ault and John Butt, p. 317.

Last night, I was meditating, absorbed in the contemplation of Nature. I was filled with wonder at its immensity, at the stars in their courses, at the mutual interaction of those countless orbs, one upon another, which people look upon unmoved. And I marvelled still more at the Mind which governs the whole mighty scheme. A man must be blind, I said to myself, not to be dazzled by such a spectacle, a fool not to acknowledge its Author, a madman not to adore him. What tribute of adoration can I pay him? Must it not be the same, wherever it is offered? Whatever thinking being inhabits the Milky Way owes him the like homage. The light shines for Sirius, even as it shines for us.[8]

This enlarging of the visible universe did not create a conflict of science and religion, but only gave added force to the old Aristotelian arguments for the existence of God as the first cause and the prime mover.

William Paley (1743–1805) added the argument from analogy that, much as we argue from what we know of the work of man as to the mind of man, so we may argue from what we observe of the work of God as to the mind of God. The classic illustration was a watch. Suppose, said Paley, I kick my foot against a stone. If I were asked how it came to be there, I might reply that for all I knew it had been there forever. But, should I stumble on a watch, I would not give that answer because the watch has manifestly been contrived for a purpose, to tell time. Such a contrivance, so marvelously designed, must surely be the work of an artificer. But, suppose I discover that the watch is able to produce another watch. I may say that the one watch is the cause of the other, but still I have to account for the first. Similarly, when I behold the ordering of the universe, I am to infer the existence of the mind of the first artificer, an intelligence vastly greater than our own, but yet not wholly dissimilar.[9]

This argumentation entails the difficulty that what we perceive

---

[8] Cf. "Religion" in *Questions sur l'Encyclopédie*, translated in Paul Hazard, *European Thought in the Eighteenth Century* (New Haven, 1954), p. 116.

[9] Summarized from the text given in J. M. Creed and J. S. B. Smith, *op. cit.*, p. 34 ff.

is not the artificer but the artifact and, if the latter is material, but
the former immaterial, how do we bridge the gap? The English
philosopher Bishop George Berkeley (1685–1753) reduced the
gap by declaring that matter itself is spirit or idea capable of direct
apprehension by the mind. And, since God is spirit, he can be
directly apprehended without recourse to inference from sensation.

But, however we arrive at God, a more serious question is,
what do we then find? We discover a great artificer who sits en-
throned above the Milky Way and lets his worlds go reeling on,
apparently heedless of the lives that come and go. Has he any
concern for us? The age of Enlightenment sought to "justify the
ways of God to man." A philosophy which sets for itself this goal
is called a theodicy. It did not originate, of course, in the eighteenth century. Every great religious system seeks an explanation
for the ruthlessness of nature and for the suffering of the just.
Here we have the ancient quest of Job. With the collapse of the
Puritan revolution, John Milton in his *Samson Agonistes* agonized
over the question why God had permitted the saints to suffer, like
Samson who was shorn, blinded, and mocked by the Philistines as
he turned their mill. The answer in this instance was simply that,
as Samson recovered his strength with the return of his hair, so
England's locks would grow again. Vastly more troublesome was
the problem of God's judgment upon all mankind. In *Paradise
Lost*, Milton saw man's plight as chastisement for pride and disobedience.

In the eighteenth century, Alexander Pope substituted for the
myth of Adam and the fall of angels the philosophical myth of
"the great chain of being," according to which all reality consists
of parts linked in a harmonious whole, provided each is willing to
play the part of a link, be it of high or low station. Man should not
complain if nature does not devote to him her exclusive care, for
she must look also to other links. Nor should man grumble that he
has not been endowed with all the excellencies of every other link.
"Why has not man a microscopic eye? For this plain reason, man

is not a fly." God has established the chain and "whatever is, is right."[10] Man is under obligation to fulfill his role as a link. To rebel against his assigned place is a sin of pride, and to fall out of place invites the doom of disorder. Pope ended with the admission of man's incapacity to find an answer. In Pope's theodicy are strains of Stoic acquiescence in fate, and of Milton's submission to the divine decrees. The German philosopher Gottfried Leibnitz had a similar view and held that, of all possible worlds, this is the best that God could have contrived.

Voltaire likewise thought so at first. Then came the Lisbon earthquake, and that was too much. He wrote:

> Come, ye philosophers, who cry, "All's well,"
> And contemplate this ruin of a world.
> Behold these shreds and cinders of your race,
> This child and mother heaped in common wreck,
> These scattered limbs beneath the marble shafts—
> A hundred thousand whom the earth devours,
> Who, torn and bloody, palpitating yet,
> Entombed beneath their hospitable roofs,
> In racking torment end their stricken lives . . .
> O wondrous mingling of diversities!
> A god came down to earth to lift our stricken race:
> He visited the earth, and changed it not.
> One sophist says he had not power to change;
> "He had," another cries, "but willed it not:
> In time he will, no doubt." And, while they prate,
> The hidden thunders, belched from underground,
> Fling wide the ruins of a hundred towns
> Across the smiling face of Portugal.[11]

In *Candide*, Voltaire gave a savage satire on this best of all possible worlds. He had no answer save that of Job, to bow before the inscrutable and then to tend one's cabbages.

[10] Alexander Pope, *Essay on Man*, ed. Maynard Mack (New Haven, 1958), Epistle II, lines 193–94 and 294.

[11] Voltaire, *Toleration and Other Essays*, tr. Joseph McCabe (New York, 1912), pp. 255–63.

Christian Faith vs. Reason

But, if the goodness of God cannot be demonstrated, but only believed, can one take solace, in any case, in the goodness of man? The century began with optimism as to man, not tainted by the fall of Adam, capable of placing Reason on her throne and of mastering in her clear light his environment and ordering his affairs in wisdom, charity, and peace. But, plainly this was not a verdict on man but a vote of confidence. Man had never yet displayed such capacity and was still far from it. Critics of eighteenth century society arose, employing in varied forms the device of Thomas More who rebuked England of his day by contrasting her society disparagingly with that of a fictional land, Utopia (derived from the Greek word meaning "nowhere"). Swift in the eighteenth century caused his Gulliver to castigate England in comparison with Lilliput. The Far East served the same end for Oliver Goldsmith who brought John Chinaman to London to laugh at wigs. Travelers who had actually visited foreign parts were so imbued with the myth that when abroad they saw only what they had gone out to see and came home to England corroborating the tales of the superiority of other lands.

And then came the myth of the *bon sauvage*, the American Indian perchance, *Hiawatha* or the *Last of the Mohicans*. In comparison, what should be said of the contemporary European? Frederick the Great talked about "that damned human race." Voltaire's *Zadig* spoke of "men as a lot of insects, devouring one another on a drop of mud." How similar to this sounds the indictment of mankind by Celsus, the pagan of the second century! But, if primitive man was so excellent, and contemporary man so depraved, how explain the discrepancy? Obviously, only by recourse again to the myth of a fall, yet not of Adam any longer, but of the original man of the Stoics who degenerated from the age of gold to the age of iron. The pagan myth supplanted the Christian myth. One finds it in Pope's *Essay on Man*. Thomas Hobbes rejected the myth, but not to the advantage of man who, at the very outset, preyed upon his fellows as wolf upon wolf. No picture of human depravity by Luther or Calvin could outweigh the indictment of man by those who lifted him out of the Christian frame.

If this then be the universe, if this then is man, experience and reason do not demonstrate either the goodness of God or man's potential for eventual redemption. These are teachings of the Christian religion, and to the Christian religion one must turn again for the answers. Christianity provides them on the basis of revelation. But how is one to know that revelation is trustworthy? The initial response of the eighteenth century was that the revelation had been validated by miracles. But, how do we know that the miracles occurred? From Locke to the end of the century this was a question of deep concern among the English Protestants. Locke said that we can know only through sensation. If it is not our own sensation, then it must be that of another. Hence the inquiry as to the credibility of the witnesses. This involves two points: the good faith of the witnesses, and the accuracy of their observation. But, there is the added difficulty that the kind of testimony that can prove a miracle must be well-nigh miraculous itself. This is the only point at which a conflict occurred between science and religion in the eighteenth century, for the new science taught the uniformity of nature's procedures, and the term natural law came to be applied not only to a universal morality, but also to the ordering of the physical world. A miracle involved a breach in the established order. It was by definition a divine intervention. If one assumed an omnipotent God, one could not deny the possibility of intervention, but to be convinced that it had actually occurred one must be supplied with quite exceptional evidence.

Thomas Sherlock, in his *Tryal of the Witnesses,* went soberly through courtroom procedures to demonstrate the credibility and the reliability of the authors of the gospels. Woolston, however, maintained that miracles simply have to be taken on faith and, to reinforce his point, magnified the difficulties. The only witness to the resurrection of Lazarus, said he, was the Apostle John who wrote sixty years after the event. Perhaps Jairus' daughter was only asleep. In any case, why should Jesus have raised a simple girl, instead of some useful magistrate or industrious merchant? Lazarus, of course, was dead, if it be true that he stank; but, who said so? Only his sister, and so on.

Voltaire and the French rationalists were full of mockery. One of the miracles of Jesus, said Voltaire, was to turn water into wine at a wedding where the peasants were already drunk. Jesus withered a fig tree that did not belong to him, because it bore no fruit out of season. He sent devils into two hundred [sic!] pigs and caused them to jump into a lake and drown in a country where pigs are not raised, and more of the same.[12] David Hume, the Scot, in thorough earnest, argued that no miracle ever could be proved because it involves the concept of causation. But causation can never be experienced. If one billiard ball hits another, we see a succession of movements. This happens with every collision, but all that we see is succession. We do not and we cannot experience and prove that one motion is *caused* by the other. This line of reasoning, however, is not so much a disproof of miracles as a flight into skepticism, since we can neither prove nor disprove causation.

The German Protestants were to wrestle with the problem more earnestly and more persistently than others. Ephraim Lessing published manuscripts which Reimarus, their author, had not dared to make public. He had adopted the procedure, sound within limits, of interpreting an historical movement in terms of its antecedents, except that a new movement must not be explained in terms of the old so completely that the rise of the new becomes inexplicable. And this is precisely what Reimarus did when he explained Christianity as so completely Jewish that nothing new remained. How then did he account for the emergence of a new religion? By fraud; for, said he, the resurrection was a trick. Lessing published

[12] The passage is given in French in Norman Torrey, *Voltaire and the English Deists* (New Haven, 1930), p. 64.

the Reimarus manuscript not to endorse it, but in the belief that its error would be vanquished by truth. Promptly, the advocates of truth tackled the problem. Heinrich Paulus, a professor at Jena, set himself to refute the charge of fraud by substituting for it the accusation of error. The disciples were not deceivers, said he, but deceived to the degree that they misunderstood what they saw, interpreting natural events as miracles. Paulus then undertook to discover what really happened to give rise to the stories of miracles. Jesus, he explained, when supposedly walking on water, was actually standing upon a submerged raft. The resurrection was a case of suspended animation, and so on.[13] The explanations were often more miraculous than the miracles and, in any case, the integrity of the disciples was saved only at the expense of their intelligence. Still more serious was the wrecking of the whole line of evidential reasoning for the validation of revelation; for, if the miracles were simply natural events misunderstood, they could prove nothing whatever about the supernatural. Thus the Protestants and rationalists of the eighteenth century handed down the problem to the nineteenth. The Catholics did not come to grips with these questions until early in the twentieth century.

Revivals

What saved Christianity at the close of the eighteenth century was the miracle of the new birth in evangelical revivals. But, before turning to them, the impression must be dispelled that the Enlightenment was a fruitless quest. As in the Puritan revolution and, indeed, in every vital new venture, achievement had failed to catch up with aspirations. In this instance, the lyrical hopes with which the century began gave way to chastened resignation. The role of the historian is to correct in like measure the exaggerations of initial optimism and of ensuing despondency. Like the Puritan revolution, the Enlightenment bequeathed positive gains. The campaign against superstition did put an end to the witchcraft

[13] Albert Schweitzer, *The Quest of the Historical Jesus* (New York, 1922).

trials that took place in the seventeenth century, particularly in
Protestant lands. The ideal of natural law as a universal ethic,
valid for all peoples, and the ideal of humanity, however tarnished
by the crimes committed in her name, serves to this day to distinguish the Western democracies from the totalitarianisms of the
twentieth century. The slogan *liberté, égalité, fraternité* contributed, along with Christian compassion engendered in evangelical
revivals, to the emancipation of serfs and to the liberation of
slaves. Charles de Montesquieu had raised a voice against slavery.
Despondency did not result in universal despair, and men like
Marquis de Condorcet could reshape the Christian hope for the
coming of the Lord into the idea of progress and, if the age came
to perceive the limitations of reason, Kant, who pointed them out
in his *Critique of Pure Reason*, proceeded to make a new start
from what he called the Practical Reason, taking as a point of
departure the moral consciousness. Although in many cases Christian terminology was supplanted by a vocabulary resuscitated
from classical Stoicism, the basic reason was to avoid confessional
strife at a time when the reformatory urge was still that of Christian reformers in the succession of men like Gregory VII, Luther,
Loyola, or Cromwell. The problems raised with regard to the
existence and nature of God, and with regard to the reliability of
Scripture, supplied the basis for passionate but fruitful wrestlings,
for years to come.

Nor are the revivalist movements to be set in complete contrast
to the Enlightenment. The compassion of the one and the Humanitarianism of the other could combine as to social reform. The
shift from the head to the heart was already manifest among the
enlightened, as for instance in the case of Rousseau. And the
revivalists, though appealing to the masses, were not uninstructed.
Jonathan Edwards had sound knowledge of the science of Newton
and of the philosophy of Locke, while John Wesley was widely
read. The program of the Enlightenment to reform by education
was endorsed by the great awakeners, albeit with a different
emphasis.

But, certainly there was a revolt among the evangelicals against the coldness of the Deists. The Scotch revivalist Thomas Chalmers said, "Moonlight preaching ripens no harvest." The German Pietists felt that the Rhine would not be set on fire by a sermon claimed to have been preached on the text, "The hairs of your head are all numbered" with four divisions: (1) The origin, style, form, and natural position of our hair; (2) The correct care of the hair; (3) Reminiscences, reminders, admonitions, and consolations derived from the hair; (4) Christian hair culture.[14] The Wesleys felt that England would not be revitalized by the argumentation of Bishop Butler, who modestly defended revelation as actually no more obscure than nature. Jonathan Edwards did not think that New England could be awakened by divines who merely composed jeremiads on the passing of the good old days.

The revivalist movements to which we now turn had a wide spread. Pietism characterized Germany and the Scandinavian countries. In England, there were Methodists and the Clapham group in the Anglican Church. In New England, the term was The Great Awakening. These were all Protestant movements.

In part, they constituted a reaction against the arid speculation and flaccid moralism of the Enlightenment and, at the same time, against the ossified conservatism of Protestant Neo-scholasticism. But every reaction is also a restoration, though never a precise repetition. Revivalism did not resuscitate the Confessionalism of the preceding era but reached back to earlier roots of experiential religion. In Germany, the revival was called Pietism. It may be traced back to the German mystics of the late Middle Ages, to Eckhart and Tauler, and to Luther in one of his phases. But, a more direct precursor in the sixteenth century was Caspar Schwenckfeld, a Silesian nobleman of courtly carriage and gracious demeanor. He was distressed by the acrimony of the religious controversies and declared a moratorium on the celebration of the Lord's Supper until there should be less heat and more light.

[14] G. R. Cragg, *The Church and the Age of Reason* (Baltimore, 1960), pp. 90, 100.

When banished from his own domains, he became a wanderer all over Europe, seeking not to gather a following but to fan among all confessions the sacred flame. Despite himself, however, a following gathered which later migrated to Pennsylvania and there still flourishes as the Church of the Schwenckfelders. In the seventeenth century, the great figure was the mystic Jacob Boehme, the shoemaker, who asked what it would profit a man to know the Bible by heart if he knew not the spirit which had inspired the book?

Revivalism in Germany

Steeped in this tradition, several figures arose within German Lutheranism, not minded to create a secession but rather to establish nuclei of fervor within the larger Church. The leaders appealed to the peasants but were not of the peasants themselves. Jacob Spener (1635–1705) was a preacher, August Franke (1663–1727) was a professor, Ludwig von Zinzendorf (1700–60) was a nobleman.

Count Zinzendorf's piety might be regarded as the medieval cult of the Passion of Christ voiced in the language of the Baroque. He rhapsodized over finding shelter in the cavernous wounds of Christ. His erotic mysticism exceeded even that of St. Bernard. The count would have done better to burn some of his effusions, but at his best he was a great lyric poet and gave a fresh impetus to congregational singing. One of his hymns is still sung in over ninety languages:

> Jesus still lead on,
> Till our rest be won,
> And, although the way be cheerless,
> We will follow, calm and fearless;
> Guide us by Thy hand
> To our fatherland.[15]

The popularity of this hymn is probably due in large measure to its restraint. Many of his lyrics are better suited to excite the

[15] Translation by Jane Borthwick (1853), reprinted in *The Hymnal* (St. Louis, Mo., Eden Publishing House, 1941).

raptures of the mystic than to voice the public worship of a congregation. Take, for instance, these lines:

> *Pure flames leaping, upward creeping*
> *Make me shine as Thou dost shine.*
> *Sweetly yearning, in love burning*
> *Make mine utter being Thine.*

> *Stoke Thy fire, O my Sire,*
> *Till the heart, mood, mind and soul*
> *By Thy blowing, all are glowing*
> *In love's incandescent whole.*[16]

The count's religion cut across class and creed. He fraternized with kings and consorted with peasants, insisting that they address him with the familiar *du*, however much it roughed his aristocratic grain. After the death of his wife, he married a peasant woman. Although of no mind to secede from the Lutheran Church, he received nevertheless on his estate non-Lutherans, Hussite refugees from Moravia or Schwenckfelders from Silesia, and was even intimate with a French Roman Catholic cardinal. This was too much for the Lutheran establishment. The count was banished and became thereupon an itinerant evangelist, but he fought for and won the vindication of his orthodoxy and was even ordained a Lutheran bishop with the consent of the king and at the hands of the bishop of Berlin. The Herrenhuters, named after his estate at Herrenhut, were recognized as a distinct Lutheran fellowship. Yet their communities tended to be separate and, in the New World, came to constitute a further denomination. Some of the group, chiefly Moravians, migrated to Pennsylvania and there founded the city of Bethlehem. They are called the Unity of the Brethren (not the United Brethren, who are another group) and, more commonly, the Moravian Church.

The effects of Pietism on the religious and social life of Germany can be discerned at least approximately. Pietism may have

---

[16] Translation by R. H. Bainton from Hans Günther Huober, "Zinzendorfs Kirchenliederdichtung," *Germanische Studien* (Berlin, 1934), p. 150.

contributed also to the rise of German nationalism. The suggestion has been made that when Pietism kindled the emotions, while Enlightenment diminished faith, the emotions were transferred from God the Father to the Fatherland. This much at least is plain, that the Romanticists, who saw a special divine afflatus in the German soul, had been reared in the Pietist tradition.

Pietism, in conjunction with Enlightenment, introduced a new way of viewing the history of the Church. In the sixteenth and in the seventeenth century, Church history had been written with a confessional intent. In the sixteenth, the *Magdeburg Centuries* (a history by centuries, printed at Magdeburg) amassed evidence in support of Protestant claims. Cardinal Baronius countered in his *Annals*. The eighteenth century strove for impartiality. This could be achieved in one of two ways. The first was by equal detachment from all movements. The men of the Enlightenment, who felt that Catholics and Protestants alike were addicted to superstitions, sometimes, like Gibbon, treated both denominations with scarcely veiled hostility, reserving warmth only for such figures as Julian the Apostate. Others, of whom the chief was Johann Lorenz von Mosheim (1694–1755), endeavored to depict all Christian varieties with judicial impartiality. His history, translated as the *Institutes of Ecclesiastical History*, enjoyed a wide vogue in England and America to the end of the nineteenth century. The other way was to approach all systems with equal empathy. This was the method of the Pietists, who fastened upon all signs of fervor in the Christian past, whether among the orthodox or the heretics, but more frequently among the heretics. Such was the point of view of Gottfried Arnold's (1660–1714) epoch-making *History of the Church and the Heretics*. This type of liberalism fostered church unity among all those kindled by the Spirit, though producing, at the same time, divisions between the kindled and the cold.

In domestic relations, Pietism appealed to the type of left-wing Protestants who subordinated the romantic element in marriage to the concept of partnership in the vineyard of the Lord. Marriages at Herrenhut were sometimes determined by lot—not that any with distinct antipathies were forcibly mated, but merely that religious obligations overrode personal predilection. The attitude to marital relations was more ascetic than in Puritanism.

From its inception, the Pietist movement issued in humanitarian endeavors. Francke founded an orphanage. Zinzendorf received refugees. In the following century, Johann Wichern organized in Germany the so-called *Innere Mission* to care for the halt, the maimed, and the blind, epileptics, lepers, unwanted children, unwed mothers, the deranged, and all those deficient in body and in mind. There was a certain confluence of the humanitarianism of Enlightenment and the compassion of Pietism. Enlightenment stressed the reasonable and opposed as superstition the hanging of witches, the treatment of the insane as possessed, and decried the irrationality of war. Pietism stressed love and compassion, opposed the killing of brothers in war, and took care of the victims of fate, fault, and folly. Wichern would have gone even further in the remodelling of society, but his followers confined themselves to measures of relief. This may be the reason why Pietism warmed the hearts of the peasants and the aristocracy but did not win the industrial proletariat who were swept into the currents of Marxist socialism. Nor did Pietism influence the German language, despite the use of the familiar form of address in religious communities. Pietism did stimulate popular education through the development of the *Volksschulen*, not only in Germany proper but also in the Scandinavian lands.

Revivalism in England: Methodism

The form taken by Revivalism in England was Methodism. It, too, was a protest against prevalent defects in the established Church. The lamentable state of the clergy in the preceding century had never been redressed. Poverty, pluralism, and absenteeism were still rife. Out of eleven thousand livings in the early eighteenth century, six thousand were estimated to have been without resident incumbents. Ecclesiastical sinecures enabled the gentry to provide for younger sons, unless war afforded greater scope in the army. The Methodists reacted against the staidness of clergymen like Bishop Butler, who told John Wesley to his face that "pretending to extraordinary revelations and gifts of the Holy Spirit is a horrid thing; yes, Sir, it is a very horrid thing!"[17] But, even more serious was the indifference of the Church of England to the growing proletariat created by the incipient industrial revolution, especially in the coal mines. Bishop Warburton said, "The Church, like the Ark of Noah, is worth saving, not for the sake of the unclean beasts and vermin that almost filled it, and probably made most noise and clamor in it, but for the little corner of rationality that was as much distressed by the stink within, as by the tempest without."[18]

Wesley's mission was to the "unclean beasts." But we must not overstress the unconcern of the Anglican Church in his day. Had there been no spark, there would have been no Wesley. In 1701, the Anglican Church had already founded the Society for the Propagation of the Gospel in Foreign Parts, meaning, thereby, the British Colonies. A devout churchman, William Law, profoundly influenced Wesley through his *Serious Call to a Devout and Holy Life.* Among the Dissenters, Isaac Watts gave an enormous impetus to congregational singing. Few hymns in the English language surpass his lines:

> *When I survey the wondrous cross*
> *On which the Prince of Glory died,*
> *My richest gain I count but loss*
> *And pour contempt on all my pride.*

The home into which John Wesley was born combined the finest strains of Anglican and Dissenting piety. His father was an Anglican priest, his mother the daughter of a Dissenting minister. She was a remarkable woman who bore nineteen children, of

---

[17] William Holden Hutton, *John Wesley* (London, 1927), p. 106.
[18] *Ibid.*, p. 110.

whom John was the fifteenth. She taught them "to fear the rod and cry softly." Every week she made time for religious instruction for each child separately. To do so, she had to be a methodist. John looked to her for guidance to the day of her death.

The Methodist movement was a youth movement. It began among a student group at Oxford. Their ascetic deportment and devotion to prayer occasioned derision, but less so than their visitations in prisons. The missionary impulse seized Wesley. He went out to Georgia to minister both to the colonists and to the Indians, whom he glorified as the *bons sauvages*. On the way over, there was a storm at sea. Wesley, badly frightened, was profoundly impressed by the composure of some Moravians, men, women, and children, who sang in the tempest. Arrived in Georgia, he discovered that the *bon sauvage* was a dirty dog. Sex upset him. He was attracted to Sophie Hopkey, and she gave him an opportunity to propose. He proposed that they sing Psalms, and she married someone else. Thoroughly dispirited, Wesley returned to England and sought out a chapel of the Moravians in London. There, in the year 1738, on the twenty-fourth day of May, at a quarter before nine, during the reading of Luther's preface to Melanchthon's *Commentary on the Epistle to the Romans*, Wesley experienced the new birth. In one of his sermons, he compared the birth in the spirit to the birth in the flesh. Prior to physical birth one is not dead, but the unborn babe, having eyes sees not, having ears hears not. Even so, before the new birth there is no knowledge of the things of God.

But when "the eyes of his understanding are opened," then he feels "the love of God shed abroad in his heart"; and now he may properly be said to live. From hence it manifestly appears, what is the nature of the new birth. It is that great change wrought in the whole soul by the almighty Spirit of God, when it is "created anew in Christ Jesus," . . . when the love of the world is changed into the love of God; pride into humility; passion into meekness; hatred, envy, malice, into a sincere, tender, disinterested love for all mankind. In a word, it is that change whereby the earthly, sensual, devilish mind is turned into the "mind which was in Christ Jesus." This is the nature of the new birth: "So is every one that is born of the Spirit."[19]

Three weeks later, he preached in St.Mary's at Oxford. The subject was justification by faith.

There are some, said the preacher, who think it is a counsel of despair to say that we cannot be saved by what we do. Why yes, to those who rely on what they can do. But very comforting to those who are self-condemned. For "whosoever believeth on Him shall not be ashamed." Here is comfort, high as heaven, stronger than death! What! Mercy for all? For Zacchaeus, a public robber? For Mary Magdalene, a common harlot? Methinks I hear one say, "Then I, even I may hope for mercy! . . . Ho! glad tidings!" "Though your sins be red like crimson, . . . return unto the Lord and He will have mercy upon you . . . and He will abundantly pardon." Only this gospel can check the immorality which has overspread the land like a flood. Will you empty the deep drop by drop? Then you may reform us by dissuasiveness from particular vices. But let the righteousness that is of God be brought in, so shall its proud waves be stopped.[20]

Here is a manifesto of social regeneration through individual conversion and, as a matter of fact, Wesley did more to make England Puritan by conversion than the Puritan movement ever had done by force of arms. His method was preaching. But soon the churches were closed to him, and he was not soothing when he rated Christians lower than honest heathen. In his father's parish at Epworth, Wesley was barred from the pulpit, and had to address the throngs in the churchyard as he stood upon his father's tomb. Then came a revival of field preaching. The medieval friars had used it, so had some of the early Protestant reformers and, in the next century, the Quakers. Wesley, on horseback, set out for the hamlets and mines. The mobs regarded a field preacher as fair

[19] *John Wesley's Sermons* (Philadelphia, 1826–27), Vol. I, Sermon XLV, Sections 4–5, pp. 402–03.

[20] J. M. Creed and J. S. B. Smith, *op. cit.*, p. 153 ff.

game. When crowds assembled, the town crier would bellow, horns would blow, a cow or a bull would be driven into the crowd. Missiles were thrown. Sometimes such attacks recoiled. One man raised his hand to throw a stone, when from the rear another caught him between the fingers. One chap had his large pockets bulging with rotten eggs. Someone clapped him from behind. Wesley comments, "He savoured not of balsam." In his diary, Wesley records that once he was riding in a coach when the mob began pelting it with stones. A large gentlewoman then sat in his lap and shielded him. Frequently, he quieted mobs by his sheer intrepidity. Once he was besieged in a house. The leader of a gang broke into his room just as the doors were shut, holding back the rest of the mob. A missile came through and hit the ruffian. He bellowed, "What shall we do?" "Pray, man!" said Wesley, and he did. Many toughs were so moved by Wesley's composure as to turn suddenly on the assailants and defy anyone to touch him. And, not a few of these bullies became the captains of the great crusade. Wesley relates how he confronted a hostile crowd. "My heart was filled with love, my eyes with tears, and my mouth with arguments. They were amazed, they were ashamed, they were melted down, they devoured every word. What a turn was this!"[21]

From village to village Wesley rode, between stops giving free rein to his horse, while he read the ancient classics and contemporary poets—across the English moors, the Scotch heath, the Irish bog, or the Welsh mountains. No one in his century knew so intimately the British Isles, and his journal is one of the great social documents of the century. At the end of his long career, when he returned to places where once he had been mobbed, the crowds now hailed him as if he had been King George.

Wesley sought out the miners in particular. At five in the morning, as they went down into the pits, he was there to deliver the glad tidings, and when, after incredible hours, they came up from the bowels of the earth, he was there to meet them. As they heard

[21] *The Heart of Wesley's Journal*, ed. Percy L. Parker (New York, n.d.), p. 176, entry for Oct. 18, 1749.

the word of redemption, tears made gutters down their blackened cheeks. For them, the new birth meant a rough time. They were called upon to mend their ways, to be sober, chaste, and humane. Drunkenness had grown more devastating because the industrial revolution had introduced distilled liquors. Beer and wine were replaced by rum. Those who spent their waking hours in the pits, not only men, but women and little children, guzzled their week's wages in the pub. To make a clean break was rugged. To suffer all week the jibes of unregenerate fellow workers was tougher. There was no better prank than to get a Methodist drunk. Witness the sport in *The Pickwick Papers* over "the red-nosed Mr. Stiggins of the Brick Lane Branch of the United Grand Junction Ebenezer Temperance Association."

Those who took the path of rectitude needed mutual support. Classes were formed, meeting weekly to recount trial, failures, and support from the Lord. This was the nucleus of an organization. By and by, in London, an abandoned cannon factory, with the roof blown off, was recapped for a tabernacle. Lay preaching was introduced. Wesley kept tab on the meetings throughout the land, and thus he became a pope without a tiara. He did not dream that he was founding a new church, but separation was inevitable, so long as the Establishment did not welcome hobnailed boots on the floor of St.Paul's Cathedral. The decisive step was the ordination by Wesley of Coke to serve as a bishop in North America. Wesley believed that, in the early Church, bishop and presbyter or priest were synonymous. He was a priest and therefore a bishop but, by the same token, Coke was also a bishop and did not need to be ordained as such. What Wesley conferred on him was really only an administrative authority, but still, to say that he was being consecrated as a bishop did not comport with the doctrine of the Anglican Church. Wesley himself never left the Church and was never disowned, but the Methodists, in time, came to recognize themselves as Dissenters. A new denomination had come into being.

Yet this was a unifying separation, since the Methodists, having some points in common with the Establishment and some with the Dissenters, diminished the gap. With the Establishment, they were generally Tory and opposed Catholic emancipation. With the Evangelicals in the Church of England they agitated against slavery. To the Dissenters they transmitted their itinerant ministry and, in polity, a measure of their "connectionalism" between congregations, rather than sheer autonomy for each. Their influence on social life in England was unparalleled. Wesley himself was a Tory in economics as well as in politics and had nothing more drastic to propose for social reform than the abolition of distilling and of breeding excessive horses for the aristocracy, since horses and hard liquor used up grain needed to feed the poor. But Wesley knew the poor. He was concerned for the poor. To his own alarm, he was making them prosperous through sobriety, industry, and thrift, and thereby introducing them to the dangers of indolence. By converting the poor, Wesley brought the British proletariat within the orbit of the Gospel, as German Pietism failed to do. Herein may lie one factor in the vast difference in the social structure of the two lands in the century to come.

Revivalism in New England

In New England, the term for revival was "awakening." There was the First Great Awakening in the 1730's and the Second after 1800, with a good many lesser awakenings in between. The American movements were in touch with those of England and the Continent. Cotton Mather was lyrical over German Pietism. A little later, the association of New England revivalism with Methodism was even more intimate. Wesley's colleague, George Whitfield, the ex-actor who could pronounce the word Mesopotamia in a way to bring tears to the eyes of the listeners, swept up and down the Atlantic seaboard leaving behind a train of wounded hearts. He visited Jonathan Edwards and was so impressed by the devoutness of Mrs. Edwards that he hoped God would find for him another such daughter of Abraham. But American revivalism needed no impetus from abroad. It has been the essence of American Christianity, from the first plantation to Billy Graham. There has been a pulse of revivals, of great harvests, successively following lean years.

At the very outset, the Church in New England consisted only of the awakened, as we have already observed. An ability to fasten upon evidence of grace was a prerequisite for church membership, and church membership was a prerequisite for full citizenship. Church and state were one, yet embraced only a minority of the community. There was at first no restiveness because the so-called strangers had never enjoyed the franchise in England on account of property qualification. But when, in the second generation, the sons of the saints could not produce the spiritual credentials, and when, consequently, even the son of a minister could not vote for an officer in the militia, there was murmuring in the new Israel. One solution was to extend the franchise, and by 1700 this had come to pass. But this did not suffice, because there were many devout and upright folk who wanted not merely a vote in the state but a share in the life of the Church, even though they could not claim an emotional conversion. To accommodate them, a second level of church membership was devised through the creation of ecclesiastical societies to handle temporal affairs. Solomon Stoddard, the grandfather of Jonathan Edwards, was even ready to go so far as to admit the unconverted to Communion in the hope of their conversion. But, vastly better would it be to convert the entire community. In that case, Church, state, and community would be bound in the bond of grace, and the Holy Commonwealth would become such a reality as it had never been in fact. This was the hope of Jonathan Edwards.

But, let it not be thought that his primary concern was for the Holy Commonwealth. His intent was to warn souls to flee from the wrath to come, that they might enjoy the blessedness of life in God. He wished for them what he had himself known.

59

"Gibbon outweighing the Bishop," a satirical print of 1788. The Bishop is saying, "Boy put on the Chymical Essays."

60a

Figure 60a is a cartoon showing the plump vicar exploiting the curates. He is saying "The Church was made for Me, and not I for the Church."

60b

Fig. 60b depicts a disorderly service in a village church, 1790, from a drawing by F. Wright.

61a

The founder of Methodism.

61b

Epworth church, where Wesley preached.

61c

Wesley preaching on his father's tomb.

61d

Wesley preaching at Gwennap pit amphitheater, where it is said he was once heard by thirty thousand.

Preaching out of doors, Wesley often faced murderous mobs such as this one at Wednesbury.

The Evangelist leader preaching a sermon on Kennington Common, in front of the gallows, on Sunday, April 29, 1739. (Engraving published by George Foster, 1739.)

63a

Always a concern of the Church, in the eighteenth century it received an added impetus through the Enlightenment, with its confidence in the power of education, and through the evangelical move-

63b

ments which although insisting on adult conversion at the same time devoted much attention to "preparation for salvation." In 1780 the Sunday School movement was initiated by Robert Raikes (1735–1811), an evangelical layman of the Church of England. Fig. 63a shows his portrait, beneath which are cuts of Sunday School scholars in England (from W. J. Townsend, *A New History of Methodism*, London, 1909).

Fig. 63b depicts a Sunday School parade in Brooklyn, N.Y., in 1868 (drawing by Theodore R. Davis in *Harper's Weekly*, June 13, 1868).

Fig. 63c shows children playing at church in eighteenth-century Germany (from Hans Bosch, "Kinderleben," *Monographien zur deutschen Kulturgeschichte*, V, 1900).

63c

A. Le Ministre, qui ce-
libre la Liturgie
B.B. Les Garçons
C.C. Les Filles.

AGAPES
des
Enfans.

DD. Les Diacres.
EE. Les Diaconesses,
qui distribuent

64

The picture is titled *Agapes des Enfans*, that is, Love-feasts of Children. In the background, below the central window, the minister (marked A) is celebrating the liturgy. He has a small table before him and is flanked by a row of sitting men on the right and a row of sitting women on the left. Toward the center of the hall, sitting on parallel rows of plain wooden benches, are boys (marked B) on the right and girls (marked C) on the left. Each bench of boys is well supervised by a man and each bench of girls by a woman. In the foreground, we see serving tables and, on the floor, baskets full of buns and tea kettles boiling on charcoal braziers. Deacons (marked D) on the right are serving the boys and deaconesses (marked E) the girls. (From S. Bandert and Th. Steinmann, *Die Welt der Stillen im Lande* [Berlin, 1925].)

65   *Yale University Art Gallery.* Jonathan Edwards *by Joseph Badger*

The sense I had of divine things, would often, of a sudden kindle up, as it were, a sweet burning in my heart, an ardor of soul. . . . I walked abroad alone, in a solitary place in my father's pasture, for contemplation. And as I was walking there, and looking up on the sky and clouds, there came into my mind so sweet a sense of the glorious Majesty and Grace of God, that I know not how to express.

The appearance of everything was altered; there seemed to be, as it were, a calm, sweet cast, or appearance of divine glory, in almost everything, God's excellency, his wisdom, his purity and love, seemed to appear in everything; in the sun, moon, . . . and all nature. . . . I often used to sit and view the moon for continuance; and in the day, spent much time in viewing the clouds and sky, to behold the sweet glory of God in these things in the meantime, singing forth, with a low voice, my contemplation of the Creator and Redeemer.[22]

Edwards was a poet in prose. He was attuned to the Enlightenment and drew from Locke and Newton. He was a theologian in the tradition of Calvin. He was an experiential Christian in the succession of the mystics. To portray him simply as dangling sinners over the pit of hell is to countenance one of the travesties of history.

Edwards set out to convert the entire community. That he should ever have supposed he could may well appear fatuous, seeing that he believed in predestination. Roger Williams had long since pointed out that, if God has already chosen some to be saved and some to be damned, there is no possibility of converting an entire community and, since all live in the community, and are governed by the state, all should share in the state, while the Church should be confined to the elect. Edwards would have only the elect in the Church, but he wanted everyone to be elect. At any rate, the preacher must proffer God's grace, for God has ordained preaching as the way in which to disclose the elect, and who was the preacher to assume that any in his congregation were not? The

[22] Jonathan Edwards, "Memoirs of Mr. Edwards' Life," *Works* (Worcester, 1808–09), I, 34–36.

sermon on *Sinners in the Hands of an Angry God* was a summons
to awake. God is indeed an angry God, said the preacher, and he
has fully as much reason to drop rebellious men into the flames
of hell as have men to fling a venomous spider into the fire. But
God is holding back to give men another chance. Only his hand
prevents them at any moment from falling into the flames. "O
sinner, consider the danger you are in. It would be no wonder if
some persons, that now sit here in some seats of this meetinghouse
in health, and in quiet and secure, should be in hell before tomor-
row morning."[23] Before the close of that sermon "there was a great
moaning & crying out through ye whole House . . . ye shrieks &
crys were piercing & Amazing. . . . Several Souls were hopefully
wrought upon yt night & oh ye cheerfulness and pleasantness of
their countenances yt received comfort!"[24] The Great Awakening
was under way.

It revivified the churches, that is to say, some of them, but it did
not restore the outward fabric of the Holy Commonwealth. Instead, it split the churches into the New Lights and the Old Lights.
To this day, in New England, villages sometimes have two Congregational churches on the green, reminiscent of the schism.

[23] *Ibid.*, VII, 501–02.
[24] Cited in Ola Winslow, *Jonathan Edwards* (New York, 1940), p. 192

XII

Expansion and Social Reform in the Nineteenth Century

D IVIDING history by centuries is always an arbitrary procedure. At no point is this more apparent than in 1800
and 1900. The second decade of the nineteenth century,
marked by the Napoleonic wars, and the second decade of the
twentieth century, memorable for World War I, would serve much
better as dividing lines between historical eras.

The developments during the two centuries can be distinguished
inasmuch as the nineteenth had seen an unparalleled expansion of
Christianity, whereas the twentieth saw some notable recessions.
The nineteenth witnessed the retardation of sect formation,
whereas the twentieth is characterized by movements toward reunification. By the close of the nineteenth, the churches in some lands
were looking to the state as the Great White Father, but during the
twentieth the state in some quarters proved to be the Great Levia-
than. Social concern and theological wrestling ran continuously
through both periods. For that reason, the present treatment will
have to be partly chronological and partly topical.

The turn of the centuries signalized for contemporaries no perceptible transitions. The clergy of New England took cognizance
of the event by preaching "centenary sermons." One such divine,
at the opening of the nineteenth century, reviewed the hundred
years past and then his own ministry of long duration to the same
congregation, though not to the same persons. He recalled that

those who first made up his flock were now sleeping on the hillside where they would very soon be joined by himself and the present congregation. And then he wished his hearers a "Happy New Year."[1] And the new year rolled on without perceptible change. There were still Deists who could titillate an audience by waxing merry over the mistakes of Moses and revivalists who could still set the prairies ablaze.

Revivalism in the New World

Revivalism continued unabated. There were two notable manifestations early in the nineteenth century, the one in New England on the frontier, the other in old England, at the University of Oxford and in the parish churches. In New England, the Second Great Awakening sought to avoid the excesses of the First, for even in Jonathan Edwards' congregation there had been swooning and one case of suicide. When reproaches against the entire movement were voiced from Boston, Edwards replied that physical manifestations neither prove nor disprove the reality of a religious experience; the test lies in the fruits of the Spirit. Some of his successors were not so discriminating, and the architects of the next upheaval advised restraint. But, let it not be thought that they were unduly restrained. Lyman Beecher, the father of Henry Ward Beecher and Harriet Beecher Stowe, when the awakening struck his congregation in Boston, described it as "fire in the leaves," and such fire easily gets out of hand. Beecher thought at first that it had when, in the middle of the century, the evangelist Charles Finney blew the gospel gales into the grass in upper New York state. That region came to be so scorched that it has been referred to as "burned-over ground."

The Western frontier was the great area for the camp meetings. Many denominations participated. None were more adept in this technique than the Methodists. There were two kinds of frontiers-

[1] Benjamin Trumbull, A *Century Sermon* (New Haven, 1801).

men to be reached: the young bucks, trigger-happy, rowdy, given
to horse stealing, gambling, wenching, guzzling, and racy profan-
ity, and there were the family type, the homesteaders who broke in
the land with incredible labor. Their lives were as hard and as
drab as those of the English coal miners. The camp meeting was
an alternative to the saloon. After reading the following account
one may understand that the expression "spiritual inebriation"
was more than a metaphor. The author, subsequently an evangelist, was, at the time, rather a freethinker. He wrote:

> The noise was like the roar of Niagara. The vast sea of human
> beings seemed to be agitated as if by a storm. I counted seven
> ministers, all preaching at one time, some on stumps, others on
> wagons, and one . . . was standing on a tree which had, in falling,
> lodged against . . . another. Some of the people were singing,
> others praying, some crying for mercy in the most piteous ac-
> cents, while others were shouting most vociferously. While wit-
> nessing these scenes, a peculiarly-strange sensation, such as I had
> never felt before, came over me. My heart beat tumultuously, my
> knees trembled, my lip quavered, and I felt as if I must fall to the
> ground. A strange supernatural power seemed to pervade the en-
> tire mass of mind there collected. . . . Soon after I left and went
> into the woods and there I strove to rally up my courage.
>
> After some time I returned to the scene of excitement, the
> waves of which, if possible, had risen still higher. The same aw-
> fulness of feeling came over me. I stepped up on to a log, where I
> could have a better view of the surging sea of humanity. The
> scene that then presented itself to my mind was indescribable. At
> one time I saw at least five hundred swept down in a moment, as
> if a battery of a thousand guns had been opened upon them, and
> then immediately followed shrieks that rent the very heavens. . . .
> I fled for the woods a second time, and wished I had staid at
> home.[2]

His time was not yet.

A circuit rider tells of an incident that occurred when he was
preaching. A major with some lewd fellows came to break up the

[2] Charles A. Johnson, *The Frontier Camp Meeting* (Dallas, 1955), p. 64.

meeting, but stayed and fell before the "awful sense of Divine power." The account concludes, "Looking around upon the scene, and listening to the sobs, groans, and cries of the penitents, reminded me of a battlefield after a heavy battle. All night the struggle went on. Victory was on the Lord's side; many were converted, and by sunrise next morning there was the shout of the King in the camp."[3]

The camp meeting was not a jag from which to recover and do it again. Those who fell rose to newness of life, and the camp meeting tamed the frontier.

The Oxford Movement

Coincidentally, revivals were going on in England in the Anglican Church. An evangelical wing, called the Clapham sect after the village where it centered, was on the order of Pietism, with religious fervour and an intense social concern. The variety of revival, however, which more profoundly affected the future not only of Anglicanism but of Protestantism in general is called the Oxford Movement (especially active from 1833 to 1841). Its leaders would have been aghast to have their revival compared to a camp meeting, for they were decorous dons. But the difference was really less in the leaders than in those whom they sought to lead. The camp meeting was directed at the frontiersman; the Oxford Movement aimed at the ancestral parishes that were not roisterous but dull, formal, and smug. The chief architect of the movement, John Keble, though a professor of poetry at Oxford, was seldom there because he spent his days mainly in a secluded country parish. His circle included notable names: Edward Pusey, Wilfred Ward and, above all, John Henry Newman. They perceived that, to bring about a revival in the parishes, there must be changes in the structure and outlook of the Church as a whole. One grievous obstacle was dependence upon the state. The prime

[3] *Ibid.*, p. 103.

minister appointed the bishops. He might be as flippant as Lord Melbourne, who swore that they died to annoy him.[4] Even in the twentieth century there was an outcry when the disquieting Hensley Henson was made a bishop by a Baptist prime minister, Lloyd George. And the Book of Common Prayer could not be revised without the consent of a Parliament filled with rabid "No-Popery" Dissenters.

The Oxford Group were prepared to go to the length of disestablishment for the sake of the Church, but where, then, was authority to be found? Not in the pew, they said, for torpid congregations are not the Church of Jesus Christ. Not in the whole people of England, for the ideal of the Broad Church to include everyone could be achieved only by reducing Christianity to a tepid minimum. No, the Church must proclaim the maximum, all the great historic affirmations, and creeds—the ancient creeds. The Church must recover her heritage, transmitted by the successors of the apostles. The attempt to discover those successors among the English bishops of that day might seem a trifle anomalous, but the real concern was not to make a shibboleth of the external succession but to revive reverence, piety, prayer, and commitment. John Henry Newman, in one of his university sermons, declared that the real religion of nature is not to be found in the optimistic platitudes of Deism but in the dark and bloody superstitions of the heathen.

> Doubtless these desperate and dark struggles are to be called superstition when viewed by the side of true religion; and it is easy enough to speak of them as superstition, when we have been informed of the gracious and joyful result in which the scheme of Divine Governance issues. But it is man's truest and best religion, *before* the Gospel shines on him. If our race *be* in a fallen and depraved state, what ought our religion to be but anxiety and remorse till God comfort us? Surely, to be in gloom —to do all we can, and try to do more than all—and, after all,

[4] Herbert Leslie Stewart, *A Century of Anglo–Catholicism* (London, 1929), p. 87.

to wait in miserable suspense, naked and shivering, among the trees of the garden, for the hour of His coming, and meanwhile to fancy sounds of woe in every wind stirring the leaves about us —in a word, to be superstitious—is nature's best offering, her most acceptable service, her most mature and enlarged wisdom, in the presence of a holy and offended God.[5]

The way to recapture the sense of the numinous was not through the camp meeting but through the worship of the parish churches, which should be restored to its pristine splendor. Not only had the Dissenters abandoned the Christian year, but the Anglicans, too, had neglected it. Keble wrote a collection of poems called *The Christian Year.* Here is a verse for Good Friday:

> *Lord of my heart, by Thy last cry,*
> *Let not Thy blood on earth be spent*
> *Now, at Thy feet I fainting lie,*
> *Mine eyes upon Thy wounds are bent,*
> *Upon Thy streaming wounds my weary eyes*
> *Wait like the parched earth on April skies.*[6]

The ancient architecture and the ancient liturgy cast a spell at a time when the Romantics were rebelling at ugly factories belching a pall of soot over the countryside. How fair were ruins in some glade of a long forsaken, cloistered choir. Isaac Williams, the poet of the group, wrote:

> *I slowly wander'd through the site*
> *Of crumbling walls, half-falling tower,*
> *Mullions and arch, which darkly lower*
> *And o'er the intruder seem to frown. . . .*
> *And through the aisled stillness deep,*
> *Strains indistinct were heard to sweep.*
> *Blest wisdom, dress'd in fancy's hue!*

[5] John Henry Newman, *Sermons chiefly on the Theory of Religious Belief, preached before the University of Oxford* (London, 1843), pp. 105–06.

[6] John Keble, *The Christian Year* (Oxford, 1827).

Such legends, if they be not true,
Speak what our nature here divines
'Mid holy sepulchres and shrines![7]

[Amid such reveries:]
I seem to walk through angel-haunted caves,
Lit by celestial light, not of the sun,
That leadeth to a kingdom far away.[8]

John Mason Neale

Proceeding from the principles of the Oxford reformers, a Cambridge group commenced a great architectural and liturgical revival. The chief figure was John Mason Neale, who inaugurated the Gothic revival by detailed studies of parish churches, revealing what once they were and the desecrations to which they were a prey. Listen to his description of the consecration of an abbey church in bygone days:

Imagine an abbey church, newly decorated . . . rood-screen, tapestry, stall, frescoed vault, gilt capital and pier in their first lustre . . . thousands of worshippers thronging the nave, . . . a mighty band of priests in chasubles blazing with gold and gems, occupying the choir, . . . bishops and abbots at the altar, . . . deacons with the sacred banners, the silver staves, the croisiers, clustering behind them. . . . The air is thick with the perfume of incense. . . . The sunbeams, rich with the lustre of stained glass, fall softly upon it. . . . A subdeacon comes forth, bearing a ponderous and mighty volume, knobbed with silver and clasped with gold, and worked, on its purple velvet sides, with threads of pearls. He opens its fair vellum pages, illuminated in quaint and gorgeous initials, with flower wreaths and clusters of gold curling down the giant pages. . . . The bishop comes forward and proceeds to denounce the punishment of those who shall sacri-

[7] Isaac Williams, *The Baptistry* (Oxford, 1848), pp. 194–95.
[8] ———, *The Cathedral* (8th ed.; Oxford, 1858), p. 124.

legiously violate the newly erected temple. . . . Let his days be
few; let another take his office; let his posterity be destroyed; and
in the next generation let his name be clean put out.[9]

Neale translated a great many of the early Greek and Latin
hymns. Fully fifteen of his renderings are common in current
hymnbooks. Among them: *Good Christian Men Rejoice; All
Glory Laud and Honor; Art Thou Weary?; Christian, Dost Thou
See Then?*; and *Jerusalem, the Golden.*

John Henry Newman

Perchance the most fertile spirit in the group, while he was in
the Church of England and again after he went to the Church of
Rome, was John Henry Newman. Witness the testimony of two
men who, as students, came under his spell, and who in later
years, though differing from him radically, could yet pay such
tribute. The first is the historian, James Anthony Froude, who
wrote:

He seemed always to be better informed on common topics of
conversation than any one else who was present. . . . Perhaps his
supreme merit as a talker was that he never tried to be witty or to
say striking things. Ironical he could be, but not ill-natured. Not a
malicious anecdote was ever heard from him. Prosy he could not
be. He was lightness itself—the lightness of elastic strength—and
he was interesting because he had something real to say. . . . He
never exaggerated; he was never unreal. A sermon from him was
a poem, formed on a distinct idea, fascinating by its subtlety,
welcome—how welcome!—from its sincerity, interesting from its
originality, even to those who were careless of religion; and to
others who wished to be religious, but had found religion dry and

[9] John Mason Neale, *Hierologus, or the Church Tourists* (London, 1843),
pp. 19–20. I am indebted to the Reverend William Baar for supplying this
passage.

wearisome, it was like the springing of a fountain out of the rock.[10]

The second testimony is from the pen of Matthew Arnold:

Who could resist the charm of that spiritual apparition gliding in the dim afternoon light through the aisles of St. Mary's, rising into the pulpit, and then, in the most entrancing of voices, breaking the silence with words and thoughts which were a religious music—subtle, sweet, mournful? I seem to hear him still saying: "After the fever of life, after wearinesses and sicknesses, fightings and desponderings; languor and fretfulness, struggling and succeeding; after all the changes and chances of this troubled, unhealthy state—at length come death, at length the white throne of God, at length the beatific vision."[11]

Newman, and some of his disciples, became Roman Catholics, perhaps because Newman was so pre-eminently the intellectual that he could not resist his ineluctable syllogisms. Keble and Pusey could not suffer any logic to sever them from the English parish church.

Missions Overseas

The evangelical revivals were chiefly responsible for initiating in Protestantism the great missionary crusade, as a result of which Christianity achieved a geographical expansion unparalleled in all preceding centuries. "From Greenland's icy mountains to India's coral strands," from the Ganges to the Limpopo, from the fjords to the jungles, from the Eskimos to the Zulus. The spirit of this great endeavor was caught by Vachel Lindsay in the lines:

> An endless line of splendor,
> These troops with heaven for home,

[10] James Anthony Froude, *Short Studies on Great Subjects* (New York, 1883), Letter III.

[11] Matthew Arnold, *Discourses in America* (New York, 1896), pp. 138–39.

With creeds they go from Scotland,
With incense go from Rome.
These in the name of Jesus
Against the dark gods stand,
They gird the earth with valor,
They heed their King's command.

Onward the line advances,
Shaking the hills with power,
Slaying the hidden dragons,
The lions that devour.
No bloodshed on the wrestling—
But souls new-born arise—
The nations growing kinder,
The child hearts growing wise.

What is the final ending?
The issue, can we know?
Will Christ outlive Mohammed?
Will Kali's altar go?
This is our faith tremendous,
Our wild hope, who shall scorn,
That in the name of Jesus
The world shall be reborn?[12]

The emissaries of this hope in the opening years of the twentieth century had for their slogan, "The world for Christ in our generation," and they did, indeed, plant Christian outposts over a vaster terrain than had been encompassed in the Middle Ages in the course of a thousand years. Christianity has not become, in consequence, the only religion of the world but it has become a world religion encompassing more of the globe than any other. There are today 850 million Christians, about one third of the earth's population, and twenty million of these are in Africa.

In the vast expansion of the nineteenth century, the Protestants were in the lead. In earlier centuries they had been far behind the Catholics. During the Reformation and the ensuing religious wars, the Protestants had been too busy converting the Catholics and

[12] *Collected Poems of Vachel Lindsay* (New York, 1913).

fighting for their own existence to be concerned about the heathen. One of the Protestants consoled himself by saying that God would use an angel to convert the Indians. As a matter of fact, the angels used by God to that end were mainly the Franciscans and the Jesuits. Although in the colonial period in New England John Eliot, David Brainerd, Roger Williams and Jonathan Edwards labored among the Redskins, by and large, the Protestants awoke to missions only in the latter part of the eighteenth century, under the influence of evangelical revivals.

A secular factor may have contributed to the shift of preponderance from the Catholic to the Protestant missions. The decline of the one is associated with the waning of the Spanish and Portuguese colonial empires, and the rise of the other with the emergence of the great colonial powers in the north of Europe, notably Britain and Holland. This fact raises the question whether the frequent allegation may not be correct that Christian missions were simply an adjunct of Western imperialism, that the missionary would call upon the natives to shut their eyes in prayer, only to let them discover the Union Jack waving over their heads when they looked up. The charge is rendered plausible by the fact that, at a particular juncture in the nineteenth century, Christian missionaries would not have been able to enter China and Japan unless the Western powers had forced the "open door." But, such a particular instance does not warrant a generalization. Over against this case may be set the wide following gained by Catholic missions in the sixteenth century in Japan without political assistance.

Undeniably, the missionaries accompanied the flag, as well they might, if for no other reason than to mitigate the asperities of colonialism. The missionaries could not, of course, engage in persistent criticism of their own governments without being sent home. But, not a few emulated Bartolomé de las Casas, who blazed out against the barbarities practised on the natives in the Caribbean in the first flush of the Spanish conquest. Far from constituting a department of the colonial office, the missionaries were, at times, restricted by Western governments, lest they put too many ideas into the heads of the natives. On the other hand, colonial governors and missionaries were often able to collaborate. The British Government in India fostered education and, in a measure, industrialization; and, with all this the missonaries were in sympathy. And many individuals in the government service were sincere evangelical Christians, who themselves acted as missionaries in off-duty hours. Missionaries themselves were willing to enter the service of such governments, though usually resigning from the mission in such a case. Not a few have served as ambassadors.

A more subtle accusation is that missionaries have sought to occidentalize their converts and have destroyed the fibre of primitive peoples through the corruptions of civilization, putting petticoats and pantaloons on Patagonians. To be sure, missionaries have sometimes been inept, but as for clothes, one should remember that the primitive peoples love to gain prestige by bedecking themselves in the incongruous castaways of European attire, even to the extent of combining epaulettes and loin cloths. As for the loss of fibre, the Hawaiians were diminishing before the missionaries came. Unquestionably, the missionaries have sought to introduce whatever they deemed to be good in their own culture; medicine, sanitation, education, transportation, and technology, especially in agriculture. As for native customs, of course missionaries have opposed suttee, the burning of widows in India. This the British Government suppressed. They have opposed child murder, prostitution, polygamy, cannibalism, and headhunting, but native literature, native drama, native music, native architecture they have sought to learn, conserve, and revive. The missionaries have reduced hundreds of languages to writing and have provided these tongues with dictionaries and grammars. The immediate purpose, of course, was to translate the Scriptures. Henry Martyn, who lived to be only thirty-one years of age, sufficiently mastered Arabic, Persian, and Hindustani to be able to translate the Scriptures into these tongues. And native literature was not neglected. Of special significance was the introduction of the printing press. William Carey, at Serampore in Bengal, working in a Baptist Mission under the Danish flag, established the first press in the land, which issued, by 1832, translations of portions of the Scripture in forty-four languages and dialects. He and his associates also translated into English a great Indian epic poem. The missionary movement, by instilling ideals of dignity and equality of opportunity, has been indirectly responsible for the rise of self-government and nationhood of many retarded peoples.

With regard to the accommodation to native cultures, there has been a difference of approach between the Catholics and the Protestants. The basic reason is that the Catholics have continued the tradition which won Europe by conversions *en masse*. Protestant missions, however, began under the influence of the great revivals, and laid emphasis, therefore, upon an individual experience of conversion followed by a period of training and testing before admission to the Church. The unhappy concomitant is that a convert entering the Church individually is cut off from his own people. His family disowns him; his wife's family divorces him. He has no recourse but to enter a European enclave. This problem has plagued the Protestants, even though they, too, have had a few instances of mass conversion in India.

The Catholic Church, which has striven to bring in communities, has felt this difficulty less acutely but has been confronted with another problem in modern, as in ancient times, because the masses bring with them their pagan beliefs and practices. In India this means caste; in Africa, polygamy; in China, the cult of ancestors; in Japan, until recently, the worship of the emperor. Then there arises once more the question of what is the inalienable core of Christianity which cannot be compromised, and what the flexible periphery which can assimilate the innocuous in paganism. Catholic missions show two great examples of accommodation. The first was in the case of the Jesuit Nobili, in the sixteenth century in India, who tried to win the leaders by living like a Brahmin and by accepting the caste principle. He believed there should be one branch of the Church for the Brahmins and a separate branch for the pariahs. Rome, momentarily, gave its approval. In China, Ricci, also an Italian Jesuit, used Confucian words for God, regarded the cult of ancestors as harmless and encouraged the pagoda type of architecture for churches. Rome approved, but banned later, certain Confucian expressions for God as well as the ancestral cult. Protestants have not been immune to these difficulties. Carey has left a description of his problems in translating the Scriptures into Bengali and Hindustani. There is no paucity of words in these languages, but the terms are fraught with meanings derived from an alien faith. The Hindu believes that the ultimate good is the loss of personal identity through absorption into the Supreme Essence, an ideal existence "devoid of positive attributes, natural or moral." Must the translator inject foreign words or can he invest the native terms with new connotations?[13] Sometimes the admissibility of pagan practices among Christians is debatable. The Presbyterians, for example, ruled in Korea against participation in the cult of the emperor, whereas other denominations considered it merely a civil rite. Often the question of the innocuous is subtly elusive; for example, a likeness of Krishna woven into a rug. Is this simply art, or is it religion? The answer may be that only after no one any longer believes in Krishna can it be regarded simply as art. But, so long as paganism is alive, it is idolatry. There is a dilemma here in which all faiths share. When the Turks took Constantinople in 1453, they plastered over the mosaics in Hagia Sophia, because they believed in Islam and disbelieved in Christianity. The Turkish government of today has uncovered the mosaics and declared Hagia Sophia a museum.

Naturally, Christianity has confronted different situations country by country. In India, the Hindus are tolerant of other religions and ideas and willing to borrow, but extremely loath to forsake a Hindu affiliation for that of another faith. In approaching them,

[13] Quotations from William Carey's journal in Clyde Manschreck, *A History of Christianity* (Englewood Cliffs, N.J., 1964), pp. 474–75.

the Church has largely adopted the policy of promulgating Christian ideals, as in the case of Gandhi, for example, who expressed great reverence for Jesus and exemplified more of his spirit than many a Christian, but was of no mind to join the Christian Church. In some lands, such as Turkey, the Church can make no other approach, for political reasons, since the government forbids open proselytizing. Roberts College at Constantinople, though manned by Christians, cannot teach Christianity.

The accessions to Christianity in India have been chiefly from among the lower castes, for whom a change in religion meant a gain in social status. Since the Church itself was popularly regarded as constituting another caste, the outcasts, by joining, acquired at least the status of caste. In China, likewise, the chief accretions have been from the lower strata. The cultivated Buddhist recoils from Christian activism, and the cultivated Confucianist from Christian religious affirmations. In Japan, however, the chief gains in recent times have been among the intelligentsia, while the masses have not been swayed.

Despite the impressiveness of the geographical spread, one cannot say that the world has been won for Christ in this generation. No serious dent has been made on the major religions, Judaism, Islam, Hinduism, Buddhism, and Confucianism. The great gains have been at the expense of primitive religions, notably animism. In the lands of prodigious missionary endeavor the percentage of Christians is small. Between the wars, the Christians in India numbered only two per cent, in China two per cent, and in Japan one-half per cent. These figures, of course, are only approximate surmises, but, even if doubled, they are still small. Christiantity is a minority religion in the world at large.[14] Of course, it always has been, but when Christians knew little about the rest of the world, they were not so aware of their numerical inferiority. It is perhaps more significant that in modern times Christianity fashioned a culture in a single instance only. This has happened in Hawaii.

[14] Alec R. Vidler, *The Church in an Age of Revolution* (Baltimore, 1961), p. 251.

Although Christianity had a momentary chance in China to influence national policy under Sun Yat-sen and Chiang Kai-shek, this was but a fleeting episode.

Christian Churches Overseas

The younger churches have not given to Christian theology a slant distinctive of their own background and situation. Thus far, they have been chiefly active in translating works from the West and in acquainting themselves with the Occidental tradition. The leaders in Japan developed an amazing zeal and skill in mastering the Western tongues and literatures to a degree vastly exceeding all that the Occidentals have done thus far with regard to the cultures of the Orient. The interchange has not brought about until now a blending of Christianity with the religions of the East of the kind which occurred in ancient Gnosticism and in the barbarian West in the period of the early Middle Ages. Such interchange has taken place today rather in the seats of long established Christianity, in Anthroposophy of Rudolf Steiner in Switzerland and in the Bahai cult in the United States. The "spiritism" of Brazil, however, is a potpourri of witchcraft and saint worship.

What the younger churches have mainly contributed is a fresh upsurge of vitality. Any religion becomes increasingly nominal once it is universally accepted by a culture and handed down from generation to generation like an heirloom. Those to whom the Gospel has come as a blinding flash have often better exemplified its spirit than those who have been reared in a light too mellow to attract the moths. One recalls the story of a Korean, whose son was condemned to death and executed by a Communist "judge," and who, when that "judge" was in straits, adopted him as his own son.

The younger churches are minorities in their own lands, and minorities have commonly a greater impact on society because, being minorities, they are able to set up and exemplify their ideals.

Henry P. Van Dusen, having recently visited the mission stations of the world, includes in his report an account of the influence of two minorities, one of very long standing, the other of comparatively recent origin. The first is at Kerala, in Travancore, India, where two Christian churches flourish, both of Syrian provenance: the Orthodox Syrian and the Reformed Mar Thoma Church. He reports:

> The moment one crosses into Kerala, he knows that he is in a "different India." He does not need to be told that the literacy rate of over 40 per cent is strikingly above that for India as a whole. . . . Nor does one need to be told that, despite the densest population in India, health conditions are extraordinarily good. . . . I am bold to suggest that Kerala is the most authentic and convincing proving-ground of Christianity in Asia. For here is a church, or rather two related churches, rooted in the life and culture of the people centuries before our pagan and barbarian ancestors in northern Europe first left their tree-huts, learned of civilization or of Christian faith. Is it coincidence that the part of India where Christianity has flourished for over 1500 years is also the area most advanced in education, health and public service?[15]

The second example is from Indonesia. Having attended a church service in the Toradja dialect, Van Dusen had occasion to observe at closer range the worshipers as they gathered about the table of the Lord.

> We looked out upon some three hundred little brown men and women and boys and girls, clean, alert, barefooted but well and becomingly dressed, spotless in their simple native costumes, hair immaculately arranged, winsome, charming, almost every face lighted by an eager sincere reverence and confident repose. The contrast to the unkempt bedraggled figures and the frightened staring faces which we had passed steadily for the preceding two days was overwhelming.[16]

[15] *Christianity on the March*, ed. Henry P. Van Dusen (New York, 1963), p. 90.

[16] *Ibid.*, p. 82.

But the work of Christian missions is not ultimately to be assessed in terms of its material and cultural contributions, nor even in terms of its numerical gains. The dedication of the missionaries is an incontrovertible testimony. One thinks of Henry Martyn who started out saying, "I will burn myself out for God," and died at the age of thirty-one, or again of David Livingstone, who penetrated Africa, the impenetrable, not to discover the Victoria Falls, but because he saw the smoke rising from a thousand villages that had not heard of Christ.

Social Reforms

During the nineteenth and the twentieth century the churches, both Protestant and Catholic, contributed to intense efforts for social reform. The persistent concern of Christians for justice in the social domain received a new impetus in the century of comparative peace in Europe, from the Napoleonic wars to World War I. In this setting, the traditional Catholic preoccupation with the social order revived, and the humanitarianism of Enlightenment combined with the ethical sensitivity of Pietism to launch many a crusade for the amelioration of social ills. In this sense, the Catholic Bishop Ketteler was active in the late nineteenth century in Germany. Among the Protestants, the Swiss Ragaz and the German Paul Tillich formed a group called Christian Socialists in the early twentieth century. In France, in recent years, the worker priests, like the early Methodists, have addressed themselves primarily to the spiritual needs of the industrial workers.

In England and the United States, the Protestants have espoused a great many reformatory movements. In general, the Anglican bishops in England were socially conservative. The Dissenters fought for relief from disabilities, favored Irish Home Rule, and sought to impose ethical checks on British imperialism. The extent of Protestant influence in this period cannot, however, be fully assessed because, in order to escape from confessional divisiveness, societies were organized with specific objectives, such as anti-slavery or anti-vivisection, drawing their membership from all faiths, or none.

The greatest evil abolished in the English-speaking world in the nineteenth century was slavery. In the case of England this meant actual slavery only in the colonies, but the slave trade was conducted by the mother country. The United States were guilty both of trading and owning slaves.

The campaign against the slave trade in England came from the Methodist and Anglican Evangelicals. John Wesley blazed against the traffic and, when told that only black men could work in the climate of the American south, gave that statement the lie on the basis of what he had seen in Georgia (that episode in his life was, after all, not fruitless). The man who for thirty years agitated in the British Parliament for the suppression of the slave trade and then for the abolition of slavery in the British dominions was the Anglican Evangelical, William Wilberforce. He was a man of one cause, and this put a great strain upon his friendship with William Pitt, the prime minister, because Pitt was willing, on occasion, to postpone abolition rather than jeopardize his entire program. Wilberforce was adamant. He appealed always to the conscience of England. The speeches of British statesmen have the ring of righteousness, from Wilberforce to Churchill. He told the House of Commons:

> Slavery battens upon vices. Does the king of Barbesia want brandy? He has only to send his troops in the nighttime to burn and desolate a village. . . . The delegate from Liverpool tells us that the apartments of the slaves in transit are "perfumed with frankincense and lime juice." The surgeons, however, tell us that the Negroes are packed so close that there is scarcely room to pass among them, and the stench is intolerable. . . . Death at least is a sure ground of proof, and upon the whole, there is a mortality of about fifty per cent. Some argue that, "If we relinquish the slave trade, France will take it up." We cannot wish a greater mischief to France. For the sake of France, however, and for the sake of humanity, I trust—nay, I am sure—she will not.[17]

[17] R. Coupland, *Wilberforce* (Oxford, 1923), p. 119.

This speech was delivered in 1779. Then came the French Revolution, and a great revulsion against social innovations took hold of the British. Not until 1808 did England renounce the slave trade. Then came the second great crusade for the abolition of slavery itself. Victory came only in 1834. There was no war, and the owners were indemnified to the amount of twenty million pound sterling. "Thank God!" said the dying Wilberforce. As his body was being laid in Westminster Abbey, eight hundred thousand slaves received the proclamation of their freedom.

In colonial America, North and South alike had slaves, whether Indian or Negro. The South used more slaves on plantations than did the North, but the North made more slaves by raids on the African coast and by their sale to the South. Protests began among the Quakers. The first American anti-slavery tract was written by the Quaker, George Keith, in 1693. The New Jersey Quaker, John Woolman, in 1757, visiting Friends in the South, would always leave with his host pay for the unrequited labor of the slaves, whereby many a conscience was quickened. By 1800 the Quakers had ceased to hold slaves. In New England, Samuel Hopkins was pastor of an opulent Congregational church in Newport, Rhode Island, on the eve of the American Revolution. This was a city of such prominence at that time that a letter from England was addressed to "New York near Newport." The wealth of the city was derived from the slave trade. Hopkins first addressed his parishioners with cold facts and ruthless logic:

> By drink we have incited the Africans to war upon each other, that the captives might be sold into slavery. They are herded together, examined as to soundness, branded with a hot iron, manacled in the holds of ships, and transported to the West Indies. Thirty out of every hundred die in transit, which means 30,000 murdered every year. Families are separated, the infirm, feeble, and females with child must work with the rest and if they fall behind, suffer the lash. Such is the oppression that they do not increase by propagation and replacement is by new importation. . . . Is it objected that immediate emancipation is impos-

sible? . . . Suppose our children were slaves in Algiers and there were not a family in the American colonies which did not have some relatives in captivity. And why are we not as much affected by slavery of the blacks? If one of our boys is impressed into the king's ship, how do his parents grieve! . . . You say, "if free, the blacks would be worse off." . . . I grant that slavery debases, but because we have reduced them to abject misery, shall we continue therein?[18]

Slavery in the North was eliminated by stages. In Connecticut, for example, there were in 1756 no free Negroes and 3,634 slaves. But, in 1850 there were 7,693 free Negroes and no slaves.[19]

But this does not mean that the Christian conscience in the South was unaroused. In 1787, the Baptists in Virginia combined evangelical fervor with Jeffersonian tenets in a resolution which condemned slavery as "a violent deprivation of the rights of nature and inconsistent with a republican government." Actually, between 1808 and 1831, the South was the center of the anti-slavery agitation. How, then, did the South come to be so solidified behind slavery?[20] Partly through fear of servile insurrection, such as the one which had occured in Jamaica, partly by reason of death or migration of the leaders of the anti-slavery sentiments, partly in reaction against the diatribes of Northern abolitionists, who "united the South and divided the North." The common assumption has been that the primary reason was the discovery by Eli Whitney, a Connecticut Yankee, of the cotton gin, which made slavery an immense economic asset in the South. But, lately this thesis has been called into question.

The Southern clergy, in any case, began to defend slavery as scriptural, and, as a matter of fact, it is not prohibited in the Bible. "Neither is polygamy," retorted the abolitionists, "but,

[18] Samuel Hopkins, *Works* (Boston, 1852), II, 553–81, abridged.

[19] Bernard C. Steiner, "History of Slavery in Connecticut," in *Labor, Slavery and Self-Government*, Johns Hopkins University Studies, XI (Baltimore, 1893), p. 84.

[20] H. Shelton Smith, Robert T. Handy and Lefferts A. Loetscher, *American Christianity* (New York, 1963), II, p. 167 and chapter xv.

should it for that reason be revived?" Three of the major denominations were split into Northern and Southern branches: the Methodists, the Presbyterians, and the Baptists. Loyalty to the unity of the Church preserved the Catholics and Episcopalians from ruptures. The Quakers were not split because they were of one mind against slavery, nor were the Congregationalists, whose terrain was solely in the North.

The anti-slavery agitation in that area stemmed directly out of the spirit of the Second Great Awakening. The "crusader in crinoline" who aroused the land with *Uncle Tom's Cabin*, Harriet Beecher Stowe, was the daughter of the revivalist Lyman Beecher. The New Englanders were divided only as to strategy, into the advocates of gradual and of immediate emancipation. The gradualists argued that there were only three ways of resolving the problem. One was secession on the part of the North. This would leave slavery intact in the South. The second was war. That was unthinkable. The third was through the persuasion of the South. This could not be achieved by violent denunciation. Then came the Fugitive Slave Law, which required the return of runaway slaves. The Northern abolitionists were abetting their escape through the "underground railroad". Some of the moderates, like Daniel Webster, pointed out that to connive in the escape of a few would only rivet the chains on the many. In the interests of ultimate emancipation, the fugitives must be returned, a course witheringly denounced by the Quaker, Whittier. Then came the Kansas and Nebraska Bill, which many in the North believed was a devious device for extending slavery into the West. The South seceded, the war came, God had "loosed the fateful lightening of His terrible swift sword." The war was a crusade.

A crusade is commonly less humane than a war waged simply to rectify frontiers. Even though Grant treated Lee like a Knight of the Round Table, the chivalry of the eighteenth-century wars was gone, the South was charred, and the end is not yet.

Christian Pacifism

The ancient plague of war was another social problem which engaged the churches acutely during the last century and a half. The eighteenth century had seen peace plans in abundance: those by Penn the Quaker, Kant the Lutheran, Comenius the Moravian, and those by Catholics, the Abbé Saint-Pierre and Jean-Jacques Rousseau. An opportunity to implement such plans was afforded by the Holy Experiment of the Quakers in Pennsylvania, which drew to itself the like-minded Moravians, Schwenckfelders, and Mennonites. Friendly relations with the Indians were all the easier to maintain there, because the neighboring Delawares did not wish to be embroiled, like the great tribes, such as the Iroquois, in alliances with either the English or the French. But, in the end, the Delawares were not permitted by other Indians to enjoy the privilege of neutrality, and the Quakers, likewise, were not free. As a colony under the British Crown, they were not permitted to create a breach in the wall through which the French could displace the English. In part, the Quakers were undone because they did not seek, like Massachusetts, to exclude from residence in their territory those not committed to their ideals. An influx of Scotch and Irish Presbyterians made the Quakers a minority in Pennsylvania, and in 1756 they withdrew from the legislature, rather than take part in the French and Indian wars.

The Puritans of New England were not tainted by pacifism. Despite some missions to the Indians, the Puritans treated them in general as Joshua did the Canaanites, and they resisted the French as minions of the Catholic Antichrist. Agitation for peace began in New England after the war of 1812, which had been very unpopular in New England, loath to sever commerce with Britain. American activism stimulated widespread efforts for peace through the technique of founding societies to that end.

The New England Non-resistance Society was pacifist out and out. The American Peace Society sought to restrain war by world government and international law. The Civil War caused a drastic setback. For the churches in the Calvinist tradition, the Congregationalists, Unitarians, Presbyterians, Baptists, and Methodists, it was a crusade to abolish slavery. For the successors of the old, established churches of Europe, the Catholics, Anglicans, and Lutherans, it was the suppression of a rebellion. After the war, the peace societies revived and became international. Their congresses did prompt disarmament conferences between governments, in which, for a time, Russia took the lead. With World War I, however, shelves of peace literature were filed for historical reference. In the United States, all save the historic peace churches rallied to a crusade to "make the world safe for democracy and to end all wars." The failure of victory to achieve ideal ends caused a great revulsion, and the churches then embarked on a crusade to outlaw war. This was implemented by the Kellogg-Briand treaties to renounce war as an instrument of national policy. World War II was fought in a mood of chastened sobriety, even though the evil to be resisted was more monstrous. In the ensuing Cold War, the dove of peace has been caged, to be released on occasion by either side in the interests of propaganda. The preservation of peace by the balance of terror elicits protests from those Christians who recoil from the use of nuclear weapons and the threat of massive retaliation and from some Humanists who think the universe would be impoverished by the extinction of the human race.

Alcoholism

Another social problem that engaged especially the churches of the United States and England was alcoholism. The evil had been accentuated, as we have observed, by the introduction of distilled liquors. Greater evils call for more drastic remedies. Prior to the eighteenth century, the Christian churches had not called for total abstinence. Monastic orders even became famous for their cordials—the Benedictine and the Chartreuse. Methodism called first for thoroughgoing renunciation on the part of the guzzling miners. In the American colonies, Benjamin Rush, a Quaker physician, recorded with scientific precision the effects of alcohol on the soldiers in the Revolutionary War. Lyman Beecher, the revivalist, was outraged by the tippling at his ordination. First came the demand for abstinence from hard liquors and, when it was discovered that alcoholics could just as readily lapse on soft, a "T" for total was added to the pledge. Hence the term "teetotal." An appeal to the state to regulate the sale and manufacture of liquor stemmed from the churches of the Calvinist tradition, with their ideal of the Holy Commonwealth. Under the influence of the Quaker, Neale Dow, prohibition was first introduced in Maine. Catholics, Episcopalians, and Lutherans supported the prohibition only because it was the law, not because it met with their approval. Catholic ethical rigorism applies to sex, not to drink. Episcopalians have always felt that, if wine may be used as a sacrament, it was not wholly to be eschewed, and German Lutherans have felt no scruples about accepting contributions from breweries. Prohibition began with local option, and was extremely effective in those areas where it was desired. But when, following World War I, national prohibition was forced upon the large cities with their steady influx of new immigrants, for whom wine and beer belonged to their normal diet, bootlegging necessitated repeal and to this day alcoholism remains one of the major social problems. No recourse apparently remains save the education of the individual conscience in the exercise of restraint, if not of entire abstinence.

Reform of the Penal System

The settlement of disputes by law and humane treatment of criminals advanced tremendously during the nineteenth century. Duelling was vigorously attacked by Lyman Beecher after Aaron Burr shot Alexander Hamilton. (Incidentally, there is no reason to regard Hamilton as a martyr, simply because he was a poorer shot.) Prison reform was initiated in the late eighteenth century by John Howard, an Anglican layman in England. Having been made a sheriff, he acquainted himself with the appalling conditions in the jails of his own jurisdiction, then moved on to investigate those throughout England and eventually throughout the Continent. During his lifetime, he traveled fifty thousand miles and expended thirty thousand pounds from his own funds. Early in the nineteenth century, Elizabeth Fry, the Quakeress, devoted herself to the care of women prisoners. On the initiative of the government, Robert Peel, the prime minister, exempted five hundred offenses from the death penalty in 1823, and deportation for crime was abolished in 1841. Peel first set up a police force in 1829, and because his name was Robert, the policemen were called Bobbies. Hitherto, the catching of thieves had been improvised by sheriffs or trading companies. In 1856, jailers were put on salaries.

These definite gains in so many areas have not by any means created a perfect social order. The attempt to prevent war by preparation for war entails grave risks and dissipates resources which might better clothe the naked. The emancipation of slaves has not ensured civil rights. Neither Prohibition nor repeal has eliminated alcoholism. But enough has been gained in these several areas to prove that social problems are not altogether insoluble.

Overpopulation and Industrialization

But, in the meantime, another problem has emerged which, next to war, is shaking the foundations of the social order and requires on the part of Christian forces profound concern for the problem itself and rethinking of the role of the Church in society and in relation to the state. This is the problem posed by the growth of population and industrialization. During the nineteenth century, America was spared a confrontation with this problem, because of the open frontier, but Europe was already profoundly affected in the early decades.

England may well serve to illustrate the European situation. Between 1811 and 1851, her population increased from twelve to twenty-one million. Cities grew. Sheffield and Birmingham doubled the number of their inhabitants; Liverpool, Leeds, and Manchester nearly trebled theirs. Large cities engendered slums, filled, in part, by those displaced from handicrafts. In 1806 Manchester had one loom. In 1818 she had two thousand. In 1835 there were eighty-five thousand looms in England and fifteen thousand in Scotland. The changes are not to be exaggerated. At the accession of Victoria, there were more women and girls in domestic service than in the mills, and more tailors and bootmakers in London than miners in Northumbria. But, still there were thousands suffering from technological unemployment, and those who had work in the factories were employed at low wages, for long hours. And not only men and women were employed in industry but small children as well.[21]

A bill introduced in 1833 seemed quite radical when it stipulated that children under nine should be excluded from factories, that those under thirteen should not work more than nine hours, nor those under eighteen more than twelve.[22] The conditions of labor were unsanitary. Such conditions induced crime, and crime was punished by death and imprisonment. Of the two, death was almost to be preferred. Prisoners were exploited by jailers whose only pay was what they could extort. The indicted and the convicted, the sick and the healthy, were all lodged together, without proper sanitary facilities. There was then a disease called "jail fever," a virulent type of typhus fever.

What were the churches to do? What could they do in the face of such conditions? First of all, they could minister to the dispos-

[21] E. L. Woodward, *The Age of Reform* (Oxford, 1938), p. 145.
[22] Robert F. Wearmouth, *Methodism and the Workingclass Movements of England 1800–1860* (London, 1957).

sessed. This task was at first assumed primarily by the Salvation Army. The Anglicans devoted themselves chiefly to the rural parishes where their constituencies lay, and the Dissenters ministered to the urban middle class. William Booth, the founder of the Salvation Army, went to the slums with a program for the soul as well as the body. Listen to this description from his book *In Darkest England and the Way Out:*

> Talk about Dante's Hell, and all the horrors and cruelties of the torture-chamber of the lost! The man who walks with open eyes and with a bleeding heart through the shambles of our civilization needs no such fantastic images of the poet to teach him horror. Often and often, when I have seen the young and the poor and the helpless go down before my eyes into the morass, trampled underfoot by beasts of prey in human shape that haunt these regions, it seemed as if God were no longer in His world, but that in His stead reigned a fiend, merciless as Hell, ruthless as the grave. Hard it is, no doubt, to read in Stanley's pages of the slave-traders coldly arranging for the surprise of a village, the capture of the inhabitants, the massacre of those who resist, and the violation of all the women; but the stony streets of London, if they could speak, would tell of tragedies as awful, of ruin as complete, of ravishments as horrible, as if we were in Central Africa; only the ghastly devastation is covered, corpselike, with the artificialities and hypocrisies of modern civilization.[23]

Booth established refuges to give food and shelter to the destitute, both men and women. Here is his description:

> Two or three hundred men in the men's Shelter, or as many women in the women's Shelter, are collected together, most of them strange to each other, in a large room. They are all wretchedly poor—what are you to do with them? This is what we do with them.
> We hold a rousing Salvation meeting . . . a jovial free-and-easy social evening. The girls have their banjos and their tambourines,

[23] Clyde Manschreck, *A History of Christianity* (Englewood Cliffs, N.J., 1964), pp. 419–23.

and for a couple of hours you have as lively a meeting as you will find in London. There is a prayer, short and to the point; there are addresses, some delivered by the leaders of the meeting, but most of them the testimonies of those who have been saved at previous meetings . . . simple confessions of individual experience. . . . There are bursts of hearty melody. The conductor of the meeting will start up a verse or two of a hymn illustrative of the experiences mentioned by the last speaker, or one of the girls from the training Home will sing a solo, accompanying herself on her instrument, while all join in a rattling and rollicking chorus. . . . Mattresses are carefully inspected every day, so that no stray specimen of vermin may be left in the place. The men turn in about ten o'clock and sleep until six. We have never any disturbances of any kind in the Shelters. We have provided accommodation now for several thousand of the most helplessly broken-down men in London, criminals many of them, mendicants, tramps, those who are among the filth and offscouring of all things.[24]

Education

Education for working men was another possibility and F. W. Robertson, the Anglican rector at Brighton, was active in this field. Experiments in various forms of cooperative labor and living interested F. D. Maurice and Ludlow. Stewardship was preached to the employers of labor, but what could they do? If a manufacturer gave decent hours and wages to his employees, how could he compete with other manufacturers devoid of compunction? Charles Kingsley, in his tract *Cheap Clothes and Nasty*, would boycott the products of sweated labor and make their sale unprofitable, but all England could not be aroused to such a renunciation of cheap commodities. One has to be wealthy in order to dispense with the labors of poverty. What then?

[24] *Ibidem.*

Labor

The only possible answer was to turn to the state, as Luther had done when he called in the prince as an emergency bishop. The state must regulate the hours of work. The state must determine the wage rates. The state must prescribe the conditions of labor. To exert pressure on the state, labor must organize and, in order that working men may have a voice in the decisions of the state, the franchise must be extended. In sponsoring these measures, various individual churchmen were active. Two Anglican laymen were notable in the struggle in labor's behalf. Richard Oastler, the administrator of a Yorkshire estate, was greatly exercised over slavery in Africa until he was made aware of a darker slavery in the factories of his own area. He then spent himself in championing shorter hours and better conditions for the workers. The great proponent of the Ten Hours' Bill, which passed in 1846, was Anthony Ashley Cooper, the Earl of Shaftesbury, a man, incidentally, of more than one single cause. He sponsored care for underground workers, child laborers, chimney sweeps, and lunatics, and worked for the abolition of slavery, the protection of animals, the reformation of juvenile delinquents, the education of poor children, and improved housing.

If social reform in England was for the most part the work of individuals, one church constitutes an exception, namely that of the Methodists—and in particular one of its branches, called the Primitive Methodists. The Wesleyan movement early became subject to the splintering process, to the advantage of social reform, because a small group is often capable of taking a more radical stand than a larger body. The Primitive Methodists had profound sympathy for those displaced by the looms. Many of their own members were among them. The so-called Luddites were trying to recover their jobs by smashing the looms. The Methodists would have no truck with violence, but they were willing to join Workingmen's Associations. Labor unions were, however, illegal until the middle of the century. The leaders of Methodism frowned on illegality, whereupon, in the five years following 1849, one-third of the Methodists seceded to the labor unions. They did not cease thereby to be evangelicals. Instead, they took with them into the labor movement their zeal, their Christian ideology, and their experience as lay preachers. Many a labor leader had his apprenticeship as a Methodist lay preacher. Methodism gave to the labor movement men of the stamp of Arthur Henderson, Ramsay Mac-Donald, and Philip Snowden.[25]

The claim has been made sometimes that Methodism prevented a social upheaval in England patterned after the French Revolution. This is saying too much. England did not have anything like the French Revolution because her revolutions had been spaced at discrete intervals. The sixteenth century saw her ecclesiastical revolution; the seventeenth the democratic; the eighteenth the industrial; and the nineteenth the urban. France had suffered from the convergence of deferred explosions. But, one might say that Methodism was one among the many reasons why England did not have a Fascist revolution in the twentieth century. Fascism imposed cooperation between labor and capital at the hands of the state. This was understandable in Germany and in Italy, where the industrial proletariat was Marxist. It was not necessarily so in England, where labor and capital still could converse in a Christian vocabulary.

But the regulation of the hours and wages of labor did not take care of unemployment by reason of technological displacement, sickness, accidents, old age, or congenital incapacity. The state must become paternalistic and take upon itself the promotion of public welfare. This was not too difficult a role for the state to assume in Germany, where Lutheranism had always looked to the sovereign to provide for the poor and had never made a gospel of individual freedom, while Pietism had quickened concern for the neighbor. In accord with these attitudes, Bismarck set an example in social legislation in the 1880's.

Nor was the welfare state difficult to accept for the Catho-

[25] Robert F. Wearmouth, *Social and Political Influence of Methodism in the Twentieth Century* (London, 1957).

lics with their long tradition of corporateness. Bishop Ketteler charged liberalism with having sanctioned "unbridled competition amongst the people dissolved into isolated individuals. . . . The tendency of our times to return to corporative forms, far from being a product of liberalism, is on the contrary a reaction against the unnaturalness of its natural law."[26] One can readily understand why Leo XIII in his great encyclical on labor, entitled *Rerum novarum*, in 1891, could endorse the welfare state and labor organizations.

To do so was more difficult for the British, nurtured as they were in the Puritan tradition of individual liberty. Despite the Restoration, England as a whole had come to believe not only in liberty of conscience, but also liberty in trade. The Utilitarians of the school of Bentham and Adam Smith had argued that a cosmic principle would cause the rivalries of self-interest, if unimpeded, to exert a reciprocal check, so that equity would result and the striving of each for himself would minister to the good of all. Plainly, this was not happening and churchmen began to renounce the philosophy of the Manchester School of *laissez faire*. A beginning of recourse to state control was made on the municipal level at Birmingham when Joseph Chamberlain, a Unitarian, was mayor, and R. W. Dale, a Congregational minister, campaigned on his behalf.

The greatest development of the role of the state as the custodian of public welfare has taken place in Lutheran Sweden and Catholic Austria. Strides in that direction have been marked in the United States. Here all the problems of the expanding population and of industrialization were precipitated only at the end of the nineteenth century, with the closing of the frontier. The answer of the churches was the "social gospel," preached notably by Walter Rauschenbusch, professor of Church History at the Rochester Baptist Seminary. The subsequent emergence of powerful labor unions has taken care of the particular evils over which he was

[26] Cited by V. A. Demant, *Religion and the Decline of Capitalism* (London, 1952), p. 44.

Held at Sing Sing, in upper New York State, August 1859 (from *Harper's Weekly*, September 10, 1859).

67a

Fig. 67a shows him as a young man, in a chalk drawing by George Richmond, ca. 1840.

Fig. 67b depicts him as an old man, in a cartoon from *Vanity Fair* for January 20, 1877.

67b

"A WOLF IN SHEEP'S CLOTHING."

Mr. Bull (*to* Britannia). "WHENEVER YOU SEE ANY OF THESE SNEAKING SCOUNDRELS ABOUT, MA'AM, JUST SEND FOR ME. *I'LL DEAL WITH 'EM, NEVER FEAR!!*"

By permission Punch, *London*

This was a matter of national concern in view of the union of Church and State. Any changes in the Prayer Book, for instance, had to be authorized by act of Parliament. That is why John Bull could be portrayed in the above cartoon from *Punch* (June 30, 1887) taking a hand to prevent Romish intrusions. A similar cartoon of Uncle Sam in the United States would have been quite unthinkable.

FUN.—June 9, 1880.

DISSENTERS STRICTLY PROHIBITED

BURIAL DISSENTERS BILL.

CHURCH *versus* CHAPEL:
A GRAVE QUESTION.

In England they were a long time in receiving redress. In the cartoon above (from *Fun*, June 9, 1880), the Lords and the Bishops are seen opposing the right of Dissenters to burial in Anglican cemeteries.

They looked with outraged wistfulness on the desecrated vestiges of bygone loveliness. The painter Joseph Turner (1775–1851) here portrays cows sheltering in the ruins of Kirkstall abbey.

70

An illustration from *The Life Boat*, a publication of the American Seaman's Friend Society, purporting to depict the fate of tipplers. A train of the Black Valley Railroad is here seen just leaving Drunkard's Curve. From an issue of 1863.

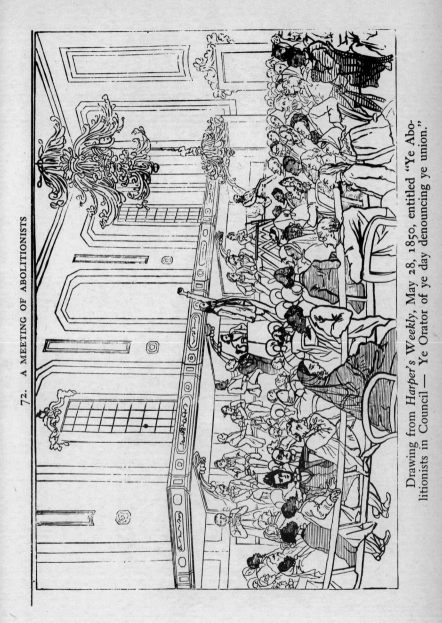

Drawing from *Harper's Weekly*, May 28, 1850, entitled "Ye Abolitionists in Council — Ye Orator of ye day denouncing ye union."

BUBBLES OF THE YEAR. FASHIONABLE PROPRIETARY CHAPELS.

By permission Punch, *London*

This cartoon in *Punch* from the latter half of the nineteenth century (Fig. 73a) satirizes the indifference of the Church to the poor. This situation spurred William Booth to the eventual founding of the Salvation Army.

73a

73b

Fig. 73b depicts William Booth preaching in the Commercial Road, Whitechapel, before the establishment of the Salvation Army.

Gustave Doré, *Over London by Rail*, 1879.

75

As drawn for *Vanity Fair*, March 30, 1872, by T. Gibson Bowles ("Jehu Junior").

76

The struggle of labor to achieve the right to organize and to strike met with opposition for a long time on the part of governments, the populace, and the churches. (We have noted that the Primitive Methodists in England constituted an exception.) After the middle of the nineteenth century, when the unions achieved legal status, the churches gradually assumed a more favorable attitude. In England Cardinal Manning and W. T. Stead, a Congregational layman and editor of the *Pall Mall Gazette*, united in support of a dockers' strike. In the United States Cardinal Gibbons persuaded Pope Leo XIII that Catholics should not be forbidden to join the Knights of Labor. However, the unions were still far from popular with the government and a goodly proportion of the population. The cartoon above purports to reflect the general resentment against a railway strike in 1894. Eugene V. Debs of the American Railway Union sits astride a drawbridge which he refuses to close, thereby tying up the traffic of the nation. (From *Harper's Weekly*, XXXVIII, July 14, 1894.)

exercised. But, in the meantime, the state has become the proponent of the New Deal and the New Frontiers. The state has an eye not only for the elimination of poverty and care for the aged, but for the conservation and restoration of natural resources, the safeguarding of public health, the preservation of beauty, the subsidizing of education, the championing of civil rights, and the promotion of the "American way of life." The role of the churches is to instill into the citizenry the ideals embodied in the American dream. The pattern of the Puritan theocracy has been revived. America thinks of herself as a nation under God, as a nation chosen by God to bring the good life to the nations. Church and state are dedicated to the same ends, but often the initiative and commonly the implementation rest with the state.

XIII

The Breaking of the Pillars
and the Apocalyptic Hope:
The Twentieth Century

PARTICULARLY to the twentieth century applies the term "an age of revolution," in this case, scientific, technological and political. It suites also the nineteenth, but the speed and the violence have now increased. More than ever, the Church has been compelled to come to grips with society. In some instances, there has been a close affiliation with the agencies of society, notably the state, in other instances there was a conflict to the blood. In some areas, the Church has gained in numbers and influence, in others she has experienced grievous regressions. Of late, the churches have been moving in the direction of uniting their efforts and their structures.

Church and State Today

We have just noticed the close collaboration which obtains in the United States between the Christian churches and the state. Certainly, in times past such an affiliation would have found embodiment in a union of Church and state. Yet there is today no other land where the separation of Church and state has so hardened into a dogma as it has in the United States. The understanding of this anomaly calls for a brief survey of the movements for the separation of Church and state in various lands. The motives have been diverse. Sometimes, the churches themselves have initiated separation, so that they might be free from state control. This happened with a section of the Presbyterian Church in Scotland. The objection was not to the Establishment as such but to the power of a lay patron under parliamentary authority to force an unwanted nominee upon an unwilling congregation. Against this system a protest was led by Thomas Chalmers in 1843, when 451 ministers out of 1,203 seceded and set up the Free Church, having first renounced their parish churches, their manses, and their endowments.

More frequently, the state has forced the separation, particularly in Catholic lands where the state has been democratic, republican or Socialist, whereas the Church has supported the *anciens régimes*, the landed aristocracy and the old dynasties, whether in power or deposed. In South America, the Church was in league with the Spanish and Portuguese elite, and separations grew out of antipathy on the part of the political order, save only in Chile. In Europe, the situation was not dissimilar, because the Church was Carlist in Spain, Bourbon in France, Hapsburg in Austria and Hanoverian in Germany. In France, the separation early in the century carried with it also the exile of the monastic orders. The situation in Spain has fluctuated, with closer relations since the victory of Francisco Franco. In Italy, the clash occurred when the Church opposed the Italian unification, because it would terminate the estates of the Church. When this came to pass in 1870, the popes made themselves the prisoners of the Vatican. Mussolini terminated the impasse by the Concordat of 1929, whereby the Church recovered political sovereignty in a territory comparable to a postage stamp, while the Church was effectively controlled because the salaries of the clergy came from the state. Since Germany was not united as a state until the advent of the Weimar Republic, the union of the Church with the state had to take place in each Protestant territory separately. In England, the Anglican

Church remains established, and in Sweden it is the Lutheran. The Communist revolution, wherever successful, has of course severed the connection.

The situation in the United States is unique, growing primarily out of the religious pluralism, which even in the colonial period characterized the Atlantic seaboard where many diverse churches were established on a territorial basis. The Congregationalists held New England and put Dissenters "over the river." The Dutch Reformed were dominant in New York, the Presbyterians in New Jersey, the Swedish Lutherans in Delaware, and the Quakers in Pennsylvania. The Anglican Church became established in Virginia and the Carolinas. Maryland was founded by a Catholic under a charter from a Protestant king. Rhode Island may be called a Baptist settlement, even if Roger Williams, the founder, was only briefly an adherent of this sect. Constraint in religion was avoided in Pennsylvania, Rhode Island, and Maryland, but conformity to the established church was enforced in the other colonies.

Gradually the system broke down. Sometimes shifts in political jurisdiction created untenable anomalies. For instance, the Dutch Reformed, being Calvinists, would not at first tolerate Lutherans in New York, but when these Dutch gained control of Delaware, they were constrained by treaty not to interfere with the Swedish Lutherans. Thereafter, it became religiously indefensible to keep Lutherans out of New York. Then the English took New York and established the Anglican Church and accorded toleration by treaty to the Dutch Calvinists. The attempt to suppress the American Presbyterian Calvinists in New York speedily collapsed. A most important factor was new immigration. The Scotch-Irish were staunch Presbyterians. The Quakers allowed them to enter Pennsylvania in numbers so large that they came to control the colony. In Virginia, they were welcomed to the Western frontiers as a bulwark against the Indians, even though the Anglican dominance was weakened. Trade and need for joint defense drew the colonies to each other and facilitated interchange of populations, while the imposition of England's Act of Toleration removed the corporal penalties for dissent. Coincidentally, the differences between the denominations were reduced. On the point of polity all tended to become congregational, even the Anglicans and the Roman Catholics, because with the great distances between settlements no central authority could be exercised. Then the great revivals shifted interest from a religion of the head, with prescribed articles of faith, to a religion of the heart, regardless of creed. In consequence, the "revived" were drawn together. But, as we noted, the Holy Commonwealth was not restored by the revivals, and the Congregational churches were split. In the meantime, the Methodists established themselves in all the seaboard colonies, thereby challenging whichever church was established.

The logic of the revivals called for separation of Church and state. If the Church were to consist of the converted only, while the entire populace could not be converted, and if the state on the other hand comprised the entire populace, then Church and state, having different constituencies, should be disengaged. And the Church should wish to have it so, lest she suffer interference at the hands of non-Christians in the state. Thus, the logic of Roger Williams and of the Baptists came to be also that of the Calvinist churches hitherto established. Coincidentally, the concepts of Enlightenment gained a great vogue among the Anglicans in Virginia, notably Jefferson, for whom the state, belonging to the order of nature, should not be confused with the Church depending on revelation. Thus, the growing religious pluralism, the logic of the revivals, coalescing with the influence of Enlightenment caused the framers of the American Constitution to forbid any national establishment of religion. Nothing was said about the states and, among them, the separation of Church and state was not completed until the 1830's.

Thereafter, a unique situation developed. The distinction of Church and sect disappeared. The Church has commonly been established, the sect disestablished, but now all religious groups in the United States were disestablished. Hence, from this point on, the American churches are commonly called not sects, but denominations. Again, the sect has frequently been dissociated from the culture, but the denominations in this country have created the culture. The Congregationalists did so in New England, the Anglicans in Virginia and the Carolinas, the Methodists in the Middle West, the Baptists in the South, the Lutherans in the central North, and the Catholics around the Great Lakes and in the old Spanish areas of the South.

This pattern persists largely into our own time. A map was published in 1962, showing the areas where a single religious body has more than 50 per cent or more than 25 per cent of the inhabitants. The Baptists have the whole of the South to the edge of New Mexico, with Methodist pockets interspersed. Methodist strength runs latitudinally across the middle of the land from Delaware to Colorado, including Ohio, Indiana, Illinois, Iowa, Kansas, and Nebraska, with large pockets in the South, the Northwest, and northern Arizona. The Scandinavian Lutherans predominate in Minnesota, North and South Dakota, and in parts of Montana. The Mormons hold Utah, southern Idaho, eastern Nevada, and western Wyoming. The Catholics are strong in the region around the Great Lakes, around New Orleans, and in the old Spanish areas: California, southern Arizona, New Mexico, the southernmost tip of Texas, which is otherwise prevailingly Baptist, Alabama, and the tip of Florida. All this one might have expected. The surprise is that the Catholics hold New England and a cardinal reigns on Beacon Hill. The reason is to be sought partly in the influx of Irish, Italian, and Polish immigrants, and partly in the migration of New Englanders to the West. But, the Catholics have also gone West and appear strongly in Montana and other areas of the Northwest. One may well be surprised that Congregationalists, Presbyterians, and Disciples hold only a few small pockets, although this is not of itself an indication of their total strength, since they have minorities in many areas that do not appear on the said map.[1] Of the total population in 1958, 66 per cent were Protestant, 26 per cent Catholic and 3.5 per cent were Jewish. The number of those professing a religious affiliation was 109,557,741, constituting 63 per cent of the entire population.[2]

American Religion

Yet with all this diversity, there has emerged an "American religion," which describes itself as Judeo-Christian and now sees itself embodied in three religious groups: Protestants, Catholics, and Jews. In point of fact, this American religion has to be Judaism: when the three speak with one voice, they have to proclaim that which they have in common, which is Judaism. Not the least Jewish element is the concept of the Holy Commonwealth. The Puritans believed themselves to be the heirs of the covenant which God made with Moses. The Mormons claim also physical descent through emigrés who left Jerusalem just prior to the Babylonian captivity and settled in the New World. The Catholics in America hail as their spiritual progenitors on these shores not Lord Baltimore but the Pilgrim Fathers. This new Israel of God is the American nation, functioning much after the fashion of Cromwell's Protectorate, which substituted for the established church a national religion resting upon three pillars: Congregational, Presbyterian, and Baptist. Now the three pillars are Protestant, Catholic, and Jewish. The nation is the manifestation of their unity, and to preserve the union a war was fought, whereas to leave a church is unexceptionable. The nation has come to be something like a church, to be joined on profession of faith. To this day, the rite of

[1] Edwin Scott Gaustad, *Historical Atlas of Religion in America* (New York, 1962).

[2] Will Herberg, *Protestant, Catholic, Jew* (Garden City, 1955), p. 47.

induction into United States citizenship includes a little homily by the judge on American ideals, with the tacit assumption that those who do not subscribe should be merely inhabitants. The United States are still a Puritan commonwealth.

Separation of Church and State

Yet, Church and state are separate and the churches wish it so. As long as they are separate they are free and their members are more devoted when they have to pay. Catholics in this country have long defended the separation, recognizing no doubt that if any church had been established it would not have been the Catholic. But, in part they have done so also on principle. They realize that for centuries the papacy has not enjoyed such prestige as it has since stripped of political power.

But, if Church and state are so intimately allied, yet in their structure so rigidly separate, what becomes of the public school? Increasingly, the doctrine of separation has been interpreted in the United States in such a way as to exclude religious instruction and practice from public schools. The Constitution has not always been so understood. In earlier days, Bible readings and prayers in public schools in religiously homogeneous communities were not taken amiss. But, with the growth in every community of large minorities, agreement on the forms of prayer has proved impossible. There are unbelievers who wish no prayer at all and, though they be few, their scruples must be respected, inasmuch as the practice of religious liberty means that the minority always wins. The solution might be perhaps in an observance of a moment's silence at the opening of the day, when each child could pray or meditate in accord with its parents' convictions.

But, the churches cannot be satisfied with such minimal practice of religion on the part of their children. Religious instruction must be either adequately given in church, synagogue, and home, or there must be parochial schools. These have been instituted by

77

The Czar and the clergy of the Russian Orthodox Church ride
upon the back of the peasant (from *The Atheist*, Moscow, 1924).

78. THE CENTER PARTY CARICATURED

Windhorst leading the clerical phalanx that is the Center Party in The Reichstag. (*Jugend,* 1907.)

78

79a

79b

79c

Despite the Concordat the Nazis harassed the monastic orders on the suspicion that they were smuggling money out of Germany (Fig. 78a). The second cartoon (Fig. 78b) has St. Peter warning the Christmas angel, who is about to descend to earth carrying a scroll of Luther's carol, to look out for flack as she comes down over the Mediterranean. Bishop Ludwig Sebastian of Speyer, who denounced the Concordat, is caricatured in Fig. 78c as "the unholy Sebastian," (a play on words, as there is a saint referred to as "the holy Sebastian"). All the cartoons are from *Kladderadatsch*, the issues of July 7, 1935, January 5, 1936, and July 11, 1937, respectively.

80a

A. Schmidhammer

The controversy had two aspects. One was to silence the Modernist scholars and the other to discourage fraternization between Catholics and Protestants. Fig. 80a depicts the first of these aspects, and is entitled "A Christmas present for the Modernists." Fig. 80b illustrates the second; the caption reads: "So you get along well with your Lutheran neighbor! Tut, tut! That will never do." (Both cartoons are from *Jugend*, 1909.)

80b

A. Geigenberger †

A MYTHICAL KICK COMING.

PRESIDENT ADAM.—Fellow Myths! We are gathered here to-day to protest against the heretical utterances of one Dr. Crapsey, who repeatedly asserts that we never existed.

From a cartoon by L. M. Glackens in *Puck*, January 30, 1907.

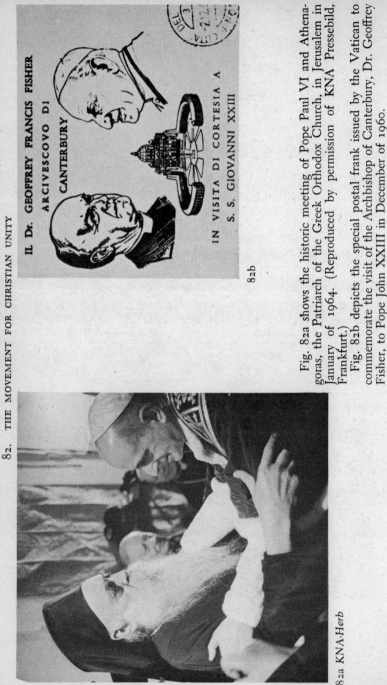

82a KNA-Herb

82b

IL Dr. GEOFFREY FRANCIS FISHER
ARCIVESCOVO DI
CANTERBURY

IN VISITA DI CORTESIA A
S. S. GIOVANNI XXIII

Fig. 82a shows the historic meeting of Pope Paul VI and Athena-goras, the Patriarch of the Greek Orthodox Church, in Jerusalem in January of 1964. (Reproduced by permission of KNA Pressebild, Frankfurt.)

Fig. 82b depicts the special postal frank issued by the Vatican to commemorate the visit of the Archbishop of Canterbury, Dr. Geoffrey Fisher, to Pope John XXIII in December of 1960.

83a

The reconstruction of churches destroyed in World War II resulted in some notable examples of the merging of old and new. In Fig. 83a, the rebuilt church of St. Columba at Cologne, we have an example of both modern architecture and the new liturgical movement. The statute of the Virgin and the little cupola above it were discovered among the ruins and have here been given the central place. The new statue of St. Columba (left) combines a feeling for medieval piety with modern technique. The abstract designs in the windows suggest rays of light and birds' wings. The altar is placed not against the wall but in the center of the chapel as a communion table. (From Martin Hürlimann, *Germany*. Reproduced by permission of Atlantis Verlag.)

83b

The Church of La Virgen Milagrosa (Fig. 83b), designed by Felix Candela and erected in Mexico City in 1955, is constructed as a continuous shell of concrete, having a thickness of only one and one-half inches with no rivets, welds, bolts or nails. "Just as the Gothic cathedrals pushed stone to the limit of its structural potential, this church pushes concrete to the limit of its plastic characteristic. . . . The campanile consists of four reinforced slabs, warped in the mid-section, pierced above, and topped by a spire and a star. . . . The interior, with its soaring vaults and triangular upward thrust, is the essence of aspiration." (Photograph and quotation from *Modern Church Architecture* by Albert Christ-Janer and Mary Mix Foley [New York, McGraw-Hill, 1962], pp. 25–26. Photograph reproduced by permission of Erwin Lang.)

a number of religious bodies, though more particularly by Catholics. If this expedient were universally adopted by the churches, the public schools would be left to the unbelievers or agnostics. The state could not view this outcome with indifference, because the public school has been its great instrument in inculcating the American way of life, in balancing ethnic differences and, at the moment, in overcoming racial discrimination. The state needs the schools. The Church, too, needs the schools. Church and state are separate. What then? A suggestion has been made to relieve parents of the double load of taxation for public schools on the one hand, and support of private and parochial schools on the other. This could be achieved by letting students of all faiths share in the common instruction of subject matters such as science, mathematics, and the like, inasmuch as they have no direct bearing on religion. However, more is involved than the cost. Such a plan would restore the state to its role as an educator. In all discussions of the subject, the fact should not be overlooked that the state does not consist of one set of people and the Church of another. The same persons have a dual role and are inwardly divided.

Whatever the solution, it should not be taken for granted that the state is necessarily the embodiment of justice or the custodian of ideals. This assumption is common, at present, in the United States, where the Supreme Court has become the conscience of the people and has taken the lead over the churches in promoting civil rights. The great cry of the integrationists is "Obey the Supreme Court." But, would they say this if this land were South Africa? In many countries the state has been ruthless in modern times in trampling on the rights of man. In these countries, the Church has been driven to utter a resounding NO.

The Church in Russia

The first instance that comes to mind is Russia and, at this point, we may take up her religious history, which we interrupted in the sixteenth century when Ivan IV took the title of Czar in 1547 and terminated the first period of Russian Church history, the Kievan, and instituted the second, called the "Moscow Period" in consequence of the shift of the capital. The new period was marked by the severance of ties with Byzantium. The Russian Church became independent but, for that very reason, more nearly reproduced the Byzantine pattern with an emperor and a patriarch of its own. The patriarchs strove to achieve a parallelism of power with the Czars, albeit in vain. The Church tended to become a department of state and, unable to exert a more profound influence on society, turned to the cultivation of the religious life by contemplation in the monasteries and the elaboration of a superb liturgy in the churches. In the seventeenth century, the Patriarch Nikon undertook to revise the liturgy after Byzantine models, but incurred thereby the rage of the Slavic conservatives, who were especially outraged because he required the priest, in giving a blessing, to use three fingers in honor of the Blessed Trinity in accord with Byzantine practice, instead of two as formerly. The point is trivial enough, but tangible trivialities often become symbols of deeper differences. Rather than worship like the Byzantines, the Old Believers seceded by the millions.

In the eighteenth century, Russia, having rid herself from Byzantine influence, fell under that of the West. The capital was moved further north to St. Petersburg and the period from then on, up to the Revolution, is called the "St. Petersburg Period" in the history of the Russian Church. Peter the Great looked to England and Germany as models, and Catherine the Great to France. In these Western lands, political absolutism prevailed and, in accord with its spirit, Peter abolished in 1699 the patriarchate, making himself the Father of the Faithful. In 1721, the government of the Church was entrusted to a committee called a *sobor*, which continued to function until the Revolution. The aristocracy took up the ideas of the Enlightenment, and the spirit of Voltaire was regnant at St. Petersburg, where for a time he resided. During the latter part of the nineteenth century, the educated classes extended the idea of the Darwinian biological evolution into a concept of social progress moving toward the Marxist goal of a classless society. Some of these intelligentsia combined atheism with the spirit of St. Francis and, divesting themselves of their goods, went to live among the peasants, not so much to raise thereby the status of peasants as to experience themselves a spiritual rejuvenation by a return to the elemental.

By the turn of the twentieth century, the Orthodox Church was immensely rich, owning nineteen million acres with an income then estimated at fifty million pound sterling a year. But, this wealth was concentrated in the hands of a few and the great majority of the parish clergy were as poor as the people. The priests were not uneducated, but were versed only in the theological and liturgical literature of the Byzantine and Slavic heritage and were not abreast of the currents of Western thought. The peasants, though not respecting the priests, loved the liturgy and, while not regarding the Czar as the Father of the Faithful, still adored the icons.

In addition to the established Orthodox Church, there were many other religious groups in Russia enjoying degrees of toleration on a descending scale. There were Catholics in Poland, Lutherans in the Baltic, and Mohammedans in the Caucasus, while Jews and Armenians were dispersed throughout Russia. In the position of pariahs in the religious caste system were the Russian sects. The largest group among them was that of the Old Believers, who had seceded in the seventeenth century. They numbered around thirteen million at the time of the Revolution. Stundists were influenced by German Pietism. Their name comes from the German *Stunde*, an hour, referring to their periods of prayer. The Molokani and Dukhobors were native sects, whose pacifism went so far that they would not even coerce the earth by ploughing. The Mennonites had entered Russia in their quest for an asylum from persecution in the West. The Baptists resulted from the dedication in the West to the great commission to proclaim the Gospel to all creatures. Although the religion of the sects was vital, their influence was not sufficiently great to give direction to the Revolution.

By 1900, the revolutionaries in Russia were of two types, the Mensheviks and the Bolsheviks. The former were moderates who sought reform by parliamentary methods. They led the first revolution of 1904, as a result of which the Czar ceased to be the head of the Church and the patriarchate was restored. Full religious liberty was accorded to all.

Communism

The Bolsheviks were the party of a new religion, a Judeo-Christian heresy, Communism. Often enough, Jewish and Christian groups have renounced private property voluntarily. Now renunciation was to be forced on the people. Jews and Christians alike have dreamed of a new heaven and a new earth. Communism dropped heaven. Jews and Christians alike believe that God is the lord of history. Communism substitutes for God the ineluctable dynamism of dialectical materialism. Jews and Christians alike have believed that, although God will bring his will to pass, nevertheless his chosen must labor arduously to implement it, whereas Communists, believing in a determinism of history, expend a colossal effort for its realization. Jews and Christians have been willing to die and to kill for their faith. Communists are utterly dedicated and utterly ruthless, reviving the methods of the Inquisition and adding to it technological refinements. Such were the men who led the Revolution of 1917, aspiring to convert Russia from a feudal to a modern industrialized state in a single generation.

To achieve this end, they felt called upon to destroy not only the Church but religion itself, the "opiate of the people." Between 1918 and 1919, twenty-eight bishops and one thousand two hundred and fifteen priests were shot. Properties were confiscated. Out of one thousand and twenty-six monasteries, six hundred and eighty-seven were liquidated. An attempt was made to destroy the Church by fomenting divisions. The old sects were less molested at first, and encouragement was given to the schism of the Renovated Church, which supported the Revolution. It has since died out. Tikhon, the patriarch of the Orthodox Church, was imprisoned and maltreated. The Church was actually purified by fire. Thousands of priests and laymen who might have saved themselves by recantation, went to concentration camps. The rites of religion were carried on with such secrecy that even a husband and wife did not dare let each other know that they were both practicing believers. The story is told of a father who took his child to be baptized, which the priest refused to do, because he had already baptized the baby when it was brought in a few days earlier by the mother. Such an incident would elude the authorities, but they could not escape a shock when the head of the largest state hospital in a certain district died and was buried in the robes of an archbishop of the Orthodox Church.[3] In 1927, a census was taken in six schools in the neighborhood of Moscow, with the result that 77.9 per cent of the boys and 46.1 per cent of the girls put themselves down as atheists; 22.1 per cent of the boys and 53.9 per cent of the girls recorded themselves as believers. Among the boys, 17 per cent were church attenders and among the girls 40.5 per cent.[4]

After the relative failure of the decade of blood, the government took a new line in 1929 and sought to eradicate religion by intensified propaganda. Measures of repression were given the air of

[3] N. S. Timasheff, *Religion in Soviet Russia 1917–1942* (New York, 1942), chapter iii and p. 81.

[4] Paul Miliukov, "Religion and the Church," in *Outlines of Russian Culture*, ed. Michael Karpovich (Philadelphia, 1942), p. 200.

responses to popular demand. Petitions from the people were stimulated for the removal of church bells and the burning of icons. Rents for the use of church buildings were raised by 120 per cent. In consequence, in 1937, one thousand nine hundred places of worship were closed. Heavier pressures were applied upon sects and upon the Catholics. Yet, this policy also fell far short of its own goal. The head of the Militant Atheists League estimated in 1937 that one-third of the adults among the industrial workers and probably two-thirds of the peasants were believers and, since the rural areas held sixty-seven per cent of the population, these figures would make the believers amount to about one-half of the total population of Russia. In 1940, an atheist journal conceded that in the cities at least one-half of the workers were believers and that in the villages hardly an atheist was to be found.

In 1939, the government adopted again a new policy. The excessive rents were dropped. Distinctions were made. Christianity was recognized as having been a great cultural force in the formation of old Russia. The icons were to be prized as objects of art, and the cathedrals preserved as museums, much as the Turks had done by restoring Hagia Sophia. The loyal support given to the state by the churches in World War II has diminished the rift. Today, the cathedrals of the Orthodox Church are said to be crowded; the sects are now classified all together as Baptists, though presumably the Catholics and the Lutherans could hardly be fitted into this category. These Baptist churches are thronged, and the preaching is powerful, but because the churches that are open are frequented, one is not to forget the many that have been closed. In the Communist satellite states the Church survives under constant harassment.

In China the Church survives, likewise. Here one cannot speak of regression in the same sense as in Russia, because there never was so much from which to regress, nor was the Church there ever wealthy. The considerable investments on the part of foreign missionary boards in schools, colleges, and hospitals have passed into the hands of the Communists. The saddest aspect of the Revolution is that those Christians who refused to meet all the demands for recantation of "foreign imperialism," have been denounced as traitors by those fellow Christians who have in conscience complied. Yet, these latter are not to be accused of abject subservience, for they could have escaped great pressures had they simply repudiated Christianity altogether. The situation offers a parallel to the imprisonment of Quakers under that devout Puritan, Oliver Cromwell.[5]

Fascism and National Socialism

The other great movements that have sought at least to curb if not to crush Christianity have been Fascism and National Socialism. Many of their methods have been taken over from Communism, but Fascism and National Socialism have had less in common with Christianity than has Communism. They have been anti-Semitic, nationalistic, and built upon class structure. Though less overtly, they have been no less averse to Christianity.

Fascism began in Italy when a resentful middle class called in the state to stop strikes and to enforce dictatorially cooperation between labor and capital. Mussolini summoned all to work rather than squander the fruits of labor in quarrels over their distribution. The champions of constitutionalism were brutally liquidated. Criticism from the Church was forestalled by the Concordat of 1929, which gave the state control over clerical salaries. Then Italy sought to recoup her economy by the conquest of Abyssinia. No open conflict of Church and state ensued.

In Germany, National Socialism grew out of longer antecedents and had recourse to more drastic measures. German aspirations toward national unity and expansion had been thwarted ever since the sixteenth century. Not even Bismarck had succeeded in unify-

---

[5] Francis Price Jones, *The Church in Communist China* (New York, 1962).

ing the German states. The greatest opposition to his efforts came from the Catholics, who did not wish to see unification achieved through the hegemony of Protestant Prussia. The Catholics formed a political party called the Center Party, which supported the House of Hanover against the Protestant House of Hohenzollern, and sought the union of Germany with Catholic Austria. Bismarck annexed Protestant Schleswig–Holstein, instead. Although the Catholic Church supported autocratic regimes in Catholic lands often enough, in Germany the Center Party was on the side of constitutionalism and, above all else, would not bargain with Bismarck as would the Socialists. Windhorst, the leader of the Center Party, would make Bismarck bellow like a bull, but he had to give in. Austria was eventually united with Germany by Hitler, but Germany was not united within herself under a strong central government controlling the territorial states. Hitler was resolved to bring about consolidation, but first he had to eliminate the Center Party and inevitably clash, therefore, with the Catholic Church.

Conflict with the Protestants was not so obviously inevitable. Hitler's attempts at extricating Germany from the toils of the Treaty of Versailles met with universal approval among his countrymen. His sallies into the Saar, the Sudetenland, and even into Poland elicited no remonstrance. His initial restrictions upon the Jews aroused no protest and his ultimate barbarities did not become generally known in Germany until after the war. But his attempts to subject all churches to the will of the state provoked intense conflict. He began innocuously enough. To the Catholics he accorded in 1933 a Concordat which conceded those liberties which, if granted, enable the Catholic Church to operate under any government, namely freedom for the celebration of the sacraments, for the education of the young, for the existence of monastic orders, and for the holding of property. In the case of Protestants, he insisted that the twenty-eight territorial churches should form one National Church. The Protestants saw no reason why they should not do at the state's behest what they might well have done earlier on Christian grounds. They fully expected that the consolidated church would be free to determine its own inner life. Then, however, Hitler began to nibble at his concessions.

The Catholic Center party in the Reichstag was liquidated and Catholic youth organizations were absorbed into the Hitler Youth, while monastic orders were prosecuted on the charge of having smuggled money out of Germany. Cardinal Faulhaber denounced the breach of the Concordat and Bishop von Galen declared in broader terms that no nation which violated the demands of justice could long endure. The pope issued the encyclical *Mit brennender Sorge*, "With Burning Anxiety."

The Protestants were promptly disillusioned when Hitler ousted the bishop of their choice and installed one of his own. Not only were the Protestant churches to be made into a department of state, but Christianity itself was to be revamped as a Germanic religion without Semitic admixtures, and those of Jewish blood, even though members of Christian churches, were to be cast out. Thereupon, four thousand Protestant ministers formed the Confessing Church which declared at Barmen in 1934 that no human *Führer* could stand above the Word of God. The Confessing Churches lost their properties. Their seminary was closed, their press silenced and, on the outbreak of war, their clergy of military age assigned to posts of greatest danger in the army, while the older leaders were sent to concentration camps.

Among the latter was Martin Niemöller, who had been a submarine commander in World War I. After more than half a year in solitary confinement, he was brought to trial under Hitler's law against "treacherous attacks upon state and party." Niemöller well knew that he was to be made an example. The place of his trial was a building adjacent to his cell and reached by a dark tunnel. A guard of impassive face came to conduct him. Niemöller was to walk ahead. Behind him, he heard only the jailer's tread and the echoes from the walls of stone. In the darkness, a sense of forsakenness and dread invaded his spirit, when he thought he heard a voice from the rear, a low voice, repeating a set of words confused by echoes. Gradually, the words took on shape: "The name of the Lord is a strong tower. . . . The name of the Lord is a strong tower." (Prov. 18:10) The voice was that of the jailer. The corridor ended. A door opened. Before the crowded courtroom stood the prisoner, unafraid.[6]

Albert Einstein paid this tribute to the stand of the churches against the Nazi persecution of religion and humanity:

> Being a lover of liberty, when the revolution came to Germany, I looked to the universities to defend it, knowing that they had always boasted of their devotion to the cause of truth; but no, the universities were immediately silenced. Then I looked to the great editors of the newspapers whose flaming editorials in the days gone by had proclaimed their love of freedom, but they, like the universities, were silenced in a few short weeks. Then I looked to the individual writers, who as literary guides of Germany, had written so much and often concerning the place of freedom in modern life; but they too were mute. Only the churches stood squarely across the path of Hitler's campaign for suppressing truth. I never had any special interest in the Church before, but now I feel a great affection and admiration because the Church alone has had the courage and persistence to stand for intellectual truth and moral freedom. I am forced thus to confess that what I once despised I now praise unreservedly.[7]

Recession and Reunification

Yet, despite the valor of Christians in social reform, intellectual questing, and resistance to tyranny, the last hundred years have witnessed great regressions, not by reason of conquest of Christian lands through unbelievers like the Mohammedans, but through corrosion from within. Those lands which once gloried in their

---

[6] Detmar Schmidt, *Pastor Niemoeller* (New York, 1959), pp. 110–11.

[7] Henry P. Van Dusen, *What the Church is Doing* (New York, 1943), p. 53.

orthodoxy, Holy Russia, the Holy Roman Empire, and most Christian France have suffered intense hostility or frigid indifference. Catholics and Protestants alike are affected.[8] France, nominally Catholic, is accounted missionary territory by the Church, despite the eminence of many of the French clergy. The popes wring their hands over South America, where in Buenos Aires, for instance, one may see a sign, "You are a Catholic. Go to Mass once a year." The Lutheran Church, established in Sweden, is said to retain less religious vitality than the Church in Russia under persecution. In England, among Anglicans and Dissenters alike, there are allegedly many who do not remember the name of the church from which they stay away. The onetime established churches in Germany, still linked financially with the state, report an active participation of only about six per cent of the nominal membership. The United States boast the highest church attendance figures in the world, yet even here the country club rates greater interest for many than the Church.

Quite likely, the recessions have had a bearing upon the present efforts of the Christian churches to consolidate their strength by reunification. But, decidedly, there are other reasons. The ultimate reason is the feeling of the impropriety of division in view of the prayer of the Lord that all might be one. Then, too, the historical law of rhythm may be operative. Throughout Christian history, periods of division have alternated with periods of solidarity. Before Constantine, the Church had about eighty divisions. During the early Middle Ages, in the West, there were no divisions worthy of mention for close to six hundred years. In the twelfth century we noted the resurgence of sectarianism, which in the sixteenth resulted in the major and lasting secession of Protestantism. Within Protestantism, the splintering reached its peak in the seventeenth century in the person of John Smyth, called the Se-Baptist because he baptized himself, in the belief that no one else living was qualified. Thereafter, sect formation diminished. In

[8] "Catholicism around the World," *Life* (Oct. 18, 1963).

England, in the nineteenth century, the Catholic Apostolic Church had only a small following, whereas the Salvation Army and Young Men's Christian Association are surely not to be ranked with churches.

In the United States, some of the older churches have suffered further divisions, though seldom with a change of the fundamental pattern. The Pentecostals are the modern protagonists of revivalism and have attracted a numerous following, in South America even more than in the north. The three new religious bodies in the United States with distinctive characteristics as over against the older churches are the Christian Scientists with the revival of faith healing, the Mormons with their linkage of the Americas to the stock of ancient Israel, and the Disciples of Christ dedicated to the reunification of the churches.

The initial impulse for Protestant reunification came from the mission fields, where the incongruity was manifest in making Southern Baptists out of northern Hindus. The revival movement also cut across the old confessional lines and tended to unite all those who had experienced the new birth in the spirit, though often at the same time to separate them from the unconverted. The theological movements of the nineteenth century drew together the liberals from all camps, though again, sometimes occasioning breaches with the conservatives. In the United States, the tendency of the Protestant denominations to stress in religion the claims of the heart rather than those of the mind enables them to work together, even though they do not always believe alike.

In this country, the divisions of churches arising from diverse national origins of the population are diminishing. For example, Danish, Swedish, Norwegian, Finnish, and German Lutherans are in the process of forming unions. Churches of the same family, such as the varieties of Methodists, have been reunited, healing the breach caused by the Civil War. The Northern and Southern Baptists have not yet come together, but the reason for the continuing separation has become theological rather than sociological; the issue now is not slavery but fundamentalism. In Canada,

Methodists, Congregationalists, and Presbyterians have formed the United Church of Canada; in North India, Presbyterians and Congregationalists have been brought together in a single Church; and Anglicans, Methodists, Presbyterians, and Congregationalists have joined to form the Church of South India. In the United States, two previously united bodies have formed a further union: the Evangelical (Lutheran) and Reformed (Zwinglian) Church united with the Congregational Christian Churches. The National Council of Churches gathers many Protestant groups into a federation for the coordination of numerous activities; so does the World Council, which includes also the Greek and Russian Orthodox Churches. The Russian Protestant sects may soon be admitted.

Recently, the initiative of Pope John XXIII in convening the Vatican Council has opened the door to a *rapprochement* between Catholics and Protestants. Yet, not even the power of the Spirit or the warmth of the pope could have called forth such a hearty response in both camps if both had not been moving, the one clockwise, the other counterclockwise, toward a point of convergence in theology and scholarship, in liturgy and in polity.

The Catholic Church Today

The changes wrought in Catholicism by the last half century have been quite marked. From the Council of Trent to the late nineteenth century, the Church held aloof from the currents of the age. During the first half of that century, political pressures induced a hardened mood on the part of the Church. The French Revolution had stripped the Church of her possessions in France. Napoleon managed the Church by manipulating the pope. With the Concordat of 1801, the pope acquiesced in the loss of the properties, but retained the right to remove bishops. However, since they were paid by the state, they became dependent upon the state. Confronted by so much opposition, the popes grew less concessive and disinclined to heed the Catholic liberals, such as Count Charles Montalembert, Father J.-B. Lacordaire, and Bishop Félix Dupanloup in France who wished the Church to espouse the cause of political liberty. In England and Germany, the liberals stressed in particular religious liberty. In 1864, Pope Pius IX condemned them all in the *Syllabus of Errors*, rejecting rationalism, Socialism, Communism, naturalism, the separation of Church and state, liberty of the press, and liberty of religion, concluding, "The Roman pontiff cannot and should not be reconciled and come to terms with progress, liberalism, and modern civilization." Dupanloup took the edge off this pronouncement by making a distinction between the *thesis*, which is what ideally should be done, and the *hypothesis*, which is actually that which will be done in particular circumstances. In other words, the pope's condemnations ordinarily would not take effect. The pope allowed this interpretation to pass. A Paris wag said that the distinction meant: "It is the thesis when the nuncio says the Jews ought to be burned; it is the hypothesis when he goes out to dinner with M. de Rothschild."[9] Modern Catholic interpreters are more disposed to say that the pope had in mind only particular varieties of liberalism, liberty, and so on.

In 1870 came the unification of Italy and the termination of the temporal power of the papacy. Just before the troops captured the city of Rome, the Vatican Council hurled a defiance against all secularisms by proclaiming the pope's infallibility. This does not mean that he cannot make a mistake, but only this, that when he speaks on faith and morals *ex cathedra*, that is officially, making his pronouncement binding upon all the faithful on pain of damnation, then and then only the Holy Spirit will prevent him from imposing error upon his flock. His pronouncement will not be due to any new revelation, but will be only an explication of that already given.

In the first decade of the twentieth century, a group of Catholic scholars adopted the methods of biblical study in vogue among the

9 A. R. Vidler, *op. cit.*, p. 152.

Protestants. They were called Modernists and were excommunicated in 1910, because they were accused of saying that an article
of faith, such as the virgin birth, can be rejected as historical fact
and then accepted as myth. They certainly reinterpreted the doctrine of infallibility as no more than the consensus of the faithful.
In recent years, some of their conclusions and most of their
method in biblical studies have been adopted by Catholic scholars.

Following the Modernist debacle, Catholic liberalism was
driven for a time into the catacombs. Scholars continued their
labors while bowing to the edicts suppressing their publications.
Père Legrange, for instance, continued his biblical studies in Jerusalem and trained a corps of scholars who have since been accorded recognition. The Church claims now no longer that the
Vulgate is the only valid translation and no longer holds that the
verse about the Trinity in I John 5:7 is authentic, as Leo XIII had
asserted. The differences between Catholic and Protestant scholars
in Old Testament studies have vanished and few remain with regard to the New Testament. The translation of the Scriptures
produced by a committee of Protestant experts, called the Revised
Standard Version, has been accepted with a few very slight
changes for use by English Catholics, and another English translation, the joint work of Protestants, Catholics, and Jews is now
under way.

Synthesis of Belief and Reason

In the meantime, the Protestants had gone to extremes in their
efforts to come to terms with modern knowledge and thought. The
conflict of science and religion belongs to the nineteenth century.
Copernicus and Galileo did not make any perceptible impression
upon Europe until the seventeenth century and, from then on
throughout the eighteenth, the new astronomy seemed to make
God only the more majestic. The single problem for the faith was
that natural law in the physical world required a special theory of

divine intervention to account for miracles. The nineteenth century introduced geology and biological evolution, and both conflicted with the Genesis. The ages of the rocks shook the Rock of Ages. Plainly, the earth was vastly more ancient than biblical chronology would admit. As worked out by Archbishop Usher, the creation supposedly took place in 4004 B.C.; but, evidently, the world was not created in six days. Some scientists attempted to harmonize geology and Genesis by expanding the days of creation to six periods, but rigorously honest biblical scholars insisted that the word used for day in Genesis, the Hebrew word *yom*, meant to the biblical writers twenty-four hours. Nor did geology give any warrant for the view that the periods were precisely six in number. The theologians would have to come to terms, but with just which theory of geology to make terms was a question. There was a debate between the Vulcanists, who attributed the earth's crust to the igneous, and the Neptunists to the aqueous principle. The theologians inclined to the Neptunists because the aqueous could accommodate Noah's flood. More disconcerting was the view of William Buckland, that successive catastrophes had wiped out all life on earth to be succeeded by new beginnings and new forms.[10] Yet out of this view could be constructed the picture of "Eternal Forethought reaching across the tottering mountains and the boiling seas," to bring into being, by his almighty fiat, the enlarging lineaments of his majestic plan.[11] This was a new version of the doctrine of creation out of nothing and, scientifically, this doctrine is not to be dismissed, for the universe does appear to be expanding. Yet, however much this particular geologic theory may be subject to correction, and however much further theological interpretation would be required, this much was plain, that the account of creation in Genesis was not science but inspired mythology.

For many, this adjustment had been already successfully achieved when Charles Darwin's *Descent of Man* gave a much

[10] William Buckland, *Geology and Mineralogy Considered with Reference to Natural Theology* (London, 1858).

[11] Horace Bushnell, *Nature and the Supernatural* (New York, 1858), p. 206.

more drastic shock, by asserting that man had not been created out of the dust of the earth in one single divine act, but had emerged from lower forms of life in the course of inconceivably long periods of organic descent. The guiding principle in this evolution had been the struggle for existence, by adaptation to environment. Only the fittest, in the sense of the most adaptable, had survived. There were larger problems here for religion than any touching upon the scientific accuracy of Genesis. What of man? If he is descended from the beasts, is he a beast? Nature is "red in tooth and claw." Must man, in this case, in order to survive, eliminate the weak? Henry Drummond, the English theologian, answered in his *Ascent of Man*,[12] that the great determinative principle in evolution is not the survival of the fittest by the elimination of the unfit, but the principle of sacrificial mother love. Another inference drawn from evolution was that advance is the law of life. The principle of progress is written into the very structure of the universe, and man is bound to move ineluctably to a nobler state. Such sublime optimism with Herbert Spencer replaced Christian apocalyptic dreams. But now, if man is descended from the animals, and the animals are mortal, when did man become immortal, or is he also mortal or, perchance, are the animals immortal? Luther certainly expected to find his dog, Tölpel, in heaven. Henry Drummond answered that life consists in correspondence with environment. After death the only environment is God. Hence, only those capable of correspondence with God can survive.[13] This is a doctrine of conditional immortality. In New England, Newman Smyth argued that, since progress is the law of life, and physical evolution has now reached its limits, further development will dispense with the body and the evolutionary process will reach its consummation beyond the grave.[14]

While Christian tenets were thus devastatingly assaulted and

[12] Henry Drummond, *Lowell Lectures on the Ascent of Man* (New York, 1894).

[13] ———, *Natural Law in the Spiritual World* (New York, 1884).

[14] Newman Smyth, *The Meaning of Personal Life* (New York, 1916).

underwent valiant reassessments, the historical foundations of the faith were being subjected to unflinching scrutiny. We have mentioned already Reimarus' dismissal of the resurrection as fraud and the rationalist explanation of miracles by Paulus. Then came David Friedrich Strauss, who claimed that the explanations of Paulus were more miraculous than the miracles. Strauss found the key in myth. If Genesis is inspired mythology, why not the Gospels? A myth is a symbol, often in story form, to enshrine an eternal truth. The eternal truth of the Gospel is that God can become man and man can become God. Christ is the most perfect exemplar. To convey this truth, stories were constructed utilizing materials from the Old Testament. John's Gospel, for instance, records that the loaves which Jesus multiplied were barley. Now, Elisha multiplied barley loaves. The story of the birth of John the Baptist by Elizabeth in her old age was modeled on the story of Sarah, the mother of Isaac, and on that of Hannah, the mother of Samuel. This entire approach does not necessarily eliminate the historicity. The concretion of God in humanity does take place in history, but no one historical event is of supreme importance.

The retreat from history could derive support also from the affirmation of F. E. D. Schleiermacher, the court preacher at Berlin, that religion consists in the feeling of absolute dependence. Georg Wilhelm Hegel sniffed that in this case the dog would be the most religious of all creatures, a rather improper remark for a philosopher who should use the language of abstraction and quite an irrelevant remark, besides, because Schleiermacher had in mind not any sort of dependence, but dependence upon God as revealed in Christ. Really, Schleiermacher was presenting to the secularized intelligentsia of his time Lutheran theology in the language of the Romantics. Man actually is dependent, weak in body, weak in spirit, weak and depraved, in need of forgiveness and strength. In contrition and with confession he must acknowledge his state and *feel* his utter dependence, that he may be helped. This is Lutheran, except that Luther distrusted feeling. Of course, Luther agreed that one must respond with feeling to God's grace, but feeling or no feeling, grace is there, and, of course, Schleiermacher never said that feeling puts it there. His primary point was that man in his dependence is ineradicably religious and that this is a fact with which science and philosophy must come to terms, just as religion must come to terms with science and philosophy.

One may see the outworkings of the stress on feeling in the English Romantics and the American Transcendentalists as well as in Horace Bushnell. Samuel Taylor Coleridge said that to enter into religion one must submit oneself "as a many-stringed instrument to the fire-tipped fingers of the royal Harper," and then, whatever "finds me" in the Scriptures is true, for "whatever finds me bears witness of itself that it has proceeded from a holy spirit."[15] Bushnell declared in New England that the key to the Bible is not logic but imagination, passion, and emotion. "The logic-chopping theologians," said he, "in the presence of Moses' burning bush would analyze the flame and put out the fire."[16] Therefore, the poets are the true theologians. But, if the poets have within them this capacity for discernment, are they really dependent upon any historical event in the past?

How far poets could go and how little they could settle is evident in England in the nineteenth century, where the poets were the theologians. William Wordsworth espoused a nature mysticism verging on pantheism.

> *And I have felt*
> *A presence that disturbs me with the joy*
> *Of elevated thoughts; a sense sublime*
> *Of something far more deeply interfused,*
> *Whose dwelling is the light of setting suns,*
> *And the round ocean and the living air,*
> *And the blue sky, and in the mind of man:*
> *A motion and a spirit, that impels*
> *All thinking things, all objects of all thought,*
> *And rolls through all things.*

[15] Samuel Taylor Coleridge, *Confessions of an Inquiring Spirit* (London, 1849), pp. 11 and 38.

[16] Horace Bushnell, *God in Christ* (Hartford, 1859), pp. 158–59.

Robert Browning had the robust faith that "God is in his Heaven and all is right with the world." Of Alfred Tennyson it has been said that at times he spoke "like an archangel assuring the universe that it would muddle through." Better one might call him an agonized seeker, holding by faith to that which none can know.

> Strong Son of God, immortal Love,
> Whom we, that have not seen thy face,
> By faith and faith alone embrace,
> Believing where we cannot prove:
>
> Thou wilt not leave us in the dust:
> Thou madest man, he knows not why;
> He thinks he was not made to die;
> And thou hast made him: thou are just.
>
> We have but faith; we cannot know;
> For knowledge is of things we see;
> And yet we trust it comes from thee,
> A beam in darkness: let it grow.

But Matthew Arnold saw the recession of faith in the melancholy roar of waves returning to the deep over the pebbles of Dover Beach, and Arthur Hugh Clough, one Eastertide, at Naples, after an agony of heart searching, brought himself to pen the lines, "He is not risen."

Poetry reflected all the answers of the age but gave an answer only at the point of demonstrating that in religion no answer can be adequate apart from feeling. But poetry and feeling cannot settle questions of historical fact, and Albrecht Ritschl, despairing of metaphysics and of ultimate answers, called for a return to history, to what we can know about the life of Christ on earth. Under Ritschl's sway, scholars dug back deeply into the sources. Adolph Harnack believed that critical acumen would be able to disengage the legendary accretions from the authentic nucleus, and one would then be able to recover the Jesus of history.

Coincidentally, early in the twentieth century Paul Schmiedel refuted the contention of those who went so far with the mythological explanation of the New Testament as to deny the very existence of Jesus. Schmiedel drew up a list of pillars of certainty, points in the Gospels which could never have been invented because in some measure contrary to current beliefs of the early Christians who wrote the Gospels. One of these pillars was the baptism of Jesus by John the Baptist. His baptism was for the remission of sins and Jesus was believed to have no sins. Again, John the Baptist had followers who were in competition with the early Church. That being so, Christians would never have invented the saying of Jesus that no one born of woman was greater than John. Since Jesus was believed to have been without sin, an evangelist would not have placed in his mouth the saying, "Why do you call me good? No one is good but God alone."[17] These and similar instances constitute a core of indisputable material by which other sayings and episodes can be tested. One notes in this entire line of argumentation that the approach is made from the viewpoint of the early Church. The New Testament gives a rich picture of the life and thought of the Christian community in the generation following Jesus and from this delineation one can work backwards.

What then did emerge? Liberal Protestantism summarized Christianity in terms of belief in the loving, heavenly Father revealed by Jesus, and belief in Jesus himself as a man of unblemished character who laid down his life in obedience to the Father's will and summoned the disciples to follow in his train.

Curiously, perhaps the first criticism of this picture came from the Catholic Modernists, George Tyrrel in Ireland and Alfred Loisy in France, who pointed out that the Protestant liberals had been highly selective in their treatment of the Gospels and had quite overlooked the prediction by Jesus that the Son of Man would come on clouds of glory before that generation had passed away. The prediction must be authentic, for no one would have contrived it when it was unfulfilled. But, if Jesus entertained such a conviction, how remote was he from a liberal Protestant ra-

[17] Mark 10:18.

tionalist! Albert Schweitzer in the Protestant camp was to make the same point.

Then came the shattering of the whole liberal picture of man with the discovery in World War I that man, created in the image of God, can sink below the level of the beasts. This was really no new insight, for this is precisely what the Bible says about man. He is fallen, depraved, vile. To be cured he must admit it, and in contrition seek and find the pardon and renewing grace of God revealed in Christ. Revealed! That was the affirmation of Karl Barth. His main contribution was to bring back to Protestantism the belief in revelation, the self-disclosure of God. Barth compared himself to a man in the first days of the airplane standing under the eaves of a second-story room and looking down on the people below, who are all seen to be looking up at something he does not see. In all the characters of the Bible he discerned this upward gaze at something coming down from above.

Barth recognized that the revelation comes to us through a book and that the book is not free from mistakes. He did not turn his back on the biblical criticism of the preceding century. Nor did he continue to grapple with the questions of historical certainty. This task fell to Rudolf Bultmann, who insisted afresh that the twentieth century could not continue using the thought moulds of the pre-scientific Christians of the first century. The Gospel must be demythologized. The coming on the clouds of heaven is mythology, the miracles are mythology, the virgin birth, the physical resurrection, and the ascension are all mythology. The Christian Gospel must be divested of its primitive garment and clothed again in terms intelligible and meaningful to the predicament of modern man.

What then remains of Christianity as a religion in the history of man? Very little of absolute certainty with respect to the words and deeds of Jesus. But, Christianity is not to be divorced from history. The Christian Church is a fact of history and the Church would never have come into being save for an unparalleled event.

The core of Christianity is *the Christ event* and the quality of faith and life which it has elicited. It is an event that calls now, as much as then, for an absolute commitment, and only to those who are so committed will the event yield its full meaning. Here is the paradox that to get faith one must first make the venture of committing oneself to faith.

But, when it comes to recasting Christianity in terms compatible with the modern world, Paul Tillich, formerly of Germany and now of the United States, points out that one cannot demythologize Christianity. One may discard a particular mythology but will be compelled to substitute for it another, because without the use of myth in the sense of a symbol one can say nothing about God save only this that he is. Literally, God is not father, sovereign, lord, king, and creator. All these words are symbols or analogies pointing to that which transcends them all, and Karl Barth says that no analogy has validity until after God has disclosed himself in Christ, just as Augustine observed that cow tracks bespeak a cow only to one who has previously seen a cow. Here then is another circle. To comprehend God one must employ analogies, and to comprehend the analogies one must first know God. All these paradoxes add up to this, that Christianity calls for a leap of faith which no analogy and no experience can ever demonstrate or validate to a degree that nothing will be risked, and that no venture remains.

But, symbols must be employed still, and they must be of a kind to convey a meaning to modern man in terms of his situation. The existentialists, whether Christian or not, insist that man in appraising his situation must start with where he is, poised between a naught and a naught, between birth, before which he remembers nothing, and death, beyond which he can see nothing, in the midst of a universe from which he is alienated. Its vastness appalls him with a sense of his littleness. What are his threescore years and ten when he looks at a piece of amber imbedding an insect trapped thirty million years ago? And how feeble is he! As

Pascal said, "There is no need for a universe to crush him, a vapor, a drop of water is enough."[18] Man then seeks to invest himself with dignity by the reflection that though the universe should crush him, yet he would be more noble than that by which he is killed, for he would know that he died. In the capacity for thought lies the dignity of man, said Pascal. Bertrand Russell, in his early years, likened the human race to men on a frozen lake with unscalable shores awaiting the thaw with unflinching dignity. Again, man is alienated from man. The totalitarian society tries to break the will of the non-conformist by wracking his body. His dignity consists in enduring torture, rather than recant his faith or betray his kind. This is the ultimate for Jean-Paul Sartre. Again, man is alienated by the work of his hands. Science has been prostituted to technology, and technology menaces its creatures with annihilation. Man is further alienated from himself. Probings into the unconscious have documented the Puritan picture of man "with a civil war in his bowels." Under these manifold strains, some maintain the pose of heroic defiance and some disintegrate. Psychiatry tries to restore the broken spirit by means of understanding: let the distraught shake off the feelings of guilt that emerge from the subconscious and face life unashamed.

Christianity endorses the diagnosis, but not altogether the prescription for the predicament of man. Heroism is noble but bleak. To eliminate the sense of guilt over that which cannot be helped is sound, but there is also in every life a personal guilt, real, though often not recognized, which needs to be seen, admitted and confessed, so that it may be forgiven. The Christian answer is not that man should be led to feel there is nothing wrong with him, but rather that something is desperately wrong. Nevertheless, God can accept him, forgive him, and treat him as if he were just, though actually he is not. This was Luther's phraseology. Casting the thought into modern terms, Tillich says that God accepts the unacceptable and, if man believes this, he can accept

[18] Blaise Pascal, *Pensées*, chap. II, section x.

himself. Tillich does not divorce this process from history, because the grace of God has been mediated through Christ at a point in time, yet forever beyond time.

Reunification of Churches

These recent developments in Christian thinking have taken place among Protestants, but can scarcely be considered distinctively Protestant. Catholics are wrestling with precisely the same issues. Nor is the thought of a Catholic liberal, lately come into his own, distinctively Catholic. Teilhard de Chardin is a biologist, philosopher, and mystic, whose conclusions about the nature and destiny of man have many affinities with those of earlier Christian thinkers, some of them Protestant. For him, as for Henry Drummond, love rather than strife is the law of life and its origins have a primordial anticipation in molecular attraction. Like Smyth, he sees the evolutionary process emerging toward ever nobler forms of life beyond the level of the physical. Pulsing through the cosmos, he feels a divine dynamism reminiscent of the vitalism posited often by the medical Humanists of the Renaissance, or again of the *élan vital* of the modern French philosopher Henri Bergson. Pierre Teilhard de Chardin is not far from Luther's doctrine of the ubiquity of Christ when he interprets the very universe as a sacrament, the visible sign of an invisible grace, enabling him to pray:

> Since once again, Lord—though this time not in the forests of the Aisne but in the steppes of Asia—I have neither bread, nor wine, nor altar, I will raise myself beyond these symbols, up to the pure majesty of the real itself; I, your priest, will make the whole earth my altar and on it will offer you all the labours and sufferings of the world.
>
> Over there, on the horizon, the sun has just touched with light the outermost fringe of the eastern sky. Once again, beneath this

moving sheet of fire, the living surface of the earth wakes and trembles, and once again begins its fearful travail. I will place on my paten, O God, the harvest to be won by this renewal of labour. Into my chalice I shall pour all the sap which is to be pressed out this day from the earth's fruits.[19]

Here, the conflict of science and religion has vanished, because the universe is no longer conceived in mechanistic terms. Similarly, the Jewish philosopher, Martin Buber, has protested against the kind of science that views the cosmos simply as an object, an *it* rather than as a *thou* with whom the spirit of man can hold a dialogue. The comprehension of the universe, many scientists are coming to see, calls not only for examination of that which meets the senses but also for an interpretation by way of intuition, vision, and illumination. In religious terminology, this is revelation. Thus the religious thinking of Protestants, Catholics, and Jews is marked by convergence with a readiness to accept the findings of the natural sciences and of biblical scholarship, and readiness to discern a self-disclosure of God in his handiwork.

Likewise, in the fields of liturgy and polity, Protestants and Catholics have drawn closer together. The Protestants of the Puritan tradition have been reviving the Christian year and remodeling their churches so as to give centrality to the altar rather than the pulpit, whereas Catholics in some instances are bringing the altar down from the chancel to be closer to the congregation as a communion table. Much of the Mass is now said in the vernaculars, with a large degree of congregational participation. Hymn singing is encouraged, even to the point of using Luther's "A Mighty Fortress is Our God." As for church music, the Catholics are appropriating Johann Sebastian Bach and the Protestants Giovanni Palestrina.

All these convergings may be interpreted as an enthusiastic response to the initiative of Pope John XXIII. Most significant is the change of atmosphere. Protestants are now addressed by Catholics as "separated brethren" and even as *carissimi fratres*,

[19] Pierre Teilhard de Chardin, *Hymn of the Universe* (New York, 1965).

and Protestants have stopped blasting the pope as Antichrist. Dialogue has become possible. Before there will ever be an organic union, many points remain to be resolved, but they are now amenable to exploration. The celibacy of the clergy need not be an obstacle, because Rome could readily extend to Protestants the same freedom as to the Eastern Uniat churches, to retain their own practices. Certain doctrines, hitherto unacceptable to Protestants, are being redefined or at least reconsidered, for example the doctrine of transubstantiation. The point is made by Catholic theologians that the scholastic distinction between accidents and substance is rendered untenable by modern physics, which looks upon matter as a form of energy. If the doctrine means that one form of energy replaces another and that the food for the body may become food for the spirit, the change appears to be functional, an interpretation which most Protestants would find acceptable.

The gravest doctrinal point is the infallibility of the pope. Protestants contend that no human being is infallible, and human formulations of belief must always be tentative, open to new light and reformulation. Moreover, to assume that someone is infallible because of election to a particular office, is to make the work of the Holy Spirit too restricted and too mechanical. Catholics reply that Protestants make too much of the point, since, as a matter of fact, papal infallibility is not workable, because, given the ambiguities of language, there is no infallible medium for the communication of infallibility. Protestants then ask why the doctrine should not be renounced and Catholics reply that great institutions change less by repeal than by reinterpretation.

Perhaps the most profound difference between Catholicism and Protestantism is in the attitude toward obedience. Catholics commend those liberals earlier in this century who bowed to the official disapprobation of their works. The example is cited of Père Legrange who refrained from publication and went on quietly with his researches at Jerusalem and with the training of a corps of scholars who now enjoy the liberties once denied to him. A Protestant might indeed emulate one who was allowed to study and to teach, but if he were exiled to some ecclesiastical Siberia where he could do neither, should he in that case withold the truth given him by God? Truth ranks above institutional unity, which after all is not incompatible with the most acrimonious contention. More to be desired are mutual respect, charity, brotherliness, and the unity of the spirit in the bond of peace. And this exists already in a marvelous measure.

The present volume has concerned itself frequently with the impact of Christianity upon the formation of Western culture. At the end, we do well to inquire whether Christianity is compatible with culture at all. In the early centuries, Celsus and Julian the Apostate, to be echoed later by Machiavelli and Lenin, asserted that Christianity is given too much to the gentler virtues to under-gird the structure of a state. From the Christian side, the Danish philosopher, Sören Kierkegaard, in the early nineteenth century, was savagely scornful of calling any culture Christian. "Everything in Denmark," he jibed, "has to be called Christian; we even have Christian brothel-keepers. But," said he, "if one considers the rigor of Christ's demands, an entire populace will never meet them. Christ said, 'Narrow is the way, and few are they that find it.' "[20] Christianity demands an absolute commitment. It can never be regarded as a mere item of interest to be reported between sports and the theatre. Christianity as a religion is not simply an object of curiosity, less fascinating perhaps than the religion of the Aztecs. Christianity is not an item in a culture, but sits in judgment upon all cultures, including those it has helped to fashion.

This conviction, as we have seen, has led some groups to withdraw from society, but much more prevalent has been the view of Augustine who saw no possibility on earth of a perfect society, yet believed in striving for an approximation. Christian rulers, said he, even if their intentions are unalloyed, cannot in view of man's fallibility avoid inequities. Yet, they should not shun the encoun-

[20] *Selections from the Writings of Kierkegaard*, tr. Lee M. Hollander (Garden City, N.Y., 1960), p. 228.

84a

There is no evidence in the theology of the younger churches of any blending of Christianity with their own earlier religious heritage. However, in their art, in the depiction of Christian themes, the younger churches have followed a long-standing tradition of placing the setting in their own locale. Fig. 84a depicts the Trinity in the pose assumed by Indian deities: seated in the roots of the Vedic tree of life. (The picture is by Angelo da Fouseca from *Exposição de Arte Sacra Missionária*, Lisboa, 1951).

84b

Fig. 84b is also from India (*At the Foot of the Cross* by Alfred
D. Thomas, taken from Daniel Fleming's *Each with his own Brush*,
Friendship Press, 1938). "This simple and effective picture combines
the pathos, the significance and the glory of the Cross. Lines give the
mere suggestion of the Himalayas and the round earth. Does this
mean that the Cross is for India and, also, for all the world?"
(Reproduced by permission of Friendship Press, National Council
of the Churches of Christ.)

84c

Marc & Evelyne Bernheim

84d

Fig. 84c shows an African priest regarding the story of Christ on the doors of St. Paul's church in Ebutte-Metta, a district of Lagos, Nigeria, carved by the pagan artist Lamidi Fakeye. Yoruba tribal figures were used, including Shango, the god of thunder, on the left in the middle panel. (Reproduced by permission of Rapho Guillumette Pictures.)

Fig. 84d is a Vatican stamp depicting the Nativity in an African kraal.

84e

Fig. 84e (from Fleming, *Each with his own Brush*) is entitled *The Lost Sheep*. "Most of the Christian paintings in Latin America are in the Roman Catholic European style even when by Indian artists. It has been difficult to find anything by Protestants. This picture is one of a dozen on the parables of Jesus by Rolando Zapata, one of the young ministers of Mexico City. His father, one of the older pastors, has always been skillful with his blackboard illustrations, and it is not surprising that his son has produced this series of entirely Mexican pictures which make the parables live before Mexican eyes." (Reproduced by permission of Friendship Press, National Council of the Churches of Christ.)

84f

Fig. 84f is by the Chinese artist Lu Hung Nien, and is entitled
And there was for them no place (from *Exposição de Arte Sacra Missionária*, Lisboa, 1951).

84g

Fig. 84g is by the Chinese artist Chang Chao Ho, and is entitled *The Flight into Egypt* (from *Exposição de Arte Sacra Missionária, Lisboa, 1951*).

84h

Fig. 85h is by the Vietnamese artist Le Van De, and is entitled *Magdalene before the Cross* (from *Exposição deArte Sacra Missionária*, Lisboa, 1951).

841

Fig. 84i is by the Japanese artist Saburo Takashima, and is entitled *The Crucifixion* (from Fleming, *Each with his own Brush*). (Reproduced by permission of Friendship Press, National Council of the Churches of Christ.)

84j

Lit-Lit Fotos

Fig. 84j is by the Korean artist Heung Chong Kim, and is entitled *The Visitation of the Magi*. (Reproduced by permission of The Committee on World Literacy and Christian Literature of the Division of Foreign Missions, National Council of Churches.)

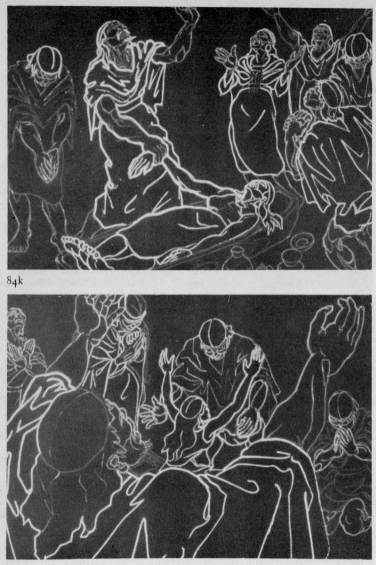

84k

84l

Fig. 84k and Fig. 84l are the last two of a series of five paintings entitled *The Raising of Jairus' Daughter* by the Chilean artist Eliseo Sau. (Reproduced by permission of "CELADEC," and the National Council of Churches.)

ter in order to preserve their own purity. On the other hand, they should not make any and every concession to the exigencies of the present, in order to get something done in a given circumstance. There are occasions when for a Christian the only possible word is a No.

What then of the future? The law of rhythm would lead one to expect that any valid element in Christianity, if obscured in one generation, will be revived in the next. There are many such rhythms. There is the cycle of the zeal of the first generation, the indifference of the second, and the resurgence of the third. There is the cycle in the expansion of Christianity of proclamation, accomodation, assimilation, corruption, and reform. The monks themselves formulated the law that religion engenders industry, industry produces wealth, wealth corrupts religion, and religion in its fall dissipates wealth. The missionary endeavor, likewise, has been marked by ebb and flow. We have noted the oscillation of sect formation and reunification. In Christian art, simplicity moved to complexity, and complexity to simplicity. The Cistercians banished the cluttered Romanesque decorations and would have no colored windows, but then elaborated in transparent windows the leaded tracery. Music moved from the Gregorian chant to elaborate settings for the Mass and back to the chant. In theology, the simple faith developed into the intricate system of Scholasticism, only to return to the simplicity of *The Imitation of Christ*. Some of these rhythms are the cycles of purity, corruption, and reform. Some indicate shifts in taste with respect to equally valid aspects of Christian thought and worship. The Christian is like a juggler who cannot keep more than four balls, let us say, in the air. One falls. In picking it up he drops another to be restored in turn.

From these observations one might infer that the history of the Church is simply a seesaw, but one is not to forget that never is a revival simply a repetition. Renewal is also re-creation and a zig-zag admits of a forward movement. But whither? Will all Christian churches ever be united? Presumably the ancient points of difference will be resolved, but new ones may emerge. Should a branch of the Church condone injustice, there would be good reason for division. Again, will all the world kneel down and confess that Christ is Lord? It might not be a gain for the world so to do were it merely to bow the knee and not rend its garments. Dean Inge well remarked that in religion nothing fails like success, and Christianity is often most truly itself when embattled against the hosts of darkness.

Hope for a Kingdom of God

But Christianity is a religion of hope. When tongues shall have ceased and knowledge shall have vanished away, hope is one of the three that abide. The Christian hope is for a kingdom of God on earth in which dwells righteousness. But the Christian hope looks also beyond the ultimate frontier, where history is no more, to that city that has no need of the sun by day nor of the moon by night, for it is lighted by the glory of the Lord, and in the city there is a river clear as crystal proceeding from the throne of God and the Lamb, and on either bank grows a tree of life whose leaves are for the healing of the nations.

Selected Bibliographies

CHAPTER IX

BIBLIOGRAPHY

Léonard, Emile G., *Histoire Générale du Protestantisme*, I, La Réformation; II, L'Établissement (Paris, 1961), 2 vols. Excellent bibliographical coverage, including periodical literature in many languages. Thomas Nelson & Sons announced an English translation.

Hillerbrand, Hans J., *Bibliography of Anabaptism* (Elkhart, Ind., 1962).

SOURCES

Hillerbrand, Hans J., *The Reformation in its Own Words* (New York, Harper & Row, 1964)

Manschreck, Clyde L., *A History of Christianity, Readings . . . from the Reformation to the Present* (Englewood Cliffs, 1964).

The Library of Christian Classics is devoting volumes XV–XVIII to Luther, vols. XX–XXIII to Calvin, including the *Institutes* in two volumes newly translated by Ford Battles and magnificently annotated by John T. McNeill. Vol. XIX includes Melanchthon and Bucer; XXIV Zwingli and Bullinger, XXV Spiritual and Anabaptist writers, XXVI English Reformers. The Concordia and Muhlenberg publishing houses are bringing out translations of Luther in 55 volumes. Most of Calvin appeared in English during the previous century through the Calvin Translation Society. The Parker Society has cared for the English reformers. For Zwingli we have *The Latin Works and Correspondence*, tr. S. M. Jackson (New York, 1912–29), 3 vols.

HISTORIES OF THE REFORMATION

The Cambridge Modern History, Vol. II, The Reformation (Cambridge, Eng., 1958), mainly political and social, excellent treatment of religious issues by Gordon Rupp.

Lindsay, Thomas M., *A History of the Reformation* (New York, 1916–17), 2 vols. Still useful for the theological aspects.

Smith, Preserved, *The Age of the Reformation* (New York, 1920 and 1960), devotes as much coverage to the age as to the religious aspect of the Reformation.

Grimm, Harold, *The Reformation Era* (New York, 1934), sets the religious issues in their political context.

Holborn, Hajo, *History of Modern Germany,* Vol. I, *The Reformation* (New York, 1959), limited necessarily to the Reformation in Germany.

Elton, G. R., *Reformation Europe* (Cleveland, Meridian Paperback, 1964), mainly political.

Chadwick, Owen, *The Reformation,* Pelican History of the Church (Baltimore, 1964), admirable survey.

Mosse, G. L., *The Reformation* (New York, Holt Paperback, 1953), brief.

Harbison, E. H., *The Age of the Reformation* (Ithaca, 1955), brief.

Bainton, Roland H., *The Age of the Reformation* (Princeton, Anvil Paperback, 1956), half text and half documents.

————, *The Reformation of the Sixteenth Century* (Boston, Beacon Paperback, 1960), does not include the Catholic Reformation.

LUTHER

Dillenberger, John, *Martin Luther, Selections* (New York, Doubleday, Anchor Paperback, 1961).

Bainton, Roland H., *Here I Stand: A Life of Martin Luther* (New York, 1950, also Apex and Mentor Paperbacks).

Ritter, Gerhard, *Luther, his Life and Work* (London, 1963).

Rupp, E. Gordon, *Luther's Progress to the Diet of Worms* (Chicago, 1951).

————, *The Righteousness of God* (New York, 1953).

Schwiebert, Ernst, *Luther and his Times* (St. Louis, 1950), new data on the role of the University of Wittenberg.

Watson, Philip S., *Let God be God* (London, 1947).

ZWINGLI

Farner, Oskar, *Huldrych Zwingli* (Zürich, 1943–60), 4 vols.

————, *Zwingli the Reformer* (New York, 1952).

CALVIN

Harkness, Georgia, *John Calvin* (New York, 1931).

Schmidt, Albert Marie, *Calvin* (New York, Harper & Bros., Torchbook, 1960).

Walker, Williston, *John Calvin* (New York, 1906).

ANABAPTISTS

Littell, Franklin, *The Anabaptist View of the Church* (Boston, Beacon Paperback, 1958).

Williams, George H., *The Radical Reformation* (Philadelphia, 1962).

Friedmann, Robert, *Hutterite Studies* (Goshen, Ind., 1961).

ENGLAND AND SCOTLAND

Gee, H., and Hardy, W. J., *Documents Illustrative of English Church History* (London, 1914).

Elton, G. R., *The Tudor Constitution, Documents and Commentary* (Cambridge, Eng., 1962).

Constant, G., *The Reformation in England* (New York, 1934–42), 2 vols., liberal Catholic.

Dickens, A. G., *The English Reformation* (London, 1964), rich in local history.

Donaldson, Gordon, *The Scottish Reformation* (Cambridge, Eng., 1960).

MacGregor, Geddes, *Thundering Scot: A Portrait of John Knox* (Cambridge, Eng., 1959).

FRANCE

Palm, Franklin C., *Calvinism and the Religious Wars* (New York, 1932).

Kingdon, Robert, *Geneva and the Coming of the Wars of Religion* (Geneva, 1956).

Grant, A. J., *The Huguenots* (London, 1934).

Zoff, Otto, *The Huguenots* (New York, 1942).

FREE SPIRITS AND TOLERATION

Bainton, Roland H., *Hunted Heretic: The Life and Death of Michael Servetus* (Boston, 1953, also Beacon Paperback).

———, *The Travail of Religious Liberty* (Philadelphia, 1951).

Jones, Rufus M., *Spiritual Reformers* (Reprint, Boston, 1959).

Wilbur, E. Morse, *A History of Unitarianism*, Vol. I (Cambridge, Mass., 1945; reprint, Boston, Beacon Press).

Leclerc, Joseph, *Toleration and the Reformation* (New York, 1960), 2 vols.

Jordan, Wilbur Kitchener, *The Developments of Religious Liberty in England* (Cambridge, Mass., 1932–40), 4 vols.

POLITICAL, ECONOMIC, AND EVALUATIONS

Allen, J. W., A History of Political Thought in the Sixteenth Century (New York, 1928).

Weber, Max, The Protestant Ethic and the Spirit of Capitalism (London, 1930).

Pauck, Wilhelm, The Heritage of the Reformation (Glencoe, Ill., 1950).

Troeltsch, Ernst, The Social Teaching of the Christian Churches (London, 1949), 2 vols.

CATHOLIC REFORM

Jedin, Hubert, A History of the Council of Trent (London, 1961), 2 vols.

CHAPTER X

THE THIRTY YEARS' WAR

Wedgewood, C. V., The Thirty Years' War (London, 1938).

Brief treatments in:

Holborn, Hajo, History of Modern Germany, Vol. I, The Reformation (New York, 1959).

Friedrich, Carl J., The Age of Baroque (New York, Harper & Row, Torchbook, 1962).

THE PURITAN REVOLUTION

Sources:

Blitzer, Charles, The Commonwealth of England 1641–1660 (New York, Capricorn Paperback, 1963).

Haller, William, Tracts on Liberty in the Puritan Revolution (New York, 1934), 3 vols.

Wolfe, Don M., Leveller Manifestoes (New York, 1944).

Woodhouse, A. S. P., Puritanism and Liberty (London, 1938).

Histories:

George, Charles and Catherine, The Protestant Mind of the English Reformation (Princeton, 1961).

Haller, William, The Rise of Puritanism (New York, Harper & Bros., Torchbook, 1957).

Hill, Christopher, The Century of Revolution (Edinburgh, 1961).

———, Economic Problems of the Church (Oxford, 1956).

Schneider, Herbert W., *The Puritan Mind* (Ann Arbor Paperback, 1958).

Wedgewood, C. V., *The King's Peace* (New York, 1956).

Willey, Basil, *The Seventeenth Century Background* (London, 1949).

Special Aspects:

Barbour, Hugh, *The Quakers in Puritan England* (New Haven, 1964).

Freund, Michael, *Die Idee der Toleranz im England der grossen Revolution* (Halle/Saale, 1927).

Gooch, G. P., *English Democratic Ideas in the Seventeenth Century* (New York, Harper & Bros., Torchbook, 1959).

Jordan, Wilbur Kitchener, *Philanthropy in England 1480–1660* (London, 1950).

Lloyd, Arnold, *Quaker Social History 1667–1738* (London, 1950).

Morgan, Edmund Sears, *Visible Saints* (New York, 1963).

Paul, Robert S., *The Lord Protector* (London, 1955).

Trevor-Roper, H. R., *Archbishop Laud* (London, 1959).

CHAPTER XI

THE ENLIGHTENMENT

Becker, Carl, *The Heavenly City of the Eighteenth Century Philosophers* (New Haven, 1960).

Brien, David D., *The Calas Affair* (Princeton, 1960).

Cragg, Gerald R., *The Church and the Age of Reason 1648–1789*, Pelican History of the Church, IV (Baltimore, 1960).

Creed, John Martin and Smith, J. S. B., *Religious Thought in the Eighteenth Century* (Cambridge, Eng., 1934), sources with introductions.

Gierke, Otto, *Natural Law and the Theory of Society 1500–1800* (Boston, Beacon Paperback, 1957), 2 vols. in one.

Hazard, Paul, *European Thought in the Eighteenth Century* (New Haven, Yale Paperback, 1954).

Stephen, Leslie, *History of English Thought in the Eighteenth Century* (Reprint, London, 1927), 2 vols.

Torrey, Norman, *Voltaire and the English Deists* (New Haven, 1930).

PIETISM

Kaiser, Gerhard, *Pietismus und Patriotismus* (Wiesbaden, 1961).

Klügel, Maria, "Wichern," *Protestantische Studien* 27 (Berlin, 1940).

Pinson, Koppel S., *Pietism as a Factor in German Nationalism* (New York, 1934).

Seeberg, Reinhold, "Das Christentum Bismarcks," *Biblische Zeit und Streitfragen* X, 6 (1915).

Tanner, Fritz, *Die Ehe im Pietismus* (Zürich, 1952).

Weinlick, John R., *Count Zinzendorf* (New York, 1956).

METHODISM

John Wesley:

Lee, Umphrey, *John Wesley and Modern Religion* (Nashville, 1936); McConnell, Francis J., *John Wesley* (New York, 1939); Piette, Maximin, *John Wesley in the Evolution of the History of Protestantism* (New York, 1937), sympathetic Catholic approach.

The Methodist Movement:

Davies, Rupert E., *Methodism* (Baltimore, Pelican Paperback, 1963); Edwards, Maldwyn, *After Wesley 1791–1849* (London, 1935); Halevy, Elie, *History of the English People in 1815*, Vol. III *Religion and Culture* (Baltimore, Penguin, 1938); Taylor, E. R., *Methodism and Politics 1791–1851* (Cambridge, Eng., 1935); Warner, Wellman, J., *The Wesleyan Movement in the Industrial Revolution* (London, 1930); Wearmouth, Robert F., *Methodism and the Working Class Movements of England 1800–1860* (London, 1957).

CHAPTER XII

THE MODERN PERIOD

Manschreck, Clyde L., *A History of Christianity: Readings* (Englewood Cliffs, N.J., 1964).

Davies, Horton, *Worship and Theology in England*, II, 1850–1900 (Princeton, 1962).

Dillenberger, John and Welch, Claude, *Protestant Christianity* (New York, 1954).

Latourette, Kenneth Scott, *Christianity in a Revolutionary Age* (New York, Harper & Row, 1958–61), 4 vols.

McGiffert, Arthur C., *Protestant Thought before Kant* (New York, Harper & Row, Torchbook, 1961).

———, *The Rise of Modern Religious Ideas* (New York, 1915).

Nichols, James H., *History of Christianity 1650–1950* (New York, 1956).

Norwood, Frederick A., *The Development of Modern Christianity since 1500* (New York, 1956).
Vidler, Alec, *The Church in an Age of Revolution*, History of the Church V (Baltimore, Pelican, 1961).

ANGLO–CATHOLIC REVIVAL

Chadwick, Owen, *The Mind of the Oxford Movement* (Stanford, Cal., 1960).
Davies, Horton, *Worship and Theology in England from Watts and Wesley to Maurice 1690–1850* (Princeton, 1961).
Simpson, W. J. S., *The Contribution of Cambridge to the Anglo–Catholic Revival* (London, 1933).
Stewart, Herbert Leslie, *A Century of Anglo–Catholicism* (London, 1929).

SOCIAL REFORM IN ENGLAND

Woodward, E. L., *The Age of Reform* (Oxford, 1938).
Coupland, R., *Wilberforce* (Oxford, 1923).
Cowherd, Raymond G., *The Politics of English Dissent* (New York, 1956).
Driver, Cecil, *Tory Radical, the Life of Richard Oastler* (Oxford, 1946).

CHAPTER XIII

THE TWENTIETH CENTURY

Macquarrie, John, *Twentieth Century Religious Thought* (New York, Harper & Row, 1963).
Schneider, Herbert W., *Religion in Twentieth Century America* (New York, Athenaeum Paperback, 1964).

NORTH AMERICA

Sources:
Smith, H. Shelton; Handy, Robert T.; Loetscher, Lefferts, A., *American Christianity*, Vol. I, 1607–1820 (New York, 1960); Vol. II, 1820–1960 (New York, 1963).

Broad Coverage:
Brauer, Jerald C., *Protestantism in America* (Philadelphia, 1953).
Herberg, Will, *Protestant, Catholic, Jew* (Garden City, Anchor Paperback, 1955).

Hudson, Winthrop, *American Protestantism* (Chicago, 1961).

James, Ward Smith and Jamison, A. Leland, *Religion in American Life* (Princeton, 1961), 4 vols. The first two volumes consist of essays by various authors; the last two are bibliographies by Nelson R. Burr.

Niebuhr, H. Richard, *The Social Sources of Denominationalism* (Reprint, Hamden, Conn., 1954).

———, *The Kingdom of God in America* (New York, Harper & Bros., Torchbook, 1959).

Mead, Sidney, *The Lively Experiment* (New York, Harper & Row, 1963).

Stokes, Anson Phelps, *Church and State in the United States* (New York, Harper & Row, 1964).

Sweet, William Warren, *Religion in the Development of American Culture* (New York, 1952).

Weigle, Luther Allen, "American Idealism," *Pageant of America* (New Haven, 1928).

Periods and Aspects:

Bridenbaugh, Carl, *Mitre and Sceptre* (New York, 1965).

Gaustad, Edwin S., *The Second Great Awakening in New England* (New York, Harper & Bros., 1957).

———, *Historical Atlas of Religion in America* (New York, Harper & Row, 1962).

Goen, C. C., *Revivalism and Separatism in New England 1740–1800* (New Haven, 1962).

Keller, Charles Roy, *The Second Great Awakening in Connecticut* (New Haven, 1942).

Miller, Perry, *Orthodoxy in Massachusetts* (Boston, Beacon Paperback, 1959).

Morgan, Edmund S., *Visible Saints* (New York, 1963).

Walker, Williston, *Creeds and Platforms of Congregationalism* (Boston, Pilgrim Paperback, 1960).

Williston, George E., *Saints and Strangers* (New York, 1945).

GERMANY

Means, Stewart P. B., *Things that Are Caesar's* (New York, 1935).

Herman, Stewart W., *It's Your Souls We Want* (New York, 1943).

———, *The Rebirth of the German Church* (New York, Harper & Bros., 1946).

———, *Report from Christian Europe* (New York, 1953).

Littell, Franklin, *The German Phoenix* (Garden City, N.Y. 1960).

RUSSIA

Spinka, Matthew, *The Church and the Russian Revolution* (New York, 1927).

Fedotoff, George P., *The Russian Church since the Revolution* (London, 1928).

Karpovich, Michael, ed., *Outlines of Russian Culture*, I, Miliukov, Paul, *Religion and Culture* (Philadelphia, 1942).

Anderson, Paul B., *People, Church and State in Modern Russia* (New York, 1944).

Bach, Marcus, *God and the Soviets* (New York, 1953).

Gorodetsky, Nadejda, *The Humiliated Christ in Modern Russian Thought* (London, 1938).

CHINA

James, Francis Price, *The Church in Communist China* (New York, 1962).

EXISTENTIALISM

Blackham, Harold J., *Six Existentialist Thinkers* (London, 1951).

————, ed., *Reality, Man and Existence: the Essential Works of Existentialism* (New York, Bantam Paperback, 1965).

Henemann, F. H., *Existentialism and Modern Thought* (New York, Harper & Bros., Torchbook, 1958).

CATHOLIC–PROTESTANT RELATIONS

Hughes, Philip, *The Pope's New Order* (New York, 1944), analysis of encyclicals.

Loewenich, Walther von, *Modern Catholicism* (New York, 1959).

Callahan, D. J., Obermann, H. A., O'Hanlon, D. J., eds., *Christianity Divided* (New York, 1961).

Küng, Hans, *The Council, Reform and Reunion* (New York, 1961).

Index

Volume II